UNRAVELLING THE SOCIAL FORMATION

Studies in Critical Social Sciences Book Series

Haymarket Books is proud to be working with Brill Academic Publishers (www.brill.nl) to republish the *Studies in Critical Social Sciences* book series in paperback editions. This peer-reviewed book series offers insights into our current reality by exploring the content and consequences of power relationships under capitalism, and by considering the spaces of opposition and resistance to these changes that have been defining our new age. Our full catalog of *SCSS* volumes can be viewed at https://www.haymarketbooks.org/series_collections/4-studies-in-critical-social-sciences.

Unravelling the Social Formation

Free Trade, the State and Business Associations in Turkey

Akif Avci

Haymarket Books
Chicago, IL

First published in 2022 by Brill Academic Publishers, The Netherlands
© 2022 Koninklijke Brill NV, Leiden, The Netherlands

Published in paperback in 2023 by
Haymarket Books
P.O. Box 180165
Chicago, IL 60618
773-583-7884
www.haymarketbooks.org

ISBN: 978-1-64259-819-3

Distributed to the trade in the US through Consortium Book Sales and
Distribution (www.cbsd.com) and internationally through Ingram Publisher
Services International (www.ingramcontent.com).

This book was published with the generous support of Lannan Foundation and
Wallace Action Fund.

Special discounts are available for bulk purchases by organizations and
institutions. Please call 773-583-7884 or email info@haymarketbooks.org for more
information.

Cover design by Jamie Kerry and Ragina Johnson.

Printed in the United States.

10 9 8 7 6 5 4 3 2 1

Library of Congress Cataloging-in-Publication data is available.

This book is dedicated to the memory of my father Ömer.
I will always remember him in the most beautiful moments
we had together. Rest in peace ...

∴

Contents

Acknowledgements

First of all, I would like to express my overall gratitude to my family. I owe them a large debt of gratitude for their pray, love, support and best wishes.

In addition, as this book is an extended and updated version of my Ph.D. thesis at the University of Nottingham, which was finalised in 2019, I would also like to extend my overall gratitude to my supervisor and mentor Prof Andreas Bieler for his precious support, guidance during this long process.

Furthermore, I am particularly grateful to my dear friends Dr. Ayşe Arslan and Dr. Bilge Şahin, for their invaluable support during this project.

Finally, and most importantly, I am gratefull to my precious wife and my lifelong comrade Eren Ezgi GEVHER AVCI.

Figures and Tables

Figures

Tables

Abbreviations

AKP	Justice and Development Party
BDDK	Banking Regulation and Supervision Agency
DEIK	Foreign Economic Relations Board
ECC	Economic Coordination Council
EU	European Union
FDIS	Foreign Direct Investments
FETO	Fethullah Gulen Terror Organisation
FTAS	Free Trade Agreements
GATT	General Agreements on Tariffs and Trade
HSYK	Constitutional Courts of the High Council Judges and Public Prosecutors
IMKB	Istanbul Stock Exchange
ISI	Import Substitution Industrialization
ISO	Istanbul Chamber of Industry
ITO	Istanbul Chamber of Commerce
MFA	Ministry of Foreign Affairs
MUSIAD	Independent Association of Industrialists and Businessmen
NAFTA	North American Free Trade Agreement
OIC	Organization of Islamic Cooperation
PWC	Post Washington Consensus
RP	Welfare Party
SMES	Small and Medium Sized Entrepreneurs
TCMB	Central Bank of Turkey
TIM	Turkish Exporters Assembly
TMSF	Saving Deposit Insurance Fund
TNC	Trans National Capital
TOBB	Union of Chambers and Stock Exchanges
TUIK	Turkish Statistical İnstitute
TURKONFED	Turkish Enterprise and Business Confederation
TUSKON	Turkish Confederation of Businessmen and Industrialists
TUSIAD	Turkish Industry & Business Associations
UCD	Uneven and Combined Development
UNCTAD	United Nations Conference on Trade and Development
WTO	World Trade Organisation

Introduction

On the Political Economy of Turkey

The collapse of the Soviet Union at the beginning of the 1990s, and the integration of China into the word trade system have transformed the process of accumulation of capital across the world. This shift in global capitalism has also transformed global value chains, dividing the process of production into segments in different countries. In this new phase of capitalism, the so-called "emerging" market economies have been a major target for transnational companies. These companies have penetrated the countries of the Global South with their industrial and financial capital. Turkey has been one of the most popular destinations for these companies to invest because of its remarkable performance in terms of its foreign trade success and its short-term economic growth in the 2000s. Accordingly, Turkey has experienced a series of structural changes in its process of capital accumulation. This was seen as confirming the neoclassical idea that free trade would lead economic and social convergence among the countries engaged in it. Thus, mainstream approaches argue that the liberalisation of foreign trade regimes and adoption of market-friendly policies will result in economic growth for both sides and an increase in foreign trade volume. This is the updated version of David Ricardo's theory of *comparative advantage* which suggests that different parties engaging in foreign trade would mutually benefit from the exchange of goods and services. Remarkably, this necessitated establishing an alliance between different social classes in Turkey and transnational capital operating in different social formations. The resultant outcome was to increase the level of integration of the countries in the Global South and to integrate them into the global value chain. However, the evidence from Southern countries, like Turkey, starkly differed from the predictions of the neoclassical theory of comparative advantage. In particular, Turkey did not catch up with advanced capitalist countries and thus the rapid growth in exports and profits in Turkey in the 2000s did not affect the underlying structure of unequal trade. It was a success for capital accumulation, but not a developmental success.

In analysing the integration of Turkey into global free trade, this book argues that Turkey has integrated into the global free trade in an uneven way, which increased the asymmetrical effects of the global free trade system on the Turkish social formation. The book also argues that integration into transnational circuits was enhanced after the 2001 banking crisis, which resulted in the intervention of the IMF into the Turkish social formation. This involved implementing market-friendly and anti-labour policies, and also increased privatization of state institutions for the sake of the transnational capital (TNC) fraction in Turkey. During this new era of global free trade, Turkish economic growth was partly based on its increased export performance in the automotive and textile sectors as well as foreign capital inflow which increased the dependence of Turkey on international financial capital and foreign direct investment (FDI). In this period, new cycles of investment have begun in Turkey and TNC in Turkey has also invested in international markets. This made Turkey an intermediate producer in global production chains, as a site where companies assemble imported resources into finished goods. This increases the dependency of the different class fractions in Turkey on the global market to reproduce the social relations of production. Turkish domestic investment is heavily dependent on capital inflows, or in other words, Turkish production is dependent on the import of low-value-added intermediate goods, especially in the automotive sector, a type of dependency which has become a characteristic feature of the Turkish economy. Turkey has become an importer of intermediate goods from countries in Asia and an exporter of finished goods to European countries. Accordingly, the share of countries in Europe and the Americas in Turkey's total export volume is 64.7 per cent (TUIK, 2019). The top export destinations of Turkish companies in 2018 are Germany (9.6 per cent), the UK (6.6 per cent), Italy (5.7per cent), Iraq (5 per cent), the US (4.9 per cent), Spain (4.6 per cent), France (4.3 per cent), Netherlands (2.8 per cent), and Belgium (2.4 per cent). On the other hand, China is Turkey's second largest import partner after Russia in 2018 (Turkey imports almost 50 per cent of its gas from Russia). This also increased the foreign trade deficit of the country, which was almost $100 billion in 2013 and $55 billion in 2018. In this new relation, Turkey did not gain persistent autonomy in relation to the countries in the so-called "emerging markets". In this free market, the integration into the different social formations through export of capital and power has created contradictions which threatened the continuity of the process of capital accumulation. This means the more the integration of Turkey into global free trade advances, the more Turkey becomes dependent on different forms of capital accumulation in these countries.

Through a set of conceptual reflections, this book defines Turkey as a late developing capitalist country in the Global South, which has submitted itself to the process of global capital accumulation in an uneven way. Capitalist classes have played important roles in the process of Turkey's integration into the world economy. This book does not only examine the contradictions between countries but also between sectors, regions, and classes engaged in production, circulation, and revalorisation processes which emerged as a

Social Relations of Production

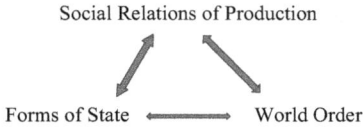

Forms of State ⟵⟶ World Order

FIGURE 1   The dialectical relations of three levels
            SOURCE: THIS FIGURE IS BASED ON THE AUTHORS' COMPILATION

result of the uneven integration into the world economy. The book pays attention to the structural peculiarities of each site in which free trade takes place, and its primary concern is to grasp the role of business associations and the state in facilitating free trade relations. The focus of this book is to examine the role of business associations in Turkey by analysing the dialectical relationship between global free trade relations and the Turkish social formation under the Justice and Development Party (Adalet ve Kalkinma Partisi, AKP) government from 2002 to the present. Thus, it provides the reader with a context within which to understand how the discussion of business associations adds to an understanding of social formations in Turkey and concludes by showing how the Turkish experience can have a general application to Southern countries.

To unpack the argument of the book, this study constructs a three-level analysis on the standard pattern of Neo-Gramscian analysis, i.e., the social relations of production, forms of state and world order (See Figure 1). The relationship between these three levels is not unilinear, and these overlapping relations provide the structure of the book (See Figure 1). Taking the social relations of production as a point of departure, the first sub-question of the book investigates the production structure in order to identify the class characteristics of the member firms of different business associations in the Turkish social formation. As a second step, the book examines the relationship between business associations and the state in order to theorise the complex relationships within the ruling power bloc in the Turkish social formation. Hence, this book analyses the role of the Turkish state in integrating business associations into global free trade relations and managing internalisation of global class relations in the Turkish social formation. Finally, it examines the integration of business associations into global free trade relations in order to highlight the historical specificity of the Turkish case among other countries in the Global South (See Table 1).

1   Class Fractions in the Turkish Social Formation

The purpose of this section is not to provide a complete historical materialist understanding of social classes in the social formation of Turkey. This section

TABLE 1   Neo-Gramscian three levels of analysis and book structure

The core research question

Social relations of production	The first level – Defining the companies from a class perspective – Integration of companies organised in different business associations into the social relations of production
Forms of state	The second level – Examining the state's external and internal functions. – Externally: Free Trade Agreements, High-level Strategic Council Meetings, regulating the legal system to help companies in expanding internationally. – Internally: Managing the contradictions among different power groups, regulating the legal system to increase the ability of capital to make different manoeuvres.
World order	The third level – Examining how business associations engage in the global free trade system, and which markets they target (the EU, Middle Eastern, and African Countries). – The internalisation of the global free trade system and global class relations in the Turkish social formation

SOURCE: THIS TABLE IS BASED ON THE AUTHORS' COMPILATION

aims specifically to define and categorise different capitalist class fractions in the Turkish social formation and to present the fragmentation of the capitalist classes in Turkey, a process necessary for studying business associations in Turkey. Although, the formations of classes take similar paths all over the world, it has different characteristics in peripheral social formations. Before analysing different class fractions among the capitalist classes in Turkey, it is necessary to point out the importance of the concept of social formation. The concept of social formation was first used by the French Marxist Louis Althusser. He differentiates Marxist analysis both from the essentialism of Hegel, which suggests that each part equally constitutes the whole, and from an economic determinism which suggests that the economic base is predominantly superior to non-economic phenomena (Jessop, 1985: 57). According to Althusser, the social totality is characterised by different levels and the unity of the whole is dominated by one level over the others. This unity in the last instance is characterised by the social relations of production, but politics is the actual site of the class struggle in a specific social formation (Althusser, 1965: 200–217). In contrast, Greek Marxist Nicos Poulantzas used the concept to analyse the different power and class forces which constitute a social formation. Accordingly, he argues that a society is composed of different modes and forms of production and more than two classes (Poulantzas [1974] 1975: 22). The classes central to Marxism, the working class and the bourgeoisie, are the dominant (but not the only) ones in a capitalist social formation. As a social formation comprises different modes of production, there can also be slaves, peasants, or unemployed people in a specific social formation. A social formation is the actual site of reproduction of the social relations of production in which class struggle is enacted (Poulantzas [1974] 1975: 23). Accordingly, this study uses the concept of social formation in a sense that includes all class and power relations within a society, but which is dominated by a specific mode of production. This concept of social formation is useful since it allows the study to analyse different business associations in Turkey which consist of different class fractions and companies with different political backgrounds. Poulantzas also suggests that the formation of social classes in a specific social formation only exist in relation to other social formations (Poulantzas [1974] 1975: 23). Here, this study examines the class fractions in the Turkish social formation in relation to the social relations of production in Turkey as well as their interaction with other social formations through engaging with global free trade mechanisms and relations of production in different social formations.

The development and formation of capitalist classes have taken different forms at different times in different social formations. In this regard, capitalist classes in Turkey do not exist in themselves or essentially, they only exist as a contingent product of class struggle. This is why this book defines the fractions in relation to their position in relations of production, relations at the state level, and their forms of integration into the global relations of free trade. The present literature on class fractions in Turkey is limited to the traditional, religious, cultural and regional dimensions in their fragmentations of capitalist classes in the social formation in Turkey, dimensions which may express or obscure the underlying class dynamics. It is fair to say that this literature does not focus on the transformation or reformation of capitalist classes in the last two decades. On the contrary, it approaches polarisations of classes or class fractions from different, cultural or regional perspectives. For instance, some authors employ categorisations such as "Istanbul Capital', 'Anatolian Capital', 'Kemalist Bourgeoisie', Islamist Bourgeoisie' and 'Secular Bourgeoisie'. At the core of their argument, there are two main camps within the capitalist classes in the Turkish social formation. The first camp is organised within the largest business association, TUSIAD, whose members mainly operate in the metropolitan cities such as Istanbul and Izmir and are loyal to democratic principles and secularism. The second fraction is organised within MUSIAD and TUSKON whose members mainly operate in newly industrialised cities in Anatolia, and are considered to be Islamic or Islamist by scholars. Similar to these approaches, institutionalist scholars studying Turkey also treat the fraction organised within TUSIAD as the constituent power of political society, while the fractions organised within MUSIAD and TUSKON are automatically located in civil society. On the other hand, some Marxist and Marxist-inspired scholars argue that, while social categories and cleavages among sects and cultures (such as religious or secular) can reflect class contradictions, the secular/religious and core/provincial binaries fail to effectively categorise capitalist class fractions in Turkey. This is because such binaries portray business associations in Turkey as monolithic entities without internal cracks and contradictions. They also focus on the business associations' domestic activities and ignore their presence in different countries.

This book argues that the effective categorisation of capitalist class fractions in Turkey requires a historical materialist understanding of the roles of the state and the market in the Turkish social formation. In this regard, the book challenges the argument that Taner Timur develops. Timur argues that the way in which Turkish state managers have tended to adopt capitalism does not fulfil the requirements of the logic of international capitalism since state intervention fettered national landowners and merchants in the national economy (Timur, 1987: 21). From the perspective advanced here, Timur does not provide an adequate assessment of the logic of the development of capitalism in different spaces at different times. He also neither explains the role of the state in the global expansion of capitalism nor the articulation of capitalism in late capitalist countries. On the contrary, this book argues that the integration of Turkey into global free trade relations and the historical consolidation of capitalism in Turkey do not indicate a rupture in the history of Turkey, but a continuity in the restructuring of global free trade mechanisms and capitalist institutions from the late Ottoman period. This seems to contradict the evidence of greater internationalisation and major social changes during the 20th and 21st centuries.

The most prominent approach to the rise of Turkish business associations, known as Weberian institutionalism, encompasses several different arguments. Most of the institutionalist approaches (Buğra & Savaşkan, 2014; Öniş & Turem, 2001; Oniş, 1997; Baskan, 2010; Atli, 2011) analyse the emergence and rise of MUSIAD with reference to centre-periphery relations within Turkey, and basically argue that MUSIAD and TUSKON dominated the centre of gravity of Turkish capital in the 2000s. They further argue that the state supported the dominant fraction of Turkish capital organised within TUSIAD, while MUSIAD and TUSKON flourished in civil society without getting direct assistance from the state. The Weberian institutionalist model has influenced many of the other approaches taken by scholars. Some Marxist and Marxist-inspired approaches (Tugal, 2009; Sönmez, 2010; Marois, 2012; Savran, 2015; Tanyilmaz, 2015) explain the differences between these business associations based on their religious stances and use the distinction between an Islamic versus a secular bourgeoisie to characterise different business associations. These Marxist approaches define these business associations as monolithic entities without internal cracks and contradictions. They translate the Weberian analysis into Marxist terms, without challenging its content. Similarly, in explaining the rise and the development of MUSIAD and TUSKON, some liberal scholars employ an identity-based theoretical approach (e.g. Yavuz, 2003; 2009; Lorasdagi, 2010; Özdemir, 2014; Koyuncu, 2014; Balci, 2003). They define MUSIAD and TUSKON as representatives of the new urban middle class which emerged at the expense of TUSIAD. Additionally, this approach explains the organisation of MUSIAD and TUSKON as a struggle against the favouritism of the state towards the "Istanbul-based capital" represented by TUSIAD (Lorasdagi, 2010; Keyman, 2007; Özdemir, 2014; Demir, Ö. & Acar, M. & Toprak, M., 2004; Hendrick, 2009; Özel, 2015). The model of class formation implied here is simplistic and inappropriate. More precisely, these scholars reduce class patterns to distributional conflicts and daily activities of businesspeople, without looking at the formation of capital. This book goes beyond these simplistic explanations that mainly distinguish among business associations based on their cultural, religious, and geographical alignments. With reference to several authors (Öztürk 2011; Ercan 2002, Gültekin-karakaş, 2009), I eschew using these concepts to define the fractions in Turkish capital since the definition of classes is not only determined by their religious, cultural and traditional stances but also by the way in which they engage in the social relations of production. Accordingly, this book defines classes in terms of their positions in the social relations of production.

This book argues that adopting a classification for the different capital fractions is crucial when studying the political conflicts and transformations in social formation in Turkey. However, this study prefers not to use concepts like 'Anatolian/Istanbul capital' or 'secular/Islamist bourgeoisie' since the composition of social classes is not only determined by their religious, cultural and traditional stances but also by the way in which they engage in the social relations of production. Rather than reducing the particular positions of different business associations to their religious and cultural attitudes, this study examines them through an empirical analysis based on their positions in relations of production, exchange and reproduction. In contrast to mainstream approaches using the earlier categorisations, this study also includes a discussion of key historical moments of capitalism in Turkey, situating the class fractions socioeconomically. Accordingly, the study argues that the dialectical relationship between global class relations and the Turkish social formation has created international differentiation between countries as well as internal differentiation in institutional and class relations, with different fractions of Turkish capital situated in different ways in this composition. Thus, this study considers social relations of production in the Turkish social formation to categorise class forces and social classes in Turkey.

With regards to the Neo-Gramscian three-level analysis, this study divides capitalist classes in Turkey into three different fractions: national, internationally oriented, and transnational. This is one of the main differences between mainstream categorisations (including some Marxists) and the historical materialist approach taken here. The national fraction of capital refers to companies which operate in one single social formation and produce for the national market. The internationally oriented fraction of capital refers to companies which produce for international markets and have a national productive base. The mode of production of this fraction is generally integrated into global capitalism through joint venture and sub-contracting agreements, which operate in more than one social formation. The transnational fraction (TNC) refers to the companies which operate in different social formations and engage in production relations in different countries. This fraction also extends the flow of capital on an extended scale and a new level. The relations of production of this fraction are not dependent on a single state. This is the largest and most powerful fraction which accounts for majority of assets and sales. The categorisation of capitalist classes in Turkey is made according to the stages in the process of their capital accumulation at which each fraction of capital is integrated into the production-realisation-valorisation processes. Thus, it is not the location of ownership of the firms which determines their spatial scale; it is the production, realisation and valorisation processes which are considered (Avci, 2021).

This study suggests that although TNC in Turkey is mostly organised in TUSIAD, there are also nationally and internationally oriented fractions within TUSIAD. The main distinction between the TNC and other fractions is that they engage in trading industrial goods, encompassing companies whose activities in the industry range from metallurgy to steel. On the other hand, although there are transnational capital groups operating in TUSKON and MUSIAD, the dominant fraction in both associations is comprised of nationally and internationally oriented SMEs. As far as the distinction between TNC and others operating in TUSKON and MUSIAD is concerned, nationally and internationally oriented fractions mainly produce in Turkey for export.

In this regard, studying business associations (BAs) in Turkey is apposite, since it is a neglected area in the literature on the political economy of Turkey and Turkish politics. For this book, I have chosen three different BAs in Turkey, namely TUSIAD (*Türk İş İnsanlari ve Sanayicileri Derneği*, Turkish Industry & Business Association), MUSIAD (*Müstakil İşadamları ve Sanayicileri Derneği*, Independent Association of Industrialists and Businessmen) and TUSKON (*Türk İşadamları ve Sanayicileri Konfedarasyonu*, Turkish Confederation of Businessmen and Industrialists). These business associations are selected because of their economic and political impacts on the Turkish social formation as well as their members' presence in global free trade relations. However, there are some other important business organisations in terms of their economic and political impacts. The ones mentioned in this study are namely: TOBB (Union of Chambers and Stock Exchange), DEIK (Foreign Economic Relations Board), ISO (Istanbul Chambers of Industry), ITO (Istanbul Chambers of Commerce), TIM (Turkish Exporters Assembly), ASKON (Anatolian Lions Businessmen Associations), and TURKONFED (Turkish Enterprise and Business Confederation). Without ignoring the importance of these business organisations, the case studies of this book are important because of several reasons. First, TUSIAD is the oldest business association, which was established in Turkey in 1971. It represents the most transnationalised fraction of Turkish business and the largest companies in Turkey, which account for almost 85% of Turkish foreign trade. The book, therefore, focuses on TUSIAD to analyse the integration of larger-scale Turkish companies into the transnational relations of production. In addition to this, the complex interplay of the relationship between TUSIAD and the state provides insight into the role of the Turkish state in the expansion of Turkish capital towards the international market and to examine the shifting patterns of power relations within the power bloc. Second, MUSIAD was established in 1990 when Turkish capital passed through different stages and transformed into money capital which was on the eve of internationalisation. This case is important as the patterns of the global free trade system after the General Agreements on Tariffs and Trade (GATT) Uruguay Round which took between 1986 and 1994 had expanded beyond trade in goods and towards areas such as services, finance and public procurements. The cooperation between the state and MUSIAD in the AKP era has allowed MUSIAD affiliates to be awarded with public procurement contracts. The shifts in the organisation of different state institutions in the AKP era also created a space for the newly emerging small and medium-sized enterprises

(SMEs) to capture state subsidies and public procurement contracts. The case of MUSIAD is, therefore, essential to understand the integration of SMEs into the total circuit of capital and the internal conflicts between individual capitals in Turkey. Finally, TUSKON was established in 2005 with a very specific focus on foreign trade. Although there are larger holdings in TUSKON, it mainly consists of SMEs. The analysis of TUSKON is important for several reasons. First, it is known to be affiliated with the Gulen Movement (currently referred to in Turkey as FETO - The Fethullah Gulen Terror Organisation) which was one of the most crucial hegemonic contenders within the power bloc in the last two decades. The analysis is, therefore, important to grasp the class struggle within the power bloc. More precisely, it will help explain the political and economic factors behind the 15 July 2016 failed coup attempt which was organised by Gulenists within the army, police and many different groups. Second, the exclusion of TUSKON affiliates from the market after the failed coup attempt in 2016 has changed the power relations between different fractions of capital and between different power groups. In this regard, the complex interplay of the relationship between the AKP and TUSKON provides insights which help to unravel the transformation of the Turkish state in the post-coup period. Third, TUSKON played a significant role in integrating Turkey into the shifting patterns of global free trade relations especially in North Africa, Central Asia and the Middle East. Overall, these business associations provide a basis to analyse how Turkey internalised the expansion of global free trade within the Turkish social formation.

Accordingly, the book argues that the Turkish state has played an internal role in mediating the competing interests of business associations in Turkey. When the Greek Marxist Nicos Poulantzas examines the expansion of US capital into European countries, he argues that European countries internalised the interests of US transnational capital in different ways in the 1960s and 1970s (Poulantzas, [1974] 1975: 50–52). This, as Poulantzas argues, changed the class relations and the patterns of capital accumulation in European countries. This book examines Poulantzas' contention in relation to the case of Turkey. The Turkish state has also played specific roles in expanding the free trade regime, most obviously signing Free Trade Agreements (FTAs) which promote and secure the operations of international capital. These bilateral agreements are another way of integrating peripheral countries into the global free trade regime which is not possible within a multilateral setting due to the competing interests of different countries (Bieler & Morton, 2014: 42). This book, therefore, examines the role of the Turkish state in the post-1994 period and the impact of its activities on transnationalised relations of production and Turkey's integration into the global free trade mechanism.

2 Theoretical Framework

The book argues in accordance with theories of imperialism and uneven and combined development (hereafter U&CD) thesis, which was initially articulated by the Russian Marxist Leon Trotsky, that every country in the world has integrated into the global free trade system in different ways at different times (Trotsky, [1930] 2000). The main argument of this book is that the expansion of global free trade relations has differentially affected the social relations of production in different geographical areas and in different historical contexts. Turkey is a case in point. Accordingly, the book argues that the expansion of different forms of capital[1] into the global relations of production has affected the integration of Turkish business associations into global free trade relations in an uneven way. Uneven development has caused differences between business associations in terms of time, scale, geographical relocation, and patterns of transnationalisation. These differences will be explained in the later, empirical chapters.

This book argues that the integration of Turkey into global free trade relations is associated with the uneven development of global capitalism. Unevenness refers to the international differentiation between countries as well as internal differentiation in institutional and class relations. For combined development, Trotsky argues that the development of backward countries leads to a combination of different levels in the historic process (Trotsky [1930] 2000). His focus is the combination of two different modes of production, established feudal and newly formed capitalist relations of production, in Russia in the late 19th century. For Trotsky, Russia did not repeat the development of the western countries but adapted industrial development in western countries to Russia's backwardness (Trotsky, [1930] 2000). This means Russia skipped over

---

1 At this stage, I shall define the term "forms of capital" which will be used through entire book. Capital is a social relation, not a thing in itself, and it takes different forms. Commercial capital is the form of capital which functions in exchange relations, in other words commodity circulation (buying and selling goods, which may or may not have been produced for the market). This is a specific part of industrial capital which acts at the level of revalorization of commodity capital. Money/banking/financial capital is the form of capital which is used to purchase means of production or provide financial assistance to invest in industry. Industrial/productive capital is the specific form of capital which constitutes the capitalist character of production: the mass production of goods for sale on the market. It transforms the techniques and organisation of the labour process in order to obtain profits, for instance through mechanisation and efficiency gains. Finance capital is the fusion of industrial and money capital, which also has a transformative impact on the social formation (Marx, [1976] 1990: 247–258).

some stages, such as craft-guilds and manufacture, that had been achieved by advanced capitalist countries, leapfrogging to the "later" stage of industriali-sation. Accordingly, Russia has developed its industry thanks to the transfer of knowledge and technology from the advanced capitalist countries (Trotsky, [1930] 2000). As a result, Russia's industry in its capitalist structure and tech-nology almost outstripped the advanced capitalist countries (Trotsky, [1930] 2000), but without thoroughly developing the associated social institutions found in the west, and with large parts of the economy and society remaining feudal or quasi-feudal. In the case of Turkey, this book uses the idea of combi-nation (in U&CD) refers to the combining of the different stages of the process of capital accumulation, in other words internationalisation of different forms of capital in the post-1980 period (and not the combination of capitalism with a different mode of production). While the powerful formations in Turkey are all capitalist, they represent different types or "levels" of capitalism which are integrated only with difficulty. Internationalisation of capital, in the Marxist sense, refers to expansion of money, commodities, and production across time and space. Thus, it is not the location of ownership of the firms which determines their spatial scale; it is the production, realisation and reproduc-tion processes which are sometimes internationalised (Bryan, 2007: 269–270). Turkey has unevenly experienced internationalisation of commercial, money and industrial capital, meaning that some parts of the economy are thoroughly internationalised, others more partially, and others barely at all. Hence, the expansion of capital globally has changed the social relations of production in Turkey. One area in which we may grasp these changes is by studying business associations in Turkey.

To analyse the role of Turkish business associations in global free trade rela-tions, and the impact of global free trade relations on the Turkish social for-mation, this book uses the historical materialist perspective which was first articulated by Karl Marx (Marx, [1976] 1990; Marx, 1973). As this approach states that everything is interconnected (Ollman, 1993), a social phenomenon becomes the product of both social structures and historical processes. A his-torical materialist study examines concepts in their structural totality as well as the dialectical relationships between structure and agency. Therefore, the analysis of free trade cannot be constructed as a separate sphere, distinct from the relationship between structure (free trade system) and agency (business associations and the state), or between the general and the specific (Ollman, 1993: 64). In other words, the structure of the contemporary free trade system and the agencies engaging in these relations are both relevant to this study. Therefore, this study does not exclude historical changes and structural totalities, which are interior to each other, from its analysis. Moreover, as it is difficult to conceptualise the whole, historical materialism suggests considering everything as constituent parts of the whole. In Bertell Ollman's words, totality "is a logical construct that refers to the way the whole [is made] present through internal relations in each of its parts" (1993: 72). This means that it is not possible to analyse the state without focusing on its different and conflicting parts. This study adopts the historical materialist approach to grasp historical conditions, class struggle, power relations, changes at the state level and the level of social structures, and international integration of business associations as part of the whole picture.

This book argues that expanding global free trade relations have affected the social formation in Turkey. In order to unpack this argument, this study initially focuses on the relations of production by engaging with Marx and Engels' own writings on free trade, which are mostly focused on the role of free trade in the global exploitation of labour, transferring surplus value globally and creating a capitalist world market which is the basis for the capitalist mode of production. Secondly, this study engages with theories of imperialism in order to grasp the necessity of global expansion of capital in the context of free trade. Thirdly, a major part of this project benefits from a neo-Gramscian analysis of the U&CD thesis to analyse unequal exchange relations in the context of free trade. This neo-Gramscian approach enables this study to examine how unevenness is always created and (re)produced at the global and regional level, and how these complex relations between countries, regions and sectors are interconnected. Accordingly, the U&CD approach provides a broader perspective through which to analyse the integration of business associations in Turkey into global relations of free trade.

In this regard, this study employs a neo-Gramscian understanding of the state with a specific reference to Poulantzas. Poulantzas' ideas on the organisation and activities of the state are influenced by the Italian Marxist Antonio Gramsci (1971: 261). Gramsci's works provided insights which Poulantzas used advance underdeveloped fields of Marxist state theory, such as to examine the political class struggle reflected within the state structures and judiciary (Jessop, 1985: 50). There are several important points one can emphasise to understand the links between Gramsci and Poulantzas, and to show how Poulantzas is used in this book. First, Poulantzas follows Gramsci in arguing that states cannot be reduced to governments. Instead, Poulantzas defines the state as a social relation in which political class struggle and reproduction of modes of production become crystallised (Jessop, 1982: 191). The actual sites of political class struggle (re)produce the capitalist society and world market at the same time (Poulantzas, 2000:25). This means states have an intertwined role in both economic and political spheres. Therefore, the relationship between the state and capital cannot be constructed as a relationship of mutually exclusive, separate entities. The state only has relative autonomy from the relations of production. The state, therefore, is not an extra-economic structure from which class struggle, classes, and forms of power are absent (Poulantzas [1978] 2000:14). This means politico-ideological relations are always intrinsic to the constitution of relations of production as they play an internal role in the reproduction of domination and subordination which involve the process of exploitation and production (Poulantzas [1978] 2000: 26–7). In this regard, the book examines the organisation of the Turkish state and how it engages in social relations of production. Second, the concept of hegemony is useful to understand the relationship between business associations and the state, and between dominated classes and the state. Poulantzas extends this Gramscian concept in a way that is applicable to understanding power struggles within a power bloc, and how the hegemony of one fraction is constituted not only at the state level but also within the dominated classes. Also, Poulantzas argues against Gramsci that hegemony should not be studied only from the class position but also in terms of the exercise of hegemony by a specific class fraction within its class or over other classes (Jessop, 1985: 321). Third, Poulantzas focuses on the institutional materiality of the capitalist state as a complex of apparatuses, an aspect which is largely ignored by Gramsci. This approach provides this study with an overarching theory through which to analyse the organisational framework of the Turkish state. In practice, the Turkish state constructs its hegemony not only through repression, but also through a fragmented network of activities in the social relations of production. Finally, and most importantly, as Poulantzas ([1974]1975: 97) argues, nation-states mediate the internationalisation of the state and capital. In this regard, the book aims to examine the role of the state in Turkey and how it manages to unite domestic capitalist classes to maintain the (re)production of international accumulation. This approach provides me with an opportunity not only to understand the relationship between Turkish business associations and the state, and also to reveal the tensions and contradictions between domestic and transnational capitalist class fractions involved in this process.

3   Synopses of Chapters

Chapter 1 of this book constructs the theoretical background in relation to free trade and the state, and critically engages with mainstream theories of political economy, namely classical-liberal, neo-classical and institutional. These approaches view free trade as producing similar, beneficial outcomes in all countries, though they differ on the role of the state. Contrary to mainstream approaches, Chapter 1 explains how free trade creates and exacerbates unevenness in global capitalism. It argues that, as a result of the uneven expansion of relations of production, free trade creates global unevenness not only between countries but also between sectors, regions, and classes engaged in production, circulation and revalorisation processes. In this regard, the chapter pays attention to the structural peculiarities of each site in which free trade takes place, and its primary concern is to grasp the role of the state in facilitating free trade relations. To do so, it initially engages with Marx' and Engels' analysis of free trade, which pays attention to the social relations of production and the global exploitation of labour. Subsequently, the chapter engages with theories of imperialism and the U&CD approach with regards to unequal exchange relations between countries. Unequal exchange refers to the trade of goods whose prices of production are not equal, which is a result of the differences in sectoral productivity in unevenly situated parts of the global capitalist system. Accordingly, it demonstrates how companies engage in production relations in peripheral countries. It argues that a global free trade system based on unequal exchange relations reproduces the social relations of production which are associated with the division of production into segments and the creation of transnational production networks. The chapter outlines how the capitalist state manages the global expansion of capital. More precisely, it uncovers the role of the state in global free trade relations which included internalisation of the global class relations in a historically specific social formation. Overall, this chapter provides an analytical framework to understand the contradictory process which intensified the conflicts, tension, alliances and compromises between the Turkish state and the BAs, which is associated with the integration of BAs into global relations of free trade.

Chapter 2 provides a chronological and systematic analysis of the development of capitalism and capitalist classes in Turkey to demonstrate where Turkey sits in the international division of labour. It also establishes links between global free trade relations and the historical consolidation of capitalism within the context of the Turkish social formation to outline the emergence of the BAs in Turkey. The chapter draws attention to the changing patterns of capital accumulation in Turkey so as to grasp the change in the social relations of production within a historical framework. This chapter demonstrates that the development of capitalism is not a linear progression and Turkey has integrated into global capitalism in a different way from core capitalist countries. The core capitalist countries integrated into the global free trade relations through the export of capital. On the contrary, Turkey has integrated through the import of industrial capital. Subsequently, the chapter provides a broader analysis of the Turkish economy, notably with respect to its dependency on foreign investments and foreign trade. Thus, it will link up with TUSIAD, MUSIAD and TUSKON whose positions in the global value chain vary greatly.

Chapter 3 provides an empirical analysis of the role of TUSIAD in the social relations of production. Accordingly, the chapter explores the emergence of TUSIAD within the context of shifts in patterns of capital accumulation in the Global South as well as the developments in Turkey. In this regard, it draws attention to the different means of capital accumulation in which TUSIAD-affiliated companies engaged in different periods. In contrast with mainstream approaches, the analysis of TUSIAD in this chapter is not only based on regional, religious or cultural dynamics but also and more precisely, the position of TUSIAD affiliates within the social relations of production. In this sense, mainstream concepts like *Istanbul bourgeoise, secular bourgeoise,* and *Kemalist bourgeoisie* are discussed and critiqued or situated in class terms. Subsequently, the chapter examines the nature of the relationship between the state and TUSIAD in order to map out the role of TUSIAD in the reproduction of hegemony throughout the different stages of the internationalisation of capital. In accordance with this aim, the chapter analyses some specific companies within TUSIAD, such as KOÇ Holding, Sabancı Holding, Anadolu Group, Cukurova Group, and ENKA Holding.

Chapter 4 argues that although MUSIAD mainly consists of SMEs which mainly operate in low-tech industries and target the Middle East and North African countries in their integration into the global free trade relations, it also has larger-scale members operating transnationally. The main purposes of the chapter are to analyse the role of MUSIAD in global free trade relations and to examine the relationship between MUSIAD and the state. Firstly, the chapter explores the ways in which MUSIAD-affiliated companies are situated in social relations of production, and at the same time, it examines how MUSIAD mediates the consolidation and survival of different class fractions. Accordingly, the chapter describes the dominant sectors in which MUSIAD-affiliated businesses operate and outlines the divisions and convergences between MUSIAD-affiliated companies and other companies affiliated with TUSIAD and TUSKON. This is crucial in situating the class positions of MUSIAD-affiliated companies. This analysis is based on how MUSIAD members are situated in the relations of production. Accordingly, this chapter focuses on the member firms of MUSIAD in provincial cities and explores the differences between larger and smaller businesses organised within MUSIAD. This analysis also provides an overview of the role of SMEs in Turkish foreign trade. In what follows, the chapter explores the role of MUSIAD in the power bloc to unpack the dialectical relationship between MUSIAD and the state. The chapter argues that the transnationalisation of Turkish capital in the 2000s changed the nature of the relationship between the state and capital in Turkey. To illustrate this, it examines the planning and promotion services provided by municipal governments in provincial cities.

Chapter 5 demonstrates that although there are larger capital groups within TUSKON, it mainly consists of SMEs which mainly operate in the health, education and construction sectors. It examines TUSKON in terms of its place in the social relations of production in Turkey in order to map out and define the class characteristics of TUSKON-affiliated companies. Contrary to mainstream approaches, the chapter does not reduce the particular class positions of TUSKON members to religious and cultural frameworks and examines TUSKON through an empirical analysis based on relations of production, exchange and reproduction. In relation to this, it initially examines the historical development of TUSKON, and examines to what extent TUSKON members engage in the process of production, exchange, and reproduction. It also explores the sectoral and regional unevenness between TUSKON members, and the larger businesses represented by TUSIAD. This analysis envelops the theoretical arguments of the uneven development approach mentioned in Chapter 2. Subsequently, the chapter examines the power and class relations which TUSKON-affiliated companies and Gülenists enter into within the power bloc. In this regard, it demonstrates the political class struggle which occurs between different BAs and power groups represented inside the state apparatus. Furthermore, the chapter investigates the crucial role of TUSKON in the hegemonic project of the AKP governments until 2013. In this regard, the chapter examines the relationship between the Gülenists and the AKP in the last two decades with the purpose of clarifying the shifting patterns of the political class struggle within the power bloc. This includes the analysis of the political and economic factors behind the 15 July failed coup attempt, and reconfiguration of the relationship between different BAs in the post-coup period. In its final section, the chapter pays particular attention to the ways in which TUSKON members integrate into global relations of free trade. In this analysis, specific companies like BOYDAK Holding, Orkide Group, and Naksan Holding are investigated to examine the international integration of TUSKON-affiliated larger-scale capitalists. In order to illustrate the space of SMEs affiliated with TUSKON and the specific forms of their integration, the chapter investigates the role of Turkish schools funded by TUSKON-affiliated companies and the effectiveness of trade bridges and conferences organised by TUSKON.

"Chapter 6, Conclusions and Reflections" provides conclusions and reflections on the study. Having provided various theoretical arguments and advanced various concepts, the chapter discusses the material findings of the book in relation to the research questions. In its final section, the chapter concludes by making proposals for future research.

CHAPTER 1

The New Phase of Imperialism and Uneven and Combined Development

The main characteristics of our time are instability, inequalities, and grow-ing imbalances between countries and classes in different social formations. This book argues that free trade generates these enormous imbalances not only between countries but also within countries, regions, sectors and classes engaging in the process of production. Accordingly, this book contends that capitalism is always in motion. What drives this motion are social relations of production, competition, and class struggle in every different social formation. Therefore, there are always shifts in global capital accumulation processes, and the way capital is transnationally realised and reproduced cannot be under-stood as just an exchange relation between national units. In other words, free trade cannot be considered merely as inter-state or international exchange relations.

Accordingly, the book uses the historical materialist (HM) perspective which was first articulated by Karl Marx to examine the dialectical relationship between global free trade relations and the Turkish social formation (Marx, [1976] 1990; Marx, 1973). This approach states that everything is intercon-nected (Ollman, 1993), so that a social phenomenon becomes the product of both social structures and historical processes. As a historical materialist study examines the concepts in their structural totality as well as the dialectical rela-tionships between structure and agency, the analysis of free trade cannot be based on the idea of trade as a distinctive sphere, separate from the relation-ship between structure (free trade system) and agency (business associations and the state), or between the general and the specific. In other words, the structure of the contemporary free trade system and the agencies engaging in trade and economic relations are both relevant to this study. Therefore, this study does not distinguish between historical changes and structural totali-ties, which are considered instead to be interior to each other. Moreover, as it is difficult to conceptualise the totality itself, historical materialism suggests considering everything as constituent parts of the whole. In Bertell Ollmann's words, totality "is a logical construct that refers to the way the whole [is made] present through internal relations in each of its parts" (1993: 72). This study adopts the historical materialist (HM) approach to grasp historical conditions, class struggle, power relations, changes at state level and structures, and international integration of business associations as part of the whole picture.

In accordance with the HM approach, this study defines free trade as a generalisation of commodity production at the world scale. In other words, free trade acts in a direction that leads to an expansion of the sphere of capitalist production and speeds up the process of capital accumulation. This, at the same time, results in the global exploitation of labour as a result of capitalists' goal of reducing the value of variable capital. This, in turn, creates an ever-expanding world market, which results in colonial expansion so as to capture more markets and resources (Marx & Engels, 1894: 235). At this stage, this study benefits from theories of imperialism in order to explain the necessity of global expansion of capital in the context of free trade. It is necessary to touch upon the significance of Lenin and his theory of imperialism. Lenin describes the features of imperialism, which are the concentration of production and growth of monopolistic firms which results in centralisation of capital, the fusion of financial/money capital with industrial capital, and the export of capital which results in the expansion of relations of production beyond national borders. He gives the example of 19th century England which applied free trade policies overseas while protecting its national economy with high rates of tariffs (Lenin, 1999: 70). The main purpose of free trade policies, for Lenin, is to utilise surplus capital in order to increase the profits of capitalists by exporting capital to backward countries (ibid, 71). Capitalism, as Lenin argues, has become overripe in certain capitalist countries. The export of capital was necessary to overcome this problem. This was achieved by subjugating the backward countries, where profits are usually high, local wages and the land rents are low, and raw materials are extremely cheap (ibid). In this regard, Lenin's central claim is that a significant amount of British capital has been invested in its colonies (ibid, 72), which thus serve as capital sinks, heading off crisis in Britain. In this connection, Lenin argues that finance capital has created an epoch for the imperial countries in which they obtained certain advantages in colonised countries. For instance, banks founded in colonised countries have played a major role in establishing links between colonial and colonised countries.

From a similar perspective, Rosa Luxemburg claims that the general sine qua non of capitalist expansion is outward enlargement in the sense of bringing non-capitalist spaces into capitalist social relations of production to ensure an increase in the surplus value (Luxemburg, [1913] 2003: 338–39). The desire of capitalists in acquiring non-capitalist areas, for Luxemburg, leads to a form of imperialism which demands unrestricted accumulation (ibid, 166: 426). Luxemburg also argues that, in the era of free trade, the primary purpose of capitalists is to capture and monopolise non-capitalist areas at home and abroad (ibid, 431). Luxemburg explains the necessity of free trade as a requirement for reproducing capital accumulation and to realise surplus value by capturing non-capitalist spaces.

Ray Kiely critically engages with these theories of imperialism, objecting that the trade between core capitalist countries was more significant than the trade between core capitalist countries and their colonies (Kiely: 2010: 77). In support of his claim, he stresses that from 1880 to 1938 only 9% of the total exports of core capitalist countries went to their colonies (ibid). Moreover, Kiely is also critical of the argument that outward expansion is the sine qua non of capital accumulation. Rather, he tends to argue that capital has continued to accumulate in home countries as well as abroad (ibid, 81). However, Bieler and Morton suggest that outward expansion is a significant tool in order for capital to overcome over-accumulation crises, while arguing that this cannot be considered as the only way to overcome such crises (Bieler & Morton, 2014: 37).

It should be noted that the post-1945 international order is very different from that of the first wave of free trade imperialism. In this period, theories of imperialism paid more attention to North-South relations rather than the relations between core capitalist countries. This is not only because of the shifting characteristics of capital accumulation, in other words, transnationalisation of productive capital, but also the role of the new agencies, namely, new sovereign states in the colonies. This term coincided with a sharp commitment to open-door free trade policies by the US and the new sovereign states on the European continent (Kiely, 2010: 91–93). In line with this thinking, the GATT was established, which became known as the World Trade Organisation in 1995. In the context of the post-1945 period, the GATT was successful in promoting free trade policies while leaving some space for states to maintain protectionist policies, such as those in Germany and Japan (Kiely, 2010:101). Overall, the expanded free trade regime after the 1994 Uruguay Round has had different impacts in different spaces as it integrated different locations of production into the global free trade mechanism at different times and in different ways.

In order to highlight the significance of imperialism theories and the uneven interactions between different social formations, the book uses the U&CD approach. In the early period of the 20th century, Leon Trotsky investigated the way in which Russia integrated into the global world economy. He argues that the vector of uneven and combined development provided the momentum in the process of Russian development (Trotsky, [1930] 2000). Trotsky's aim was to provide a comprehensive and connected explanation of human history, on the one hand, and of Russian development, on the other. The starting point for Trotsky was the "most general law" of human development, which is "unevenness" (ibid). For Trotsky, it is important to pay particular attention to the dialectical relations and interactions in the development of societies, and the differences and multiplicities between them, which create and reproduce the conditions of unevenness. By doing so, it is possible to capture the cultural and class relations not only between societies but also within societies. As a second universal characteristic of global development, Trotsky makes use of the concept of combined development (ibid). According to his analysis of global development, it is crucial to focus on the plurality of the existing sociological forms and internal relations of societies, which are also in a dialectical interaction with other societies (Ashman, 2012:62). The development of any given society is determined by its "interactive relations with other developmentally differentiated societies" (Anievas & Nisancioglu, 2015: 48). The lacuna that this approach attempts to fill is how societies change, how they interact and how a dialectical relationship is created between them (Anievas & Nisancioglu: 2015: 44). However, this approach does not overlook the significance of internal dynamics embedded in any given social formation. Moreover, U&CD arguments contend that the international is "itself part and parcel of [the] wider socio-historical development process" (ibid). This implies that countries are economically and socially integrated into the world market in different and unequal ways (Trotsky, 1936, PT I).

Extending this theory further, Samir Amin explains how the conditions of U&CD and the relations of unequal exchange between unevenly developed parts of the world have been constructed. Historically speaking, he outlines two different stages of the outward expansion of capitalism, in other words, how the early capitalist countries managed to integrate the latecomers into the global capitalist economy. The starting point for Amin is that once the early capitalist countries have completed the process of primitive accumulation whose essential feature is unequal exchange, the essence of unequal exchange results from differences in the prices of production, and different rates of productivity (Bieler & Morton, 2014:40). These differences, in turn, are the result of the uneven development which has characterised the global development of capitalism. Accordingly, as the rate of surplus value is higher in the backward countries, international trade is based on the exchange of products produced at an unequal cost. Amin argues that the process of outward expansion was necessary for capitalists in order to exploit new regions (Amin, 1976: 187). This was an attempt to overcome the negative consequences of the tendency of the rate of profit to fall. It was achieved through the export of capital to peripheral spaces where global capitalists enjoyed low wage costs and high rates of surplus value. As Smith additionally argues, the low wage advantage is not the only factor attracting transnational companies to peripheral spaces. As can be seen in the case of the Bangladeshi garment industry, transnational corporations are also attracted by the flexibility of workers, the absence or weakness of independent trade unions, and the low rates of taxation by the local governments (Smith, 2016, 24). In the case of Turkey, it is the geographical proximity of Turkey to the European market which reduces transaction costs. More importantly, capital is also attracted by the declining price of labour in recent years which is the result of the dramatic depreciation of Turkish lira against the US dollar. In short, through these unequal exchange relations, capitalists have managed to transfer surplus value between different locations of production.

These unequal exchange relations, which are the direct consequences of capital accumulation and reproduction of the relations of production, have led to the revival of international capital in the age of monopoly capitalism. This brings us to the conclusion that uneven development is the consequence of free trade policies which are carried out 'behind the backs' of actors (Kiely, 2010: 188). This is to say that uneven and combined development and the way in which free trade operates in a globalised capitalist system develops the advanced countries at the expense of the rest. In line with this thinking, it becomes evident that agents (states, multinational/transnational companies, and international financial institutions) play a crucial role in creating a comparative advantage for countries in the Global North while hampering countries in the Global South (Kiely, 2010: 188).

1   Free Trade/Transnationalisation of Production and the Role of the State

This chapter initially pays attention to the social relations of production and the global exploitation of labour. Subsequently, the chapter engages with theories of imperialism and the uneven and combined development (U&CD) approach regarding unequal exchange relations between countries. Unequal exchange refers to the trade of goods whose prices of production are not equal, which is a result of the differences in sectoral productivity in unevenly situated parts of the global capitalist system. Accordingly, this theory demonstrates how companies engage in production relations in peripheral countries. It argues that a global free trade system based on unequal exchange relations reproduces the social relations of production which are associated with the division of production into segments and the creation of transnational production networks. The section outlines how the capitalist state manages the global expansion of capital, more precisely, it uncovers the role of the state in global free trade relations which included internalisation of the global class relations in a historically specific social formation. Overall, this section provides an analytical framework to understand the contradictory process which intensified the conflicts, tension, alliances and compromises between the Turkish state and the business associations (BAS), which is associated with the integration of the BAS into global relations of free trade.

After the completion of the GATT Uruguay Round in 1994, free trade policies have pushed neo-liberal restructuring across the world (Bieler, Hilary, Lindberg, 2014). The relationship between core capitalist countries and countries in backward conditions has been reconfigured in this era, which has led to the global centrality of transnational corporate production (Hart-Landsberg, 2013: 14). The Uruguay Round brought about the most substantial reforms of the free trade system since the establishment of the GATT. One of the main objectives of the Uruguay Round was to make the world trading system transparent, or in other words, liberalise the system. Hence, the expansion of capital after the completion of the Uruguay Round does not simply refer to the expansion of exports of goods, but also international copyright, services, and investment (Bieler & Morton, 2014: 42). Moreover, the Uruguay Round has weakened government control over foreign trade policies and opened up key sectors of national economies to uneven international competition.

There has been a departure from the previous production strategies adapted by transnational corporations. For instance, the sphere of industrial production has spread mainly to Third World countries (Hart-Landsberg, 2013: 16–18). This process was associated with the division of production process into segments and the creation of cross-border production networks, which resulted in a shift in the dynamics of global accumulation. Capital thus invested in Third World countries to "locate the labour-intensive production segments of these goods" in low-wage, low-cost localities when manufacturing textiles, electronics, and technologically advanced goods (ibid: 83). There was also an attempt to cheapen the cost of production. The importance of production in the Third World was highlighted by the fact that around 50 percent of foreign direct investment went to the Third World in 2010 (UNCTAD, 2011: 3). Furthermore, transnational corporations have cooperated closely with 'partner' manufacturers in order to produce parts and components of a final product through their control over the production process (Hart-Landsberg, 2013: 18). For instance, the required parts and components of an Apple product were produced in four different countries: Japan, South Korea, Germany, and the US (ibid, 21). These products are then shipped to China in order to export to other countries.

Since most countries in the Global South produce and export primary commodities, while importing high-tech products, the gap between countries widens (Ashman, 2010:190). More importantly, on the one hand, the capitalist countries in the Global North continue to exercise enormous power over high-value sectors and high-skill-based technological production. The countries in the Global South, on the other hand, still provide lower wages and supply high surplus labour, yet struggle with high barriers to entry (Kiely 2012: 165). This suggest that technologically advanced firms automatically benefit from free trade. As mentioned earlier, if disadvantaged firms enter free trade relations without any preparation for this challenge, they will most likely become suppliers of cheap labour and resources (Shaikh, 2007: 10). Historical evidence on the development of free trade demonstrates that the early capitalist countries implemented protectionist foreign trade policies in the early stages of development. Emphasising the specificities of the development of capitalism in these countries, it must be acknowledged that they have adopted free trade policies only once the capital accumulation process has been completed within their national territories (Shaikh, 2007:7). Hence, their implementation of free trade policies must be understood as a way of overcoming barriers to capital expansion. Historical evidence from England, Germany, Japan, and the USA demonstrate beyond doubt that the expansion of capitalism in the countries in the Global North - with some exceptions - has demanded the protection of national borders from external markets. As Engels ([1848] 2000: 4) has already pointed out in his introduction to the Marx' speech on the question of free trade:

> Protection at home was needless to manufacturers who beat all their foreign rivals, and whose very existence was staked on the expansion of their exports. Protection at home was of advantage to none but the producers of articles of food and other raw materials, to the agricultural interest, which, under the existing circumstances in England, meant the receivers of rent, the landed aristocracy.

The above passage confirms that one aspect of unevenness arises due to the implementation of free trade policies. The process of adaptation and integration of the rest of the world into these unequal exchange relations should be conceived as a historical necessity for capitalism in overcoming recurring crises of capital accumulation. This neither creates a convergence among countries, nor improves the conditions of workers in backward countries. Instead, it considerably widens the gap between the countries in the Global South and North, and results in subjugation of other classes by transnational classes.

In the post-1994 period, the classical argument that free trade brings development was rephrased "if the countries in the Global South open up to free trade they will automatically catch up with the countries in the Global North" (Bieler, 2012: 10). However, most of the countries in the Global South deindustrialised in the era of neoliberal free trade, and this increased their import dependence. This shows that universalised unequal exchange relations create and deepen the unevenness between the various parties engaging in the trading process (Ashman 2010: 188) and leaves not only countries but also classes dominated and subjugated. This unevenness in global development, as well as unequal distribution of income, would lead to an economic convergence among the early capitalist countries as late capitalist countries tend to diverge because of the uneven and combined dynamics of global capitalism which are reinforced by free trade relations (Saad-Filho, 2015:65). In other words, this ultimately brings into existence an ever-growing disparity between rich and poor countries. This is simply a reflection of free trade policies, which reproduce unevenness and instability rather than convergence and equilibration.

2   Internationalisation of the State and Its Internal Functions

In Marxist theory, the state is considered a form of social relations through which class and power relations are expressed. This is why neither states, nor markets, nor classes can be taken as independent, singular units and determinant factors in themselves, but only as part of a relational system. Therefore, states cannot be discursively constructed or examined as entities separate from the other parts constituting the social relations of production but should be viewed as internally related, rather than treating each social force as a 'variable independent of one another' (Bieler & Morton, 2008: 116). This methodological and epistemological approach is called 'the philosophy of internal relations' (Ollman & Badeen, 2015: 3; Ollman, 2015: 10). Positing the axioms of this philosophy will help this study to theorise the state with its relational and different clashing parts and to frame the relationship between the state and capital as an internal one rather than an external one. As the nature of the state cannot be separated from intra-class and inter-class struggles within and outside the power bloc, an analysis of the state requires focusing on the dialectical relationship between dominant and dominated classes as well as within the dominant classes. This then requires an analysis to place a special emphasis on how the relationship between dominant and dominated classes is constituted, formed, and reproduced within the internal structures of the state in order to grasp the dialectical relationship between the different class fractions forming and shaping the state.

Poulantzas argues that the relationship between class forces within the power bloc is not static, and the state, in turn, is not a neutral agent between these classes. Instead, it is a "material condensation" of the relations between classes and class forces (Poulantzas [1978] 2000: 73). The term "power bloc" is used to refer to an arena which designates an alliance among dominant classes and fractions (Poulantzas [1974] 1975: 24). This is to say that social classes and class struggle are not exclusively constructed prior to the state, or to the production process which is related to the ideological, political, economic and social practices of the state (Poulantzas [1978] 2000: 37; Bieler & Morton, 2006:169). Poulantzas, therefore, stresses that the state is a social relation and one of the actual sites of political class struggle which reproduce the social relations of production (Poulantzas, [1978] 2000:25; Jessop, 1985: 336–37).

The most significant reconstruction of Poulantzas is the separation of the political sphere from the economic, which constitutes the *relative autonomy* of the state in terms of establishing the unity of dominant classes as well as constituting the relationship between dominant and dominated classes. Relative autonomy means that the state plays an intertwined economic role in relations of production and in the class struggle, yet simultaneously to this, it maintains a distinct socio-political role in the process of (re)production of the world market and capitalist social relations (Marois, 2012:27). As Poulantzas argues, there is today an enhanced role for the state in the public sector, taxation, and state credits, which are the ways in which the redistribution of surplus value is determined, and allocation of money is realised (Jessop, 1985: 350). The relative autonomy of the state along with class unity of the state apparatuses in the capitalist mode of production necessitates a rigid separation of the conflicting fields of the class struggle. This separation poses a great challenge for class unity for both the dominated popular masses and for some fractions of the dominant classes (Poulantzas, [1968] 1978:91–92; Poulantzas, [1978]2000:127). As the dominant classes are not able to act as a uniform and single entity due to their contradictory and conflicting interests, the crucial role performed by the state apparatuses are, therefore, managing class contradictions and securing the cohesion of dominant classes, while disorganising the dominated classes (Poulantzas, [1968]1978:54; Jessop, 1982:186). In the same vein, capital also cannot be expressed as a singular, homogeneous or total entity within the state. It is safe to say that state policies might favour some fractions of capital while undermining other fractions. This approach gives the state a distinctive and unifying role which is not only maintained or controlled beneath the state's bureaucratic apparatuses (government, military, judiciary etc.), but also through the power of the dominant ideology that operates through universities, mass media, family and so on (Poulantzas [1978]2000: 127).

The integration of American capital into an international process of accumulation in Europe and other countries in the post-war era, or in other words the internationalisation of trade and Foreign Direct Investments (FDI), constituted new dynamics in terms of the role of the state in the economic sphere and contributed to the restoration of global financial markets under the hegemonic leadership of the USA (Panitch & Gindin, 2004:18). This hegemony was not challenged by the revival of European and Japanese capital, despite the tensions and contradictions between the USA, Europe, and Japan. Rather, in Poulantzas' words, "the question for them is to reorganize a hegemony that they still accept ...; what the battle is actually over is the share of the cake" (Poulantzas, [1974] 1975:87). In this period, the internationalisation of capital and global integration was achieved through FDI and cross-border networks established by American corporations (ibid.: 19). In short, the internal structure of the state and classes in core capitalist countries have been influenced by American FDI. Capitalist classes in different countries, as Poulantzas also argues, have interacted with the international capital flowing into their country of origin to maintain and reproduce their social formations in the US-led global order (Panitch & Gindin, 2004:20).

The role of the state in the era of the internationalisation of capital has been reconfigured regarding both formations of social relations and imperialist production chains, which are fundamentally characterised by uneven development (Poulantzas, [1974] 1975: 39). This uneven and combined characteristic of capitalist development in the monopoly capital (imperialist) stage refers to the specificity of each social formation, and the role of the state in this process. As Poulantzas ([1974] 1975: 42–43) clearly states:

> This specificity is a function of the forms that the dominance of the capitalist mode of production at the international level assumes over the other modes and forms of production that exist within a social formation.

It is in this context that the internationalisation of the state's functions become important. Nation states have played primary roles in establishing and reproducing "the social relations and institutions of class, property, currency, contract and markets" as well as mediating the international process of capital accumulation (Panitch & Gindin, 2004: 17). As Poulantzas argues, the era of internationalisation of capital neither surpasses nor bypasses national states (Poulantzas [1974] 1975: 73). Most present nation-states do not have a high capacity to control the internationalisation of capital accumulation. However, they enjoy some capability to influence capital accumulation within national borders (Bryan, [1987]2007:254). The important class relations for the reproduction of the national type of production and accumulation are created and secured 'within the space of the nation and using the nation-state' (ibid.). This new relationship between capitalism and states can be understood as the internationalisation of the state, since each national state became responsible for "managing its domestic capitalist order in a way that contributes to managing the international capitalist order" (Poulantzas [1974] 1975: 73). This phenomenon referred to the internationalisation of capital which was internalised within each state in different forms at different times (Bieler & Morton, 2006: 170).

The intervention of the state in the economy, in turn, operates in favour of dominant fractions of capital and against other fractions (Poulantzas [1974] 1975: 71). For instance, national or international capital is always given support by national states, such as public subsidies, tax reductions and so on. This is a way of locking-in and smoothing the process of internationalisation, concentration and expansion of capital. As the internationalisation of capital not only increases global integration, but affects domestic social formations, it has also led to significant changes in domestic class structures (Kiely, 2010: 141). As a result of the deepening of markets and increased competition in the era of neoliberalism, the internal fabric of states and the crucial role that states should perform have been reconstructed and shifted at the expense of the productive forces. This US-led global project of encouraging the free flow of capital across the world demanded the establishment of new formal and informal mechanisms in different forms in different regions and countries (Panitch & Gindin, 2004: 22; 2012: 224). The development of such mechanisms within the internal structures of individual nation states is performed by the states themselves.

Anchored within the broader debate relating to the role of the state in global free trade relations in the era of neoliberal globalisation, the concepts of the space of the state and the space of capital have become contested. The debate revolved around whether the state still fulfils its internal functions or whether, in contrast, the transnationalisation of capital has superseded the space of nation-states. Indeed, transnationalisation of capital has different impacts on different types of states, such as governance states, export-oriented developmental states, metropolitan capitalist states, or rentier oil states, but states still operate as localised power containers that mediate the contradictions between the fractions of capital within a particular territory (Jessop, 2010: 40). In this regard, it remains crucial to recognise the continued importance of the state's national space regarding its role in internalising transnational/international[1] capital's interests within the domestic structures of state institutions.[2] Before the role of the state is discussed, the "transnationalisation of capital and state" should be outlined.

"The globalisation of the production process" is viewed as *transnationalisation of production* (Robinson & Harris, 2000: 11).[3] This means that the shift or transformation of the organisation of production in the late 1970s divided the process of production into segments, and created transnational networks in different provinces, countries and regions (Bieler, 2000: 20). In particular, the growing number of transnational corporations (TNCs), and the relationship between world export chains and FDI can be perceived as the most significant processes which demonstrate the increased significance of transnational production networks (Bieler, 2006: 49–50). However, this does not automatically mean that transnationalisation of production leads to a borderless global market; rather, it is to emphasise that the outflow of FDI and the growth of TNCs are part and parcel of the globalisation process (Bieler, 2000: 22). According to Robinson, transnationalisation of capital has led to the emergence of a Transnational State (TNS), which is responsible for mediating

---

1   Leo Panitch and Sam Gindin argue that the internationalisation of American capital did not spawn a "transnational capitalist class," loosened from any state moorings or about to spawn a supranational global state; "national capital," in the shape of firms with dense historic linkages and distinct characteristics, did not disappear, as international capital still "saw the American state as the ultimate guarantor of capitalist interests globally" (Panitch & Gindin, 2012: 11:345).

2   It is also crucial to highlight the fact that transnational capital's interests are internalised in different forms in different countries, in ways which are characterised by uneven development. Further, geopolitical rivalries between states need to be taken into account in order to underline the fact that class struggle does not only exist at the state level but also at the international level (Bieler & Morton, 2013: 44).

3   For further information, see Bieler, 2000: 20–22; 2006:49–54; Robinson & Harris 2000; Sklair, 2001; Gill, 1993: 21–49; Robinson, 2004: 39–40; Cox, 2008. From a different perspective, Bryan ([1987]2007) argues that "First, capital does not move in the form of production. Production can be relocated by changing the site of the productive process, but what moves physically in this process is money (loans and investments) and commodities (the factory), not production as a social activity. Marx clearly identified production as a break in the circulation process, not as a form in which capital circulates (Marx, [1885]1978: 118). Second, the internationalisation of capital should not be reduced to the spread of transnational corporations (including transnational banks). This is only an institutional appearance, not the essence of a relocation of production and the mobility of money and commodities internationally." (259). With this in mind, the differentiation between fractions of capital (national-international-transnational) should be made according to the stages in the process of their capital accumulation at which each fraction of capital is integrated into the production-realisation-valorisation processes.

and guaranteeing capital accumulation at the global scale (Robinson, 2000: 2; 2001: 157). In line with this thinking, the nation-state is considered as a collective authority for the global ruling class; the nation-state thus became absorbed into the structure of global capitalism; and the new TNS organises new class relations between global capital and global labour (Robinson, 2001: 158). The main argument of the TNS thesis is that:

> capital has become increasingly liberated from the spatial barriers of the nation-state as a result of new technologies, the worldwide reorganisation of production, and the lifting of nation-state constraints to the operation of the global market taking place under globalisation.
>
> ROBINSON, 2004: 39–40

However, this is not borne-out in practice. In contrast to Robinson's conceptualisation of TNS, "transnationalisation of capital" neither effaced each state's national and internal functions nor spawned a transnational state. Neither the space of state action nor the space of capital can be taken as global/transnational or superior to each other, but the point should be to "appreciate in which [ways] capitalism operates through nodal rather than dominant points" (Bieler & Morton, 2013: 35). It is true that the transnationalisation of capitalist relations has affected the structures of the state, but it has not led to the supersession of nation-states (Bieler & Morton, 2013: 33). As Poulantzas clearly argues, as a result of the internationalisation (transnationalisation) of capital, all nation-states came to accept and to create the necessary internal conditions for the maintenance of international accumulation, such as fiscal policies, oppressive labour by laws and regulations, and removal of all restrictions to the expansion of capital (Poulantzas, [1974] 1975: 47). Another problematic aspect of the TNS concept is that it reduces the role of the state to a transmission belt (Kiely, 2010: 143), repeating the errors of instrumentalism. Robinson, therefore, argues for a reductionist view of the state, which views class relations as external to the nation-state. He also tends to exaggerate the role of "transnational capital" in its relationship with nation-states, and consequently, overlooks the role that nation-states play in deepening and increasing the speed of integration (Kiely, 2010: 144).

As a pillar of the historical materialist approach and the philosophy of internal relations, which suggests that all entities are internally related to one another, the state itself is a relation by which the interests of transnational capital are interiorised (Bieler & Morton, 2008: 116). Drawing on the works of Poulantzas, and Gramsci before him, it is necessary to conceptualise the state as a condensation of class relations without underestimating the relationship between the state's internal functions and international market conditions, and 'global capitalist relations of production' (Bieler & Morton, 2013: 38). Gramsci argues that the state is present in both civil society and political society, the totality of which is called the integral state (Gramsci, 1971: 269). Poulantzas later developed the Gramscian concept of the integral state into an analysis of economic relations (Jessop, 2014). It is in this context that the internal relations between the state and capital, the state and market and the political and the economic are taken into account (Bieler & Morton, 2013: 38). The political field of the state is therefore studied as part of an analysis of the role of the state in reproducing social relations of production and in responding to global structural changes in the modes of capital accumulation through the realisation of transnational capitalist interests. More precisely, nation-states are responsible for constituting and maintaining the necessary internal conditions to maintain international accumulation, "such as stable prices, constraints on labour militancy, national treatment of foreign investment and no restrictions on capital outflow" (Poulantzas [1974] 1975: 20). This means transnationalisation of capital is not understood as a process which surpasses the state but involves "a process of internalisation within which interests are translated between various fractions of classes within states" (Bieler & Morton, 2003: 487).

This means new transnational class forces and the state are not exterior to each other, but rather, their relationship is represented through class struggle within the state form (Bieler & Morton, 2013: 42). Individual states have become more complex and contradictory due to the varying interests of the different fractions of capital. Inter-class and intra-class struggles are still crystallised within and through the forms of individual states (ibid., 43). Seen in this light, international or transnational capital are not always superior to nation-states. Rather, this internationalisation or transnationalisation of capital is *"founded on an induced reproduction of imperialist power dominant in each national formation and its own state"* (Martin, 2008:245). The state's public functions have been internationalised with respect to capital, and transnational class forces need state support more than ever before to extend the base of production of capital. In other words, policy-making channels of state institutions have become responsible for the formation of local expressions of the transnational process of capital accumulation and managing the reconfiguration of class forces and inter-class and intra-class struggles between various fractions of capital (Bieler & Morton, 2003: 477:489).

Despite the reductions in the sovereignty of nation-states in the face of globalisation, many states not only deal with multi-level governance but also with generating and managing extraterritorial spaces such as export processing zones, offshore financial centres and tax havens (Jessop, 2010: 42). This is achieved at the spatial scale of state power which is also characterised by U&CD (Bieler & Morton, 2013: 36). In order not to fetishize the impact of globalisation on the structures of states, it can be argued that state-capital relations "require some form of separation of a profit-oriented, market-mediated economy from a juridico-political order that secures key extra-economic conditions for accumulation and social cohesion" (Jessop, 2010:41). Although some nation-states are not fully able to articulate their interests in international/supranational organisations such as NAFTA, NATO, the G8, or the European Union, and end up subject to supranational power as a result, nation-states remain significant for managing and organising microsocial conditions for the maintenance of capital accumulation (ibid., 43). When capital moves freely through the global market, different nation-states pursue different strategies to regulate economic activities, thereby internalising the interest of transnational capital within their structures.[4] For example, the Turkish government is limited in its use of protectionism by adherence to the WTO, and in its labour policies when it aspired to EU membership, but the regulation of trade and labour in the Turkish territorial space remains mainly the Turkish state's responsibility in the global system. In this sense, FDIs and operations of TNCs are mediated by each nation-state in different ways since each country has specific social and economic environments.

3   Conclusion

This chapter argued against the mainstream approaches to free trade, namely, classical, neoclassical and institutional, which mostly argue that free trade is a win-win situation for all parties engaged in it. While classical and neo-classical theorists are against state intervention in economic activities, institutional political economists draw attention to the necessity for state intervention in the arena of foreign trade and suggest a need for extra-market coordination which is based on an interaction between the state, market, private sector actors and other institutions. Overall, mainstream theories overlook the global unevenness not only between countries but also within them, mask the exploitation involved in the process of production and overlook the unevenness between

---

4   For instance, the French president is opposed to signing the Trans-Atlantic Trade and Investment Partnership agreement between the EU and the USA, which would have significant impacts on the internal structures of the French social formation (Foreign Policy, 03 May 2016). This illustrates that the relationship between the state and transnational capital is not always unilateral.

productive workers engaging in this process. In contrast, Marxist theory contends that it is not comparative advantage that determines unequal exchange relations between unevenly developed parts of the world. From the U&CD perspective, there is unevenness between countries, regions and sectors as well as within the units of capital in one sector and among fractions and circuits of capital. U&CD theory is centred on how global free trade has led to the subjugation of some countries by others as well as some classes and class fractions by others. This means that countries are economically integrated into the world market in unequal and differentiated ways. The neoliberal agenda, which Kiely refers to as a new phase of neoliberal free trade imperialism, divides the capitalist world into peripheries and cores.

This chapter also argued that because the prices of commodities in backward countries are lower than the prices in advanced countries, this makes advanced countries internationally more competitive. In this sense, the neoclassical assumption of "convergence" or "catch-up" is far from accurate. This is crucial to explain why countries in the Global South continue to grapple with the challenges of development and long-term growth. In short, as global development is uneven and combined, free trade not only made the countries of the Global South increasingly dependent on the countries in the Global North but also intensified inequality among the classes in different social formations engaging in the production process.

Accordingly, this chapter examined the role of the state in free trade relations as theorised in international political economy to provide a theoretical and analytical basis for a historical materialist understanding of the concept of the state and the dialectical relationship between the state and the capital. The chapter argued that neoclassical-liberal and institutional approaches are problematic as they define the state as an abstract entity or as a monopoly on the legitimate use of physical force. More precisely, it argued that mainstream approaches do not analyse the class character of the state and thus states' various operations and strategies in mediating the interests of the fractions of classes within the power bloc. In short, these inabilities of mainstream approaches arise out of their treatment of the state as singular, monolithic, or a sovereign subject, which lead them to consider the relationship between state and capital as external. Rather, the chapter argued that the state is a moment in the various class struggles. Thus, the state is considered as a social relation involving the reproduction of the social relations of production.

Drawing on the writings of Poulantzas, the chapter argued that state theory ought to concentrate upon the relative autonomy of the state apparatuses and the class struggle within the political and economic spheres. Poulantzas, in this regard, proposes that the state enjoys relative autonomy vis-à-vis social classes and fractions of classes, and in addition to this, the state does not only engage in relationships within the power bloc but also between the dominant and dominated classes. The state is not an instrument in the hands of the bourgeoisie, and does not directly represent the interests of dominant classes within the power bloc; however, the state cannot be considered separately from the relations of production. To mediate the interests of the dominant classes, and to control the dominated classes, the state also organises hegemony over the dominated classes by seeking their active consent. In this regard, this study attempts to theorise the state without lapsing into an instrumentalist account or a transnational state theorization. It is also argued that, although the transformation of the relations of production brought major challenges to the nation-state, the economic, political and ideological functions of national states are still important. Internal structures of domestic economies have become more important as a result of the withering-away of most obstacles to capital mobility (Savran, 2008: 35). This consolidation of states' internal functions has become more apparent in the wake of the 2008 global financial crisis in terms of resolving social, political and economic problems (ibid.). This is evident in the large subsidies given to bankrupt companies so as to recreate the necessary conditions for capital accumulation. Overall, the role of the state in the era of transnationalisation and internationalisation of capital has been restructured and updated in terms of both mediating the conflicting interest of dominant classes within the power bloc and internalising the interests of transnational/international capitalist classes. In this regard, it can be argued that the internationalisation of capital neither vanquishes nor bypasses the nation-state, but instead, passes through it. This is why states cannot be excluded from an analysis of capitalist social relations of production. Thus, capital needs states for a particular purpose: securing social and economic conditions for the reproduction of capitalist social relations of production.

In terms of the role of business associations, cross-border production within the process of internationalisation of capital has been the primary objective of transnational companies. This evidently demonstrates that internationalised capital does not only penetrate into host countries as merely an abstract investment, but also transforms the social forms within the host country and strengthens the leading pro-imperialist class fractions within each social formation. In this sense, the current system of free trade cannot be analysed in separation from the relations of production and circulation of capital in this structure. Business associations are in a close relationship with the state in terms of reproducing the relations of international production. This reproduction has been realised through the signing of FTAs, which aimed to internationalise the relations of production, dividing production into segments and locating the separate stages in two or more countries, thereby creating global production networks. While the FTAs are transnational, the conditions for signing and enforcing an FTA are internal to each state. In summation, the analysis of the role of business associations in free trade cannot be pursued without reference to the uneven and combined patterns of international free trade which create unevenness in the global capitalist system. The engagement of business associations in the global value chain process still leads to the exploitation of resources in countries in the Global South as well as the classes engaging in relations of production in these countries. It is for this reason that the role of the state in these global relations of free trade must also be analysed, in order to unearth the significance of business associations, which will be discussed in the next chapter.

The subsequent chapters will present an analytical and critical basis to uncover how the relationships between transnational/international/national capital and the state in Turkey have been constructed. This question occupies a central space here. The process described in these chapters is what impels the movement of capital towards the countries in the Global South. Further, these chapters will also explore how the interests and operations of transnational/international capital have been internalised within the Turkish state structure and how the relationship between the Turkish state and capital has been reconstructed during the internalisation process. This is important so as to provide a solid account of how the process of internationalisation and transnationalisation of capital might relate to the history of neoliberalism, and the specificity of the social relations of production under the umbrella of imperialist production chains which are fundamentally characterised by U&CD and the internalisation of productive capital. This is explored in Turkey, in particular, by examining the relationship between the state and business associations.

CHAPTER 2

A Historical Materialist Analysis of Capitalism in Turkey

The aim of this chapter is to demonstrate the effectiveness of a historical materialist approach to business associations in Turkey as a means to explain the development of capitalism in Turkey and its impact on the Turkish social formation. It starts from the examination of historical and material factors to grasp how business associations have emerged, developed and engaged in capitalist relations in a particular manner in the Turkish social formation. To this goal, the chapter focuses on the historical consolidation of capitalism in the Turkish context and the shifts in the global free trade regime. Using a neo-Gramscian analysis, it places emphasis on *the changes in social relations of production, the shift in state-capital relations* and *the internalisation of global free trade relations* within the context of the Turkish social formation. It also explores what the discussion of business associations adds to an understanding of social formations in Turkey and concludes by showing how the Turkish experience can have a general application to business associations writ large.

The chapter divides capitalist development in Turkey into four different but connected periods which are: (i) the defining role of uneven and combined development - commercial and agrarian capital-based accumulation until the late 1950s, (ii) industrial capital-based accumulation based on the Import Substitution Industrialisation (ISI) model until the 1980s, (iii) export-led capital accumulation in the post-transition period and (iv) transnationalisation of Turkish productive capital. This periodisation is based upon the shifts in the capital accumulation models which have directly affected by the shifts in the global process of capital accumulation. In order to grasp the change in the social relations of production within a historical framework this chapter draws attention to the changing patterns of capital accumulation in Turkey. As the change in social relations of production in Turkey has been marked by a specific shift in the patterns of the global free trade regime, this chapter also discusses the changes in global patterns of capital accumulation and the ways in which Turkey integrates into global free trade relations. As mentioned in previous chapter, this study argues that the development of capitalism is not a linear progression and every society in the world has developed in different ways at different times. The present chapter models the articulation of the capitalist mode of production in Turkey, a process which involves both the organisation of class relationships and the process of state formation. It also provides an overview of the differences between different companies operating in different business associations engaged in social relations of production in different time periods, and the global/regional unevenness among business associations engaging in global free trade relations. It concludes with a final assessment and an overview of the empirical cases examined in this book.

1   The Making of Capitalism in Turkey: The Defining Role of Uneven and Combined Development

The development of capitalism has taken different forms in different countries at different times. It has also taken a unique form in the case of Turkey which has also unevenly integrated into global capitalism. It is crucial to emphasise that with the dissolution of the previous mode of production and transition to the capitalist mode of production, Turkey has followed an uneven path. The indicators of uneven development are as follows. First, the Ottoman Empire in the late 19th century did not have true industry of the kind then prevalent in Europe. The integration of the Ottoman Empire into the global capitalist system has started with the "Balta Limanı Trade Agreement" signed between the Ottoman Empire and Great Britain in 1838. This agreement signifies the beginning of systematic interaction between European imperialism, in the form of British industrial capital, with the commercial bourgeoise in the Ottoman Empire. Additionally, the place of the Ottoman Empire in the global capitalist system was a typical peripheral position as an exporter of raw materials and importer of industrial products, meaning it was economically speaking a semi-colonised country in the 19th century. With this characteristic backwardness, it provides a good example of a Smithian or Ricardian mercantile country which has specialised and had comparative advantage in non-industrial products, and thus did not develop a proper industry. Secondly, the catalyst for capitalist development was the commercial bourgeoisie in the Ottoman Empire as a late-developing capitalist country (Savran, 2010:57). In other words, primitive accumulation in the Ottoman Empire happened in the commercial capital cycle, which had a disintegrative impact on pre-capitalist relations (Öztürk, 2011: 41). Moreover, the sugar and wheat industries developed first, in contrast to advanced capitalist countries which had long specialised in industrial production in different sectors (Boratav, 2014: 21). For Korkut Boratav, huge amount of foreign debts, and economic capitulation to European countries, also demonstrated that the Ottoman Empire was unevenly integrated into the global capitalism (Boratav, 2014:21). Thirdly, the absence of substantive political independence of the Ottoman state in the late 19th century also provides evidence of uneven development of capitalism in Turkey. The Ottoman state in the late 19th century was dependent on imperial states in its fiscal, monetary and administrative spheres. Thus, it is accurate to say that the Ottoman Empire was dominated politically, economically, socially and culturally by the imperial powers, in a similar manner to what would later be called neocolonialism. Finally, the role of the state in the development of capitalism in Turkey is different from its role in the early capitalist countries in Europe. For instance, while the state has co-developed with the industrial/imperial capital in advanced capitalist countries, the Turkish state has played an important role in the formation and development of national industrial capital (Savran, 2010: 96).

These patterns of late development also affected the establishment of business organisations in the Ottoman Empire. Although there were almost 100 chambers of agriculture and industry in 1889 and 160 by 1908, they were not robust enough to make a tangible impact on the economy or state (Koralturk, 1999: 293). However, there had also been some prototypes of business associations in the late Ottoman period. These associations were mainly organised outside the chambers and were established to bring entrepreneurs together, encourage them to work in collaboration with each other and to encourage the Ottoman state to increase its level of industrialisation (Koralturk, 1999: 297). The very first examples of these associations were Boykotaj Sendikasi (1908) (The Boycott Union), Tuccar-i Osmaniye Heyeti (1908) (Ottoman Merchants' Committee), Cemiyet-i Mutesebbise (1909) (The Entrepreneur Society), Istanbul Musluman Tuccar Cemiyeti (1914) (Istanbul Muslim Merchant Society), and Milli Fabrikalar Cemiyeti (1917) (The Society of National Factories) (Koralturk, 1999: 297). These are the first examples of business associations which were established to influence the economic policies of the state. However, they failed to directly influence government policies until the establishment of the biggest and the most influential association: TUSIAD. As the commercial bourgeoisie was previously the dominant fraction in the capitalist classes, the industrial bourgeoisie only managed to establish its own organisation in 1950[1] (Koralturk, 1999: 292–6).

The Republic of Turkey was founded in 1923 in the aftermath of national upheavals. After the foundation of modern Turkey in 1923, the main motivation of the Turkish state was to remove all political, social, legal and economic

---

1   The first chamber of industry was established in Izmir in 1951, and the second in Istanbul in 1952 (Koralturk, 1999: 296).

obstacles so as to establish and develop capitalist relations of production. In this endeavour, the state abolished Islamic law and the caliphate, enacting a transition to modern law based on rule of law, secularism and a parliamentary regime. This means the legal system of the country was harmonised with the European capitalist countries, which hastened the process of transition to a capitalist mode of production in every geographical region of the country. The process of capital accumulation had already started in 1908 and continued under the İttihat ve Terakki (Union and Progress) Party governments (aka the Young Turks). The establishment of the Republic, therefore, did not represent a radical shift in terms of the mode of capital accumulation. However, its establishment represents a break with the Ottoman state in terms of the state form. The new state after the revolution was equipped with crucial institutions in order to influence capitalist relations of production and class relations in the country. In this period, there was also a civil war between different social groups represented by different power-groups in the country. This means it was not only foreign countries which the Kemalist cadres fought against; it was also domestic power groups. Sungur Savran argues that this Kemalist revolution completed the unfinished task of the Young Turks by destroying the Ottoman state (Savran, 2002: 6). This means the establishment of Turkey represents a bourgeoisie revolution which had roots in 1908 revolution made by the Union and Progress Party (Young Turks) against the Ottoman state. Korkut Boratav defines the establishment of the new Republic in 1923 is an 'unfinished bourgeoisie revolution' or as 'first steps to create a national capitalism' (Boratav, 2014:21). The Cumhuriyet Halk Partisi (CHP, Republican People's Party) became the first political party of the new state and ruled the country until 1950 within a one-party system. This means the state has taken a new form and a new set of relationships were created in the power bloc.

The class composition of the Turkish republic in its early years included a weak working class, a large peasantry and a dominant commercial-agricultural bourgeoisie which was also not strong enough to act independently as a class force. The primary motivation of the dominant classes in this period was to strengthen the incorporation of Turkey into global capitalism, mainly by establishing trade relations, as the bourgeoisie was weak *vis-a-vis* international competitors (Gulalp, 1985: 334; Savran, 2002: 6). This was a necessity for the new Turkish state, as a late-developing capitalist country, in order to engage in global value production and capital accumulation processes. In this regard, one of the most important steps, taken by the Kemalist state in January 1923, was to create the Economic Congress of Izmir, which was organised in order to tackle problems in certain sectors such as credit, production, taxation, customs, and communications. The dominant classes represented in this Congress were the mercantile bourgeoisie and the landed classes. This Congress, there-fore, involved a new alliance between the state and capital and a new period in state-capital relations (Yalman, 2002: 26). In this time, an active role in the process of capital accumulation was allocated to the state, a situation which has continued ever since. Parallel to the resolutions which arose out of the Congress, the establishment of the Turkiye Is Bank in 1924, and the Turkiye Sinai ve Maadin Bank (Turkish Industrial and Mines Bank) in 1925 further helped Turkish capitalists to flourish. These banks also played a mediating role between national capitalist classes and the state and between national and international capital. In other words, they became a centre of power which internalised global class relations inside the country. As a consequence, 66 of 201 companies established in Turkey between 1920 and 1930 were foreign-capital-affiliated companies (Boratav, 2014:42). However, during the decade, the new state also did not have full control of its national borders and foreign trade regimes due to the sanctions imposed by the Treaty of Lausanne signed in 1923 between the Ottoman Empire and the Allied Forces.

In the aftermath of the 1929 global economic crisis, and at the end of the five-year regime of economic sanctions imposed by the Treaty of Lausanne, Turkey made a deliberate attempt to shift its mode of capital accumulation to a more industrial base. This capital accumulation model involved creating state-owned enterprises (SOEs), which aimed at promoting state-capital rela-tions through public tenders and subsidised credits (Marois, 2012: 47). Parallel to this policy agenda, Sumerbank (1933), Halkbank (1938) and Etibank (1935) were established to finance these SOEs through financial support and trade credits (Marois, 2012: 48). Korkut Boratav defines this period (1930–1939) as protectionist and statist industrialisation, or in other words, a state-led inward-looking development strategy (Boratav, 2014: 59–81). This strategy was also a response to the recession in raw material importation and the decline in trade volumes on a world scale after the 1929 global economic crises (Gulalp, 1985: 333). The global recession reduced raw materials prices more than prices of industrial products and also narrowed export earnings. This global crisis provided incentives for late-developing capitalist countries like Turkey (and countries in Latin America) to implement protectionist foreign trade policies and to shift towards industrial capital-based accumulation as Turkey was still an exporter of raw materials and an importer of industrial products until 1929. In this period, the Kemalist state was the chief actor in terms of constituting patterns of capital accumulation, which included issuing import quotas and export-based foreign credits, and overvaluing the Turkish currency (Shick and Tonak, 1987: 337). The state also established Turkiye Cumhuriyeti Merkez Bankasi (CBT; Central Bank of Turkey) in 1931 to internalise the capitalist financial system and to fund Turkey's national development strategies in the context of narrowing export earnings (Marois, 2012: 48).

The years between 1930 and 1939 saw a sustained process of industrialisation in Turkey while advanced capitalist countries have suffered from the 1929 global recession. In this period, industrialisation was put into effect through strong state intervention, mainly through ISI policies. This period was defined by the internalisation of commodity circulation (Gulalp, 1985: 335), and represents a break with the previous periods in terms of patterns of industrialisation. State intervention also worked for the benefit of firms producing for the domestic market (Boran, 1962: 90–98), and those are the winners of state tenders. On the other hand, the outward-oriented sections of the commercial bourgeoise in Turkey lost their domination among the capitalist classes due to the decline in foreign trade volume. Industries also made the most of the opportunities provided by the implementation of the Law for the Encouragement of Exports (Teşvik-i Sanayii Kanunu). This is to say that the statist policies of the 1930s gradually led to the emergence of an industrial bourgeoisie (Boratav, 2014: 62), which was to dominate the circuits of capital and establish TUSIAD later.

State-led development had lost its momentum by the end of the decade, and there had been a break in industrialisation policies because of the outbreak of World War II. In this period, the Turkish state intervened in the economy by confiscating the land and animals of the non-Muslim bourgeoisie. In addition to this, the implementation of a Capital Levy (Varlik Vergisi) in 1942 aimed at taxing profiteers (Keyder, 1987: 37). Due to the application of this levy, non-Muslims were forced to sell their properties at a loss since the tax was not affordable. In fact, this was a way of transferring capital controlled by non-Muslims to the emerging Turkish-Sunni-Muslim bourgeoisie. In the years of the war economy, agrarian and commercial capital achieved an unprecedented rate of accumulation because of shortages at home, speculation and black-market trade (Gulalp, 1985: 336). Hence, Turkey succeeded in creating an industrial bourgeois class, which came to replace the commercial/comprador bourgeoisie in terms of internalising the global class relations in the Turkish social formation (Boratav, 2014:61). But this new class also struggled to win autonomy from political power (Schick & Tonak, 1987:338).

As each transition between different phases of capital accumulation necessitates a shift in the social relations of production, it also entails a restructuring of the class relations, which determine each pattern of accumulation (Gulalp, 1985: 333). On the state level, there was a change in the power bloc in the early 1950s (Oğuz, 2008: 90). This period also witnessed a contradiction between the industrial bourgeoisie who were in favour of protectionism in foreign trade, and the commercial bourgeoisie who were in favour of a more liberal trade regime. This conflict within the power bloc was mirrored in the national Chambers of Commerce and Industry which were the semi-official business organisation of the local chambers of commerce based on geographical representation. Consequently, the Chambers of Industry separated from the Chambers of Commerce. Further to this, a new law was passed setting up the TOBB (Turkiye Odalar ve Borsalar Birligi, Union of Chambers and Stock Exchanges), which is the general representative of all chambers (Oğuz, 2008: 91).

The global process of capital accumulation has shifted from protectionism towards free trade in the post-WWII period. In Turkey, the commercial and agricultural bourgeoisie which dominated the total circuit of capital in the war years due to the increasing demands on agricultural and industrial products demanded by the state. This caused the state to abandon protectionist foreign trade policies (Boratav, 2014:95). Between 1946 and 1953 the Turkish state removed barriers to foreign trade and opened its borders to international capital and foreign aid. In this period Turkey joined the IMF, the World Bank, the OECD, and the NATO. In the late 1950s, there were serious contradictions between the biggest landowners, a privileged stratum within the Democrat Party, and rich merchants in the towns, and a second contradiction emerged between the state and capital because of state intervention in the economy (Keyder, 1987: 40). This contradiction can also be explained with reference to the increasing foreign trade deficit which forced Turkey to restructure its pattern of capital accumulation. Parallel to these developments, the pattern of capital accumulation shifted from commercial and agrarian capital towards industrial capital, giving industrial capitalists greater power within the overall power bloc. As a result, there was a need to adopt the necessary legal and political superstructure to meet the needs of the changing patterns of capital accumulation (Savran, 2002: 11).

2   Industrial Capital Accumulation Based on the ISI Model until the 1980s

The historical development of capitalism in Turkey involved a further change in the patterns of capital accumulation in the post-1961 period which focused on production for the national market. This was a response to the over-accumulation of commercial capital in the previous years, a global decline in demand for Turkish exports, and the recovery of the European agricultural sector, which led to reductions in global agricultural prices, and resulted in a foreign exchange crisis for Turkey (Oğuz, 2008: 91). As a consequence, Turkey shifted its capital accumulation model towards an inward-looking one by the mid-1950s, which was based on increasing manufacturing capacity to replace imported products.

In order to overcome the balance of trade crisis, the Turkish state made some attempts at reducing imports throughout this period, such as issuing import quotas and tariffs. The transition from commercial capital accumulation to industrial capital accumulation gained momentum in the aftermath of the military coup on 27 May 1960, which represented an attack on the existing power bloc by statist, Kemalist military officials, supported by the Istanbul bourgeoisie who were neglected during the DP period for the sake of the majority of small capitalists and the agricultural bourgeoisie. In other words, without ignoring the other political reasons for the coup, one factor was that the industrial bourgeoisie was disaffected with the agriculturally-centred policies of the DP, 'which subsidised the peasantry at the expense of industry' (Schick and Tonak, 1987: 342). Overall, protectionist foreign trade policies in the 1960s and 1970s based on inward-looking capital accumulation provided a suitable environment for productive/industrial capitalists to concentrate their capital inside national borders. As a result, smaller and weaker fractions of capital were captured by the bigger and stronger capitals which had advantages in terms of producing more cheaply and employing more workers in the process of production. This mirrored the process of monopolisation of capital in the advanced capitalist countries, and led to a situation where big family-based holding groups, such as KOÇ, SABANCI, and CUKUROVA, emerged as the hegemonic fraction within the power bloc (Gulalp, 1985: 330). As an illustration, a few firms employing more than 200 workers dominated the Turkish economy with their presence in the industrial production occupying almost 71.5% in 1967 (Özgür, 1972: 183–84, quoted in Öztürk 2011: 87).

The newly established industrial bourgeoisie constituted the main capital groups which established TUSIAD in 1971. As argued in the previous section, the dominant fractions of Turkish capital (the agrarian and commercial bourgeoisie) had benefited from state policies in the previous years. In this period, certain sections of the commercial and agricultural bourgeoisie transformed themselves into industrial capitalists so as to internalise and benefit from the new patterns of capital accumulation (Gulalp, 1985: 337). By 1971, industrial production accounted for 60% of the national economy, rising from 30% in 1962 and 48% in 1967 (Ercan & Tuna, 2007:405). This period not only saw the emergence of productive capital in Turkey, and corresponding transformations of the capitalist state, but also provided a conducive atmosphere for the big holding groups in Turkey to centralise and concentrate their capital by buying smaller export and import firms (Ercan & Tuna, 2007:383).[2] In this time, the domestic market was protected by state policies, which also shielded capitalist classes in Turkey from competition from foreign firms. This protection was given in two different ways: (i) through public enterprises providing cheap materials for the private sector, and (ii) through state-private sector partnership. In particular, the establishment of the State Planning Organisation (Devlet Planlama Teskilati; SPO) in 1960 fostered protectionism in foreign trade and state intervention in the economy. The state policies in this period protected certain fractions of capital in their initial period of capital accumulation and later helped them to monopolise the means of capital accumulation. Industrial capital also achieved a certain capital adequacy through its ownership of banks (Oğuz, 2008: 93). This period also saw the establishment of the *conglomerates* which brought various fractions of capital together in the form of holding companies.

There were some contradictions during the ISI period. For instance, imports of raw materials increased from 33.4% of total imports in 1950 to 62.4% in 1979. Despite ISI, production was still heavily dependent on imports. This contradiction arose via partnership agreements, joint ventures and licence agreements between transnational firms and sectors of the national bourgeoisie such as KOÇ Holding (Eralp, 1980: 618). This centralisation resulted in domination by a few big capitalists over the mass of smaller capitalists (Öztürk, 2011: 117). For instance, in 1969, 236 of the 251 most-consumed products in Turkey were produced by only three big corporations (Öztürk, 2014: 233). This was also a consequence of the uneven integration of Turkish capital into global free trade relations. Furthermore, Turkey produced relatively low-tech products in these years and did not get the chance to compete in the global market. In late-developing capitalist countries like Turkey, the appropriation of surplus value usually occurs in the sphere of exchange, and this causes a relatively low rate of appropriation of surplus value in the sphere of production. As capitalists wish to produce more surplus value rather than making commercial profits, Turkish capitalists desired to move towards a productive capital-based model of capital accumulation rather than producing marginal surplus value through assembly production. However, the rate of industrialisation was slow, and export volumes did not provide the necessary currency flows to enable Turkey to move up the value chain (Öztürk, 2014: 231). Equally importantly, export in this period was focused on agricultural products (Boratav, 2014: 120–122), and

---

2   KOC, SABANCI, ECZACIBASI, ANADOLU GROUP and many more are the examples of the monopolistic industrial firms, which established TUSIAD. This will be discussed in detail in the following chapters.

production was heavily focused on intermediate goods rather than finished products. As a result of the fact that Turkey restricted the inflow of foreign capital in this period, there was a currency crisis which showed to some extent the structural limitations of the ISI strategy (Gulalp, 1985: 339). As a generalisation, it is possible to say that the 1971 military intervention was a response to this currency crisis and aimed at reconstructing the patterns of capital accumulation once more (ibid. 340). The primary objective of Turkish military intervention, in general, has been to mediate the struggles between and within different fractions of classes in times of crisis (Savran, 2002: 3).

The form and the rhythm of development of capitalism in the 1960s and 1970s demanded that Turkish capital reproduce the capitalist mode of production in a specific form, or in other words, that it liberalise the foreign trade regime since the capital accumulation process had reached its domestic limits and had to find new markets to sustain the appropriation of surplus value. At this stage, the core capitalist countries started to shift the process of production towards more peripheral spaces (Bieler & Morton, 2014: 39), including Turkey, which provided the advantage of low wages. This period was the beginning of internationalisation of Turkish capital and the end of the ISI strategy (Öztürk, 2014: 230). This is to say that the hegemonic fraction of Turkish capital (mostly composed of the member firms of TUSIAD) was ready to expand internationally.

3   Transition to Neoliberalism: Integration into Free Trade and the Changing Role of the State

The transition to neoliberalism involved a departure from protectionist foreign trade policies to a free trade regime. There were two significant phases of this transition. The first was the inward-oriented capital accumulation period in which big domestic corporations exploited the advantages of the ISI strategy. Hence, they increased their capacity to control the total circuit of capital. This phase was an era in which TUSIAD members maintained hegemony over other fractions of capital. The second stage was the export-driven internationalisation period in which Turkish commercial capital integrated into global free trade relations. As mentioned in the previous section, the ISI period represented a transition to productive capital accumulation, which is a direct consequence of the transnationalisation of productive capital in the advanced capitalist countries, in other words, the expansion of the global free trade regime to peripheral spaces. It also involved the emergence of a national bourgeoisie in Turkey at a moment in which the dialectical relationship between capital and the state became crystallised. The transition to neoliberalism, and the resultant internationalisation of Turkish commercial capital, was a structural necessity for Turkish capital as the inward-oriented capital accumulation model had reached its domestic limits in the late 1970s. As a result of internationalisation, barriers to capital accumulation were overcome. The main pillars of the economy in this period involved promoting strong state subsidies, wage suppression, management of the exchange rate, and regulated capital movements (Oğuz, 2008: 105). This explains the fact that a new set of relationships were constructed in the social relations of production. Hence a considerable number of big corporations in Turkey have intensified and increased their ability to manage and influence the total circuit of capital inside the country.

The transition to neoliberalism in Turkey was accompanied by the implementation of neoclassical-inspired, market-oriented structural reforms, which started in the late 1970s, within a context of global capitalist crisis. Since the revalorisation of the total circuit of capital was negatively affected by the long depressive wave of crisis in advanced capitalist countries, the individual capitalists in these countries had to search for new outlets for their commercial, money and industrial capital (Panitch & Gindin, 2004:18). There was therefore a need to restructure the global division of labour between advanced and late-developing capitalist countries (Poulantzas, [1974] 1975:87). The internationalisation of Turkish capital in the 1980s was thus an outcome of the inherent crises of capitalism in the advanced capitalist countries which arose in the 1970s as well as the decrease in the appropriation of surplus value inside the country. Capital export and international integration through foreign direct investment (FDI) were the main ways of expanding the global free trade regime into peripheral spaces (Panitch & Gindin, 2004: 19). The IMF was also restructured in this period. It became an institution which pressurised and coerced peripheral countries to integrate into global free trade relations (Sawaya, 2018:150). In the case of Turkey, in 1979, the IMF launched a financial assistance package to save the Turkish economy from collapse because of the failure of the Turkish government to repay interest payments (Marois, 2012: 65). This intervention paved the way for departing from an inward-looking accumulation model to an outward-looking one, which aimed at liberalising the Turkish foreign trade regime and restructuring the role of the Turkish state in economic activities (Yalman, 2012:23).

The period between 1981 and 1987 is a distinctive phase in which the Turkish economy integrated into the global capitalist financial system by removing all the barriers to foreign trade. Free market principles have been the determining rule in the market, and the state implemented a policy in order to increase its commodity and service exports (Yeldan, 2011: 39). This was accompanied with a global agenda of free trade which expanded beyond trade in goods and towards trade in services, finances and agriculture (Bieler and Morton, 2014: 41). The military regime maintained earlier policies designed to promote deeper global integration after the 12 September 1980 military coup and civilian governments also continued these policies in the 1980s (Yalman, 2002: 39). This transition process was initiated by the "24 January Decisions" undertaken by a neoliberal technocrat, Turgut Ozal, who worked as a consultant for the World Bank and Sabancı Holding in 1970s. He was then prime minister and president between 1983 and 1993. One of the main targets of the "Decisions" was to weaken the organised labour movement and cut prices (Boratav, 2014: 147). The neoliberal turn was crystallized in tthe 1982 Constitution (Savran, 2002: 15). Liberalisation of foreign trade, therefore, gained momentum in the 1980s and constituted the basis for the neoliberal policies of the next decades (Savran, 2002: 15). On the other hand, in the later stages of the ISI strategy, Turkish industrial capital accumulation based on durable consumer goods production became almost unsustainable, which made an investment in productive capital necessary (Ercan, 2002: 24). This is because of the competitive disadvantage of Turkey in industrial production which automatically suffered from imbalances and foreign trade deficits as Turkey entered into global free trade relations in an uneven way. The Turkish commercial bourgeoisie, therefore, shifted towards an outward-oriented capital accumulation model to overcome the barriers to competition in global markets.

The new capital accumulation model in the 1980s posed some serious difficulties for the big Turkish companies which were not exactly armoured and ready for global competition. For instance, Turkish exporters failed to achieve a regional diversity in their share of foreign trade partners. European countries became the largest export market for Turkey in the 1980s (due to geographical proximity as a low-wage producer), while external economic relations with countries in the Middle East, Africa and Asia remained stagnant. More importantly, Turkish exporters were not able to achieve an increase in the export of industrial goods. Instead, they shifted their trade towards the service sector in accordance with the prescriptions of the GATT Uruguay Round. As a result, cracks and contradictions emerged among different fractions of Turkish capital regarding the ways in which to integrate into the global process of capital accumulation (Ercan, 2002: 22). These contradictions will be highlighted in the empirical chapters.

As the state is an actual site of political class struggle and the reproduction of social relations of production (Poulantzas, [1978] 2000:25), the state restructured intra-capital relations and the relationship between the state apparatuses and particular fractions of Turkish capital. These contradictions arose out of the transition to neoliberalism which did not develop independently from the outside control of the IFIS. However, these reforms were not directly imposed from outside (Marois, 2012: 99). Touching on Poulantzas, this suggests that the Turkish state cannot be seen as simply a tool in the hands of IFIS (Poulantzas [1978] 2000: 37). Rather, the Turkish state apparatuses under the control of the military regime, and the larger fraction of Turkish capital represented by TUSIAD actively engaged in this process due to their willingness to integrate the Turkish economy into the global neoliberal economic system. By doing so, the state managers demanded the support of a bourgeoisie who were loyal to these neoliberal adjustment policies (Yalman, 2002: 39), otherwise the policies would have been subverted from within or reversed when the crisis was over. The internal relations within the state structure are significant to analyse the role of the state in integrating into global relations of free trade (Figure 2). Accordingly, an alliance between Turkish state managers and TUSIAD was formed in support of neoliberal policies (Boratav, 1990:199–229).

Chapter 3 demonstrates that TUSIAD was willing to operate in a market-oriented economic system but also wanted to maintain its privileged relations with the Turkish state apparatus in the 1980s (Marois, 2012: 101). Different branches of domestic capital also supported neoliberal, market-oriented policy reforms. For instance, Chapter 5 argues that MUSIAD and TOBB which represent the interest of SMEs supported this project (Öniş, 1997:758 & Marois,

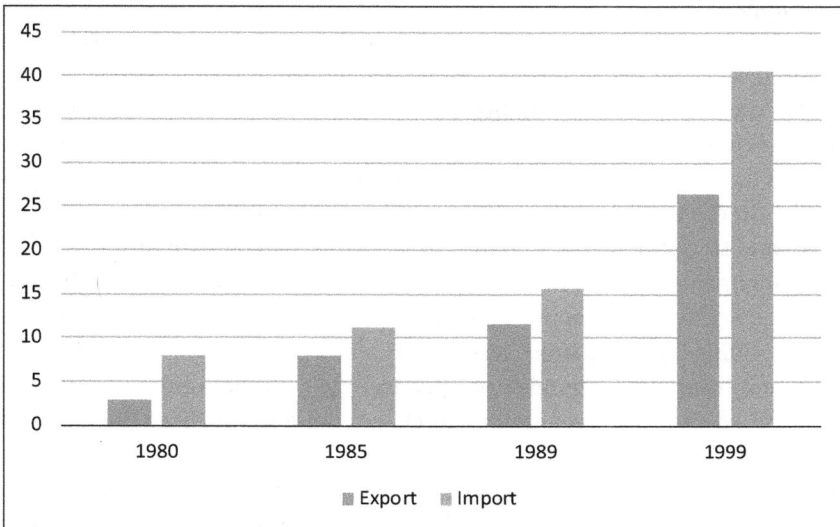

FIGURE 2   Turkish foreign trade statistics in the post transition period (US$ Billions)
SOURCE: TUIK, 2019

2012: 101). However, state interventions mainly worked for the benefit of the larger fractions of Turkish capital. As an illustration, exports increased from 3.3% of GDP in the 1960s to 16% between 1980 and 1997. A significant amount of this increase was realised through international subcontracting agreements in labour-intensive sectors (Ercan, 2002: 33). This brings us to the conclusion that, as mentioned in Chapter 2, state policies might favour some fractions of capital, while undermining other fractions (Bryan, [1987]2007: 274). As the transition to neoliberalism demanded cooperation between state apparatus and the larger fractions of capital, so at different times in different ways, support was provided by the military regime and its successor civilian governments for TUSIAD and MUSIAD, by implementing market-friendly policies. This provides a typical example regarding the state's role in organising different fractions of capital. This neoliberal restructuring, strengthened after the establishment of the 1982 Constitution, was designed to protect the power of the state apparatus and the business elites' privileged access to this apparatus.

The 1982 Constitution not only built closer relationships between the state apparatus and capital, but also changed the form of the Turkish state. This was a process which attempted to put an end to class-based politics (Yalman, 2002:38) by disorganising labour and disbanding the trade unions (Ozbudun, 2000 & Sakallioglu, 1991). As Poulantzas and Jessop argue, because the dominant classes are not able to act as a uniform and single entity due to their contradictory and conflicting interests, the crucial role performed by the state apparatuses is, therefore, managing class contradictions and securing the cohesion of dominant classes, while disorganising the dominated classes (Poulantzas, [1968]1978:54; Jessop, 1982:186). Indeed, the restructuring of the state in the aftermath of the military coup appears 'as an integral part of [the] new hegemonic strategy' (Yalman, 2002: 39). The existing hegemony was in crisis in the 1970s because of the increased strength of organised labour movements. On the other hand, conflicts between capital fractions became intensified, and thus, the military regime appeared as the guardian of the survival of the bourgeoisie (ibid.). In this regard, the state under the control of the military was relatively autonomous and hence was able to unite the power bloc, while dividing the dominated classes.

From a historical materialist perspective, the state does not only manage the contradictions between dominant classes but also mediates the relations between dominant and dominated classes to pursue its hegemony (Bieler & Morton, 2013: 41; Jessop, 1985: 57). In the Turkish case, some important legal changes influenced the power relations within and outside the power bloc and led to significant shifts in class relations. The military government, for its part, implemented new laws to control the labour movement and to decrease the number of unionised workers. The density of union membership was the highest it has been in Turkish history in the late 1970s (Akkaya, 2002: 64). This meant that class struggle between workers and capital owners was much more visible in every sphere of social life. For this reason, it was essential for the fractions of capital and state authorities to put an end to class-based politics (Akkaya, 2002: 69). As a means to this end, the stand-by agreement signed with the IMF covering 1980–83 and the agreements made with the World Bank for Structural Adjustment Loans reduced opposition from the society and social forces (Ercan, 2002: 25). This intensified the contradictions between the working class and capital on behalf of the capitalist classes. In short, this transition was a reaction of the dominant classes to suppress the working class which developed rapidly throughout the 1960s and 1970s.

The goal of weakening of the organised struggle of labour required the state to introduce hierarchical spinoff mechanisms to mediate the conflicting interests of the capital fractions and substitute for direct confrontation. For instance, the floating of interest rates after the 24 January Decisions removed the barriers to mobility of international money, which deepened the gap between big fractions of capital and SMEs. The military regime also established the Export Promotion and Implementation Department, gave Export Promotion Licences to exporters, and to set up an Export Promotion Fund. All of these measures aimed at mediating the conflicting interests of capital fractions and constructing the bourgeoisie's hegemony in the aftermath of the transition to neoliberalism, which involved the adoption of the Thatcherite slogan: "There is no alternative".

With Decree No. 32 implemented in 1989, the control over capital movements was lifted and capital groups were allowed to establish private banks, liberalise their interest volumes and foreign exchange controls, all of which have facilitated the growth of the Turkish bourgeoisie (Ergüneş, 2007: 240). On the other hand, this Decree has left Turkish capital unprotected against international capital movements (Ercan, 2002: 32). This has also increased the inflow of short-term capital and loans. At the same time, it cheapened the price of imports, but had an adverse impact on export. In this context, the process of money capital accumulation has witnessed three main periods. The first was the integration of idle resources inside the country into the capital accumulation process. As the obstacles to establishing private banks were lifted, these private banks have started to engage in foreign trade and import foreign currency into the country (Ergüneş, 2007: 251–53). The second was the international money capital-led period, which was mainly dependent on external finance and global capital movements. This process also related to the shift in the global free trade regime in the 1990s, which sought to internationalise the global finance sector. Accordingly, it was intended to enhance the ability of money capital to carry out strategic manoeuvres (Ergüneş, 2007: 255). As an illustration, the share of public banks in the Turkish banking sector has decreased from 45.3% in 1981–85 to 33.6% in 1997 (Ergüneş, 2007: 258). The third period was the era of the restructuring the economy on behalf of international capital, which worked mainly to the benefit of the industrial bourgeoisie (Ergüneş, 2007: 259). This has crystallised the contradictions among capital fractions (Gültekin-karakaş, 2007: 287). There were several significant dimensions to this contradiction. Firstly, favouritism towards the finance sector resulted in a dramatic increase in the volume of interest, which increased the value of variable capital (money expended on labour-power). In relation to the first dimension, favouritism in finance has led holding banks - established in money capital form - to become more competitive in relation to industrial capital, capturing capital which might otherwise be invested in industry. For instance, there were 32 holding banks in the top taxpayers list in 1999. Thirdly, the reforms encouraged international money capital to invest in Turkey. This led to an increase in the currency value and provided some advantages to those particular big capital groups which can shift between different sectors (Gültekin-karakaş, 2007: 287–88). The reforms thus favoured large over small capital, mobile over fixed capital, and money capital over industrial capital.

The 1990s witnessed the transformation of the industrial bourgeoisie into finance capital in the classical Marxist terms, which involves the fusion of industrial, commercial and money capital (Savran, 2002: 18). This resulted in a struggle between two fractions of capital in Turkey, namely the first and second generations of capitalist classes.[3] In fact, the emergence of the second generation of the Turkish bourgeoisie coincided with the transformation of the industrial bourgeoisie into finance capital. State policies in this period have worked to the benefit of some fractions of capital but weakened other fractions. Policies on rent transfers to banks through state borrowing adopted in the 1980s and 1990s have led to monopolisation in certain sectors as it has

---

3 In the next chapters, the book will provide a detailed conceptualisation of capitalist fractions in Turkey. For the present I will only mention this: the first generation of bourgeoisie refers to the capitalist classes who entered into the process of capital accumulation before the other fractions of capital. This fraction basically consists of the member firms of TUSIAD. The second generation of bourgeoisie refers to the ones who entered the process of capital accumulation later than the first generation. This basically refers to the member firms of MUSIAD and TUSKON. I refrain from using concepts like "secular bourgeoisie" or "Islamist bourgeoisie" as the definition of classes is not determined by their religious stance, but the way in which they engage in the process of capital accumulation. This will be detailed in the later chapters.

served as a mechanism of resource transfer to big capital (Oğuz, 2011: 7). As SMES were not allowed to receive state loans, they were eliminated from many sectors (Yeldan, 2011: 144–155). The big holdings preferred to invest in the banking sector rather than in manufacturing as it was more profitable to invest in banking. The aim of the policy was capitalist development, and it was presumably anticipated that financialisation would generate later industrial growth. However, it did not have a serious impact on Turkey's industrial development since holding companies preferred to enjoy high rates of interest coming from state borrowing rather than developing a systematic strategy based on labour productivity. Touching on the arguments made in previous chapters, the appropriation of surplus value based on high-value-added sectors and high-tech sectors remained insignificant,[4] and therefore, this pattern of capital accumulation was ultimately unsustainable (Gültekin-karakaş, 2007: 277).

In this period, Turkey signed stand-by agreements with the IMF in order to reproduce the financial system of the country. Turkey borrowed 20.5$ billion from the IMF. The reform packages implemented by the IMF and the Turkish state in the late 1990s and early 2000s also led to financial instability, as hot money flowed to and from the Turkish financial system. The dependence of the Turkish financial sector on external money flows and IMF credits resulted in the 2001 banking crisis. In the light of this event, the state and capital sought new reforms to enable the big holding companies to compete in the global market. Both MUSIAD and TUSIAD as representatives of commercial and industrial capital were in favour of reforms in the banking sector for different reasons. TUSIAD, for its part, represented firms which were mostly already in the process of integration into global capitalism and thus demanded reforms compatible with international norms and principles, which would pave the way for their integration into larger-scale markets. On the other hand, MUSIAD was in favour of reforms favouring internal sectors for the sake of SMES (Gültekin-karakaş, 2007: 296). Concomitant international developments also increased the extent to which the Turkish bourgeoisie was internationalised, for instance, the demise of the USSR in 1991, the Customs Union agreement signed with the EU in 1996, and the East Asian Crisis in 1997. After the collapse of the Soviet Union, Turkish capital has expanded towards post-Soviet countries in Central Asia and the Caucasus. In 1999, after the Helsinki Summit of the European Council, Turkey was accepted as a "candidate state destined to

---

4 According to Saygili, low value-added sectors constitute 40% of the total value added in industrial production between 1990 and 1997, while high value-added sectors constitute 5.5% of the total value added (Saygili, 2003). This means that the Turkish industrial sector was still labour-intensive in the 1990s.

join the Union". The relations with the European Union were also an integral part of the internationalisation of Turkish capital in the 2000s, which will be detailed in the following chapters. Overall, the reform packages and liberalisation policies since the 1980s have weakened market conditions in Turkey. In other words, the shift from ISI to an export-led development model deregulated the market. As a result, Turkey was hit by a severe banking crisis in 2001.

4   Transnationalisation of Productive Capital and the AKP

By the end of the twentieth century, Turkey had entered a new phase of neoliberalism in line with the policy principles of market-oriented internationalisation (Ercan & Oğuz, 2006: 648). The first two phases of integration of capital have occurred in the circulation sphere including commercial and money capital, while the third and last phase, the transnationalisation of capital, crystallised in the sphere of production. This reflected the emerging principles of the global free trade agenda relating to the GATT Uruguay Round. This also relates to the emerging Post-Washington Consensus (PWC) which is a new phase of neoliberal capitalist development which emerged in the wake of the East Asian economic crisis in 1997. As the global trade in goods and services were in decline in the aftermath of the 2008–9 global financial crises, "developing countries" like Turkey were still urged to integrate into the global economy by increasing foreign trade and FDI (Rogers, 2010: 18). In this period, Turkey has placed itself in a new location in the global free trade system.

The policy prescription of the PWC era centres on the institutionalist idea that active and regulatory states can efficiently solve the stagnation arising in the total circuit of capital due to neoliberal free trade (Rogers, 2010: 11). In short, it is suggested that capitalists are not themselves able to manage the contradictions and errors in the market; therefore, there was a need for more regulatory and proactive government and supervisory institutions to enhance private-sector-driven growth (ibid.). On the other hand, this period also saw the transnationalisation of Turkish productive capital including commercial and money capital. It should be noted that this process was part and parcel of the internalisation of the operations of transnational capital within the context of the Turkish social formation. Indeed, the hegemonic fraction of Turkish capital and the state authorities knew that patterns of capital accumulation had to be standardised in line with the dynamics of the global accumulation regime. As the money capital-based accumulation period was based on low-wage exploitation, it was essential for Turkish capitalists to move into higher value-added accumulation and increased mechanisation (Gültekin-karakaş

& Ercan, 2008). In this context, a shift in the patterns of capital accumulation was vital in order for Turkish productive capital to strengthen its competitive power and integrate into global free trade relations (Gültekin-karakaş, 2009b: 126).

The transnationalisation of productive capital was not only a demand of Turkish capitalists, but also an economic prerequisite for continued accumulation, since the process of money capital accumulation has reached its limits, and it was required in order to integrate Turkish capital into the global accumulation process (Ercan, 2002: 6). The AKP came to power in 2002 after general elections in November, in the period following the banking crisis. The distinctive feature of the pre-AKP period was the lack of any hegemonic power which was able to unify the interests of Turkish capital (Oğuz, 2016: 93). The dominant classes have unified under the hegemony of one fraction of a given class or a fraction within the power bloc which is able to secure and advance the interest of all fractions, and bring various class fractions together, while disorganising the popular masses. In Turkey, the AKP appeared as a new hegemonic power within the power bloc. Thus, it obtained the support of different social forces within and outside the power bloc. These fractions of capital sought to expand into new markets. For instance, the EU membership process was supported by an alliance between TUSIAD and the state in the early 2000s (Keyman & Öniş, 2007: 40). EU membership was perceived as essential to integrate into the global free trade relations (Yaka, 2011: 81). On the other hand, Turkey's foreign economic relations have witnessed a shift during the AKP era in the context of the restructuring of the Ministry of Foreign Affairs under the rule of Ahmet Davutoglu. This was accompanied by the improvement of bilateral political and economic relations with neighbouring countries. However, the main aim, partially conditioned by the 2001 financial crisis, was to foster a deepening of neoliberal restructuring in the aftermath of the crisis.

5   Regional Expansion of Turkish Capital through Free Trade Agreements

In order to solve the stagnation arising out the 2001 banking crisis, and in accordance with the transnationalisation of productive capital, Turkey signed free trade agreements (FTAs) with different countries around the world. As mentioned in Chapter 2, these FTAs were a response to the expanded free trade agenda in the aftermath of the GATT Uruguay Round, which furthered bilateral trade agreements at a time when further multilateral agreement was stymied (Bieler & Morton, 2014: 42). In line with the shift in the global free trade agenda, these FTAs did not only include trade in goods, but also services, agriculture and finance (Ersoy, 2013). For instance, the Turkey-South Korea FTA signed in 2013 included trade in goods, services, investment, agriculture, and intellectual property rights (Ministry of the Economy, 2014). Turkey signed FTAs with 36 different countries including Tunisia in 2005, Morocco in 2006, Egypt in 2007, Albania in 2008, Georgia in 2008, Serbia in 2010, Montenegro in 2010, Jordan in 2011, Chile in 2011, and Malaysia in 2015, and negotiations are proceeding with 17 other countries/blocs (RMT, 2020). In the field of political relations, Turkey has also conducted High Level Strategic Cooperation Council Meetings with Lebanon in 2010 (MFA, 2011a), with Iraq in 2009, on subjects ranging from security to energy (MFA, 2011b), with Greece in 2016 (MFA, 2016a), through the fifth meeting with Gulf Cooperation Council High Level Strategic Dialogue (MFA, 2016b), and many more with different countries. Further, Turkey and Egypt organised a "Turkish-Egyptian Business Forum" which was held in 2010. Prior to the political and economic destruction in Syria starting in 2011, Turkey established new relations with Syria through organising common cabinet meetings, signed a free trade agreement and lifting visa requirements for Syria in 2009. As a result, the volume of trade between Turkey and Syria almost doubled from $1.4 billion to $2.2 billion in 2010. However, Turkish imports from Syria declined to $51 million in 2015 because of the deterioration of the bilateral political and economic relations with this country and its collapse into civil war. Turkey reduced a range of trade barriers with Lebanon and Jordan in 2011 to advance a set of economic goals aimed at creating a free trade area (Tur, 2011). More significantly, the construction of post-war Iraqi Kurdistan provided a cross-border opportunity for Turkish businesspeople to expand their investments. Hence, Iraqi Kurdistan became Turkey's second largest trade partner by 2011.

As the real form of motion of capital from one place to another creates new conditions of production and results in differentiation (Palloix, 1977:3), the transnationalisation of productive capital has caused some significant changes in the regional patterns of the AKP's foreign economic relations in the early 2010s, which were accompanied by the diversification of Turkey's foreign trade partners. Tables 2 and 3 demonstrate that there has been a substantial increase in the share of Near and Middle Eastern and Organization of Islamic Cooperation (OIC) countries, and a dramatic decline in the share of European Union (EU) countries as Turkish foreign trade partners during the selected period. In 2006, the Near and Middle Eastern Countries received only 13.2% of Turkish exports, but by 2015 the ratio had increased considerably to 21.6 %. Similarly, OIC countries have become a popular destination for Turkish foreign trade. Between 2006 and 2015 Turkish exports to these countries rose from 17.5% to 29.7%. On the other hand, the proportion of Turkish exports sent to the EU countries has decreased from 56.3% in 2006 to 44.5% in 2015, although the absolute value of these exports increased in a context of rapidly increasing exports. Although there has been a dramatic increase in the share of non-EU countries in the Turkish foreign trade, the EU countries still occupy a central place in the share of Turkey's foreign trade partners. This shows that relations with EU countries remained an integral part of the expansion of Turkish capital towards world markets, and at the same time, the EU membership process involved fiscal adjustment (Öniş & Bakır, 2007: 152). Also, Turkish finance capital has moved its investments from labour-intensive sectors to capital-intensive sectors within the period of the transnationalisation of productive capital (Yukseler & Turkan, 2008: 13). This happened because of the continuing pressure on the Turkish bourgeoisie that was brought about by competition from China and India which have greater advantages in labour-intensive sectors (Saygili et al., 2010: 7).

Moreover, there has been an attempt to offset the intra-regional and intra-sectoral unevenness of the process of production. To this end, the Turkish state has announced the "Eighth Five-year Development Plan" (2001–2005) suggesting that Turkish industrialists must focus on producing high value-added products which have become indispensable for Turkey's development (SPO, 2000: 21). The policy aim is to encourage companies to shift their production from low value-added sectors to high value-added sectors (Arslan, 2021:6). This policy led to a concentration of new investments in higher value-added sectors, even though established sectors also experienced growth.

As an illustration, the annual increase in agricultural exports was 5.1% percentage between 1996 and 2007, while the increase was 15.6% for industrial goods, and 24.3% for sectors producing capital-intensive goods such as electronic devices, motor vehicles, and communications devices (Yukseler & Turkan, 2008: 24). This suggests that commercial and money capital, which previously concentrated on the appropriation of absolute surplus value through labour-intensive production, have started to engage in the extraction of relative surplus value through specialisation in high value-added sectors and increasing labour productivity (Gültekin-karakaş, 2009b: 100).

In line with this shift, in the AKP period, Turkey has received FDI in greater quantities than any time in its history (see Figure 3). The resultant FDI inflow, which has transformed the Turkish social formation, is one of the most important stimuli for the integration of the Turkish economy into the global capitalist system in the AKP period, as there has been a sharp growth of international money inflow coming into Turkey. In this period, new cycles of investments

TABLE 2   Export by country groups and years, share in total (%)

	2006	2008	2009	2011	2012	2015
European Union*	56.3	48.3	46.2	46.4	39.0	44.5
Near and Middle Eastern	13.2	19.3	18.8	20.7	27.8	21.6
Organization of Islamic cooperation	17.5	24.7	28.0	27.7	36.2	29.7
African countries	5.3	6.8	10	7.7	8.8	8.6

* Including the UK

SOURCE: AUTHOR'S COMPILATION BASED ON TUIK DATA, 2016

TABLE 3   Exports by country groups and years, value: Billion $

	2006	2008	2009	2011	2012	2015
European Union*	48.1	63.7	47.2	62.5	59.3	63.9
Near and Middle Eastern	11.3	25.4	19.1	27.9	42.4	31
Organization of Islamic cooperation	15.0	32.5	28.6	37.3	55.2	42.7
African Countries	4.4	9	10.1	10.3	23.5	12.4

* Including the UK

SOURCE: AUTHOR'S COMPILATION BASED ON TUIK DATA, 2016

have begun in which a new type of value has started to accumulate in the production process. As Hart-Landsberg (2013: 16–18) argues, this is also an outcome of the capital accumulation crisis in advanced capitalist countries since they have expanded their base of production in late-developing capitalist countries via the operations of TNCs (Gültekin-karakaş; Hisarciklilar; Hayta, 2013: 307). According to the ISO 500 List, 126 of the 500 leading companies involved in FDI in Turkey were joint ventures with foreign companies (ISO, 2017: 45). However, Figure 3 also demonstrates that there has been a radical decline in the inflow of FDI coming to Turkey in the aftermath of the 2008–9 global financial crisis. To overcome this threat and to turn the crisis into an opportunity, Turkey implemented economic policies designed to encourage foreign capital to invest in Turkey.

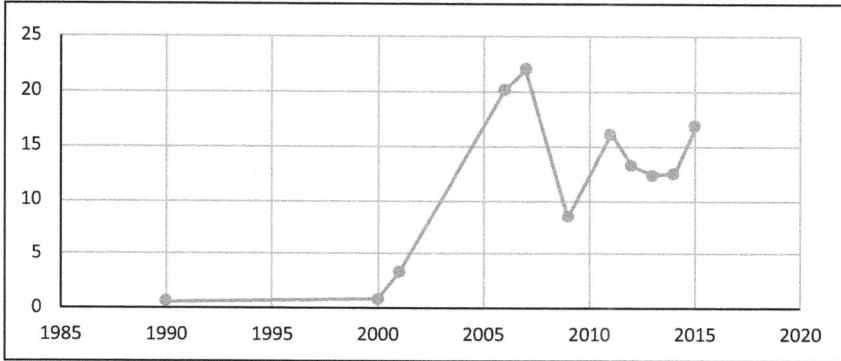

FIGURE 3   Foreign direct investment, net inflows (BoP, current US$)
SOURCE: AUTHOR'S COMPILATION BASED ON WORLD DEVELOPMENT
INDICATORS, CREATED ON 27/10/2016

As Oğuz also argues (2011: 16), Erdoğan's speech which he delivered in the aftermath of the crises provides a solid background to the reactions of Turkey to the economic crisis.

> We say that whatever you call it, money or capital or labour does not have a religion, does not have a country, and does not have a nationality. Money is like mercury: whenever it finds the proper environment, a safe environment for itself, it immediately flows there. That is a reality. If you prepare that environment, it will flow to you, and if you fail to do that then it will turn its direction and go somewhere else. This is why we were determined to provide that environment. For that purpose, we also try to increase the flexibility of the labour market and to improve and strengthen the R&D and innovation capacity to expand knowledge and communication, the IT technologies, and to ensure high value-added production capabilities in the industrial and service sectors.
>
> ERDOĞAN, 3rd April 2009

In this context, the AKP period is unique regarding the increase in FDI and foreign trade, which is a consequence of the growth in manufacturing, foreign direct investment, and exports (See Figure 3). These developments can partly be explained by the fact that domestic and foreign investments were highly encouraged and promoted by the AKP government at a rate unprecedented in Turkey's economic history (Özkale & Yüksel, 2016: 2).

This resulted in a fourfold increase in Turkey's foreign trade (Figure 4), in addition to a threefold increase in the size of the Turkish economy and its

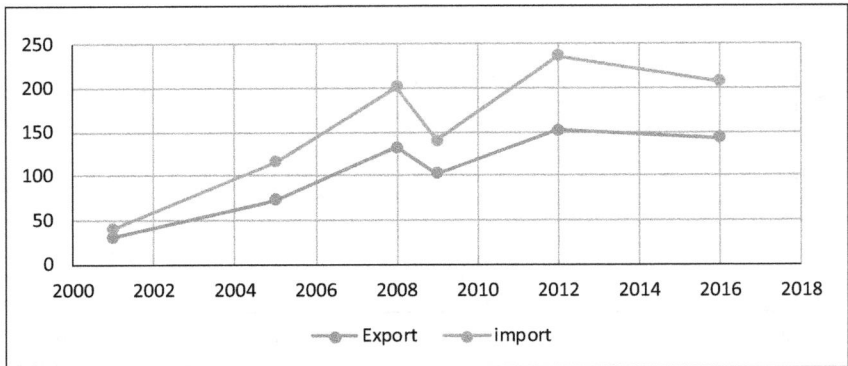

FIGURE 4   Turkish foreign trade over time
SOURCE: AUTHOR'S COMPILATION BASED ON TUIK DATA (2019)

per capita GDP (Öniş & Kutlay, 2013: 1412). The reforms in the PWC era have also encouraged large domestic companies to expand internationally and to integrate into the global value-production process. Consequently, the AKP government took a more active role to improve the functioning of the economy through the PWC reforms.

6   The Role of the State in the Expansion of the Base of Production

As Poulantzas argues, the state plays a crucial role in expanding the space of production and accumulation of capital (Poulantzas, [1978]2000: 213). In the case of the Turkish state, this was achieved through regional policies that aimed to increase the global competitiveness of Turkish capital via the domination of industrial capital within the power bloc (Oğuz, 2013: 200). The diversification and proliferation of Turkey's trade partners, or in other words, the transnationalisation of productive capital provided some fractions of Turkish capital with opportunities to find new spaces to operate, and hence to appropriate more surplus value. On the other hand, the AKP government provided public subsidies for SMEs after the 2008–9 global financial crisis and refused to sign a new stand-by agreement with the IMF (Oğuz, 2013: 205). In this regard, the AKP turned the crisis into an opportunity to increase foreign and domestic investments, while establishing a new mechanism to control productive forces.

Although there has been a substantial increase in Turkish foreign trade volume and diversification in trade partners, the foreign trade deficit has reached almost $100 billion by 2015 (See Figure 4 above). Also, contrary to the mainstream argument that free trade will create more job opportunities for the workers of each country engaged in it, unemployment in Turkey has risen to 13.2% (4.194 million workers) in 2020 (TUIK, 2021). Even though Turkey liberalised its foreign trade regime and engaged in free trade relations, this did not create more job opportunities and a balance of payments. Rather, Turkish exporters are highly dependent on imported products in the leading export sectors such as the automotive, durable consumer goods, textile and garment industries (See Table 4).

Table 4 demonstrates the production structure in Turkey until 2008 was a breaking point for many countries hit by the global financial crisis. This shows that, during the 2000s, Turkey was heavily reliant on imports of intermediate goods in as components for producing industrial products. Turkey has moved up the value-chain in this and the subsequent period, but its industry remains concentrated in low and intermediate value-added sectors. By 2016, the share of intermediate-low tech products in Turkey's production was 39.3%; low-tech products was 37.4%; intermediate-high tech products was 19.5; and high-tech products was 3.7% (ISO, 2017 13; 94). Among the top 500 industrial companies, the share of intermediate-high technology products (chemical products, electronic devices, motor land vehicles, and medical supplies) in Turkish exports was 51.5% in 2016, while the share of high-tech products was less than 5% (ISO, 2017 : 94). This reflects the Turkish foreign trade strategy of "buying from

TABLE 4   The share of goods in Turkey's export and import (%)

Years	Share in export (%)			Share in import (%)		
	Industrial goods	Intermediate goods	Consumer goods	Intermediate goods	Industrial goods	Consumer goods
2001	42.7	8.5	48.7	66.1	20.9	12.7
2002	40.6	7.7	51.2	73.2	16.8	9.2
2003	39.1	9.2	51.1	73.0	16.3	9.5
2004	41.1	10.3	48.3	71.7	16.3	11.3
2005	41.2	10.9	47.4	69.3	17.8	12.4
2006	44.2	11.0	44.2	70.1	17.4	12.0
2007	46.1	12.8	40.7	71.4	16.7	11.5
2008	51.3	12.7	35.7	72.7	15.9	11.0

SOURCE: SAYGILI, S. (ET. AL. 2010, P.7)

Asian countries, selling to European countries" (Yukseler & Turkan, 2008: 15), positioning Turkey as a semi-peripheral intermediary between low-wage Asian producers and European consumers. This strategy leads to extreme dependence on imports of low-value-added goods. Table 4 demonstrates that Turkish exports of industrial products are dependent on the import of intermediate products within the selected period. For instance, the share of intermediate goods in Turkish imports in 2008 is 72.7%, while the share of industrial products in Turkish exports is 51.3%. As Table 4 demonstrates, Turkey mainly engages in the export of industrial and consumer products based on cheap labour and assembly production for TNCs. This has increased the share of intermediate goods in imports. This reflects the diversification of the global manufacturing process into segments in different countries, with Asia monopolising low-end industrial production, while Turkey integrates itself into the global value chain as an intermediate-good importer and finished-good exporter (see Table 4). In the process, Turkish firms shifted their patterns of capital accumulation by decreasing the value of variable capital, by lowering employment and lowering real wages, and by increasing the productivity of labour.

This process was accompanied by the internationalisation of the state's function in the 2000s. The reform packages implemented after the 2001 Turkish banking crisis aimed at restructuring the social relations of production in Turkey so as to eliminate all the remaining trade barriers and remove all obstacles to the international operation of capital (Gültekin-karakaş, 2007: 284–285). They also aimed at standardising capital accumulation patterns in all sectors from energy to finance. This meant there was also a need to restructure the state apparatuses. Therefore, another significant transformation is noticeable in the role and structure of the state. As predicted by Poulantzas ([1974] 1975: 73), the internationalisation of Turkish capital neither surpassed nor bypassed the Turkish state. Rather, the capacity of the Turkish state was increased so as to control and manage the regional expansion of various members of the Turkish business associations. The transformation of the state apparatuses, therefore, appeared to be as a response to, and a result of the 2001 banking crisis, which showed that the government at that time was not able to overcome the problems in the economy, such as overaccumulation, balance of payment deficits, high inflation rates and so on. Therefore, the state's executive branches and institutions were restructured to play a more active economic role to maintain the global expansion of capital (Marois, 2012: 167). The transformation of the regular state apparatuses was demanded, so as to facilitate changes at the level of the relations of production and accumulation. The structure of the state was reconfigured to pave the way for the internationalisation of capital, and thus, the state was also internationalised during this process.

The formation of neoliberal authoritarian statism in Turkey in the PWC era was crystallised under the rule of the AKP government through the rise of independent regulatory agencies and the strengthening of the executive branch of the state vis-a-vis the administrative and judicial branches. With reference to Poulantzas ([1974] 1975: 73), this was an attempt to manage "its domestic capitalist order in a way that contributes to managing the international capitalist order". There was also internalisation of the global class relations inside the Turkish social formation through implementing IMF reforms. One of the most crucial steps in this context was banking reform in the aftermath of the banking crisis in 2001 (Oğuz, 2008: 118). This was essential for the continuity of productive capital-based accumulation. As the previous rent transfer mechanisms relying mainly on state borrowing had contributed to the collapse of the banking sector in Turkey at the beginning of the 2000s, there was a need to shift funds from state debts towards fixed capital investments (Oğuz, 2008: 119). It is thus fair to speculate that the IMF was concerned that the capital accumulation model based on state borrowing would further undermine the whole process of capital accumulation in Turkey, and, given Turkey's existing level of internationalisation, this would have a spillover effect onto other countries (Gültekin-karakaş, 2009b: 98). The banking system, therefore, had to be standardised in accordance with international banking standards (Gültekin-karakaş, 2009b: 95), removing a major channel for rent-extraction (and thus for state management of contradictions among capitalist fractions and favouritism towards particular fractions). This said, it is notable that these reforms were not directly imposed by the IMF, as Turkish state authorities were themselves enthusiastic to adopt these changes, even at the expense of some fractions of capital (ibid., 112). This shows that the Turkish state is not simply a tool in the hands of imperialist institutions. Rather, it still enjoys relative autonomy in the national space. Consequently, the Banking Regulation and Supervision Agency (Bankacilik Duzenleme ve Denetleme Kurumu, BDDK) established in 1999 has made critical attempts to restructure the banking system. In the aftermath of the 2001 banking crisis, Kemal Dervis, who was the former vice-president of the World Bank, was appointed as the Minister of the Economy in order to restructure the banking sector and the economy in line with international norms. A new economic program called 'Transition to a Strong Economy' was announced, with officials suggesting that immediate reform was needed in critical sectors including telecommunications, energy, agriculture, and finance/banking (Marois, 2012: 168). This was a direct result of developments in the global free trade agenda in the post-Uruguay Round which expanded global trade from trade in goods to services, finance and agriculture. Dervis partially stated that the aim was to separate the economy from the political sphere, a goal which meant accelerating the process of state restructuring in accordance with neoliberal market principles (Marois, 2012: 168). In tandem with this, the Central Bank of Turkey was also reconstructed by granting it independence from the Turkish government.

The establishment of YOIKK (Yatırım Ortamını İyileştirme Koordinasyon Kurulu, The Coordination Council for the Improvement of the Investment Environment) exemplifies the intensification of the relationship between the state and capital (Akçay, 2013: 29). This Council is responsible for organising the relationship between different fractions of capital and the state and at the same time organising links between the international bourgeoisie and Turkish capital. The economic functions of the state are constructed in certain state bodies which are charged with the depoliticisation of the decision-making process. Moreover, The Turkish Sugar Authority (Şeker Kurumu), Energy Market Regulatory Authority (Enerji Piyasası Düzenleme Kurumu), Public Procurement Authority (Kamu İhale Kurumu), Competition Authority (Rekabet Kurumu), and Saving Deposit Insurance Fund (Tasarruf Mevduatı Sigorta Fonu) were strengthened in order to operate on behalf of the market rather than politics (Bedirhanoğlu, 2013: 54). The strengthening of the executive branch aimed at eliminating the contradictions within the state structure so as to put neoliberal policies into practice (Bedirhanoglu, 2013: 52). This reconstruction has yielded dramatic changes in the relations between state financial apparatuses and capital-labour relations in Turkey. As Poulantzas argues, authoritarian statism plays a strong role in economic activities, such as the restructuring of industry, and selective aid to individual capitals (Poulantzas, [1978]2000: 212–13). In line with this, changes in the law gave the state financial apparatuses the ability to support some fractions of capital, while disorganising the popular masses. Legal regulations made by the AKP governments have provided opportunities to some fractions of the capitalist classes to invest inside and outside the country. Further to that, legal and institutional obstacles to privatisation were eliminated in accordance with "the new orientation of Turkish capitalism towards productive capital accumulation" (Ercan & Oğuz, 2015: 117). One example of these opportunities came through the changes to the Public Procurement Agency (Kamu İhale Kurumu), which aimed at opening public tenders to international competition through the cooperation between state apparatuses and business associations, such as MUSIAD and TUSKON (Ercan & Oğuz, 2006: 647).

As the state itself is a relation through which the interests of capital are interiorised (Bieler & Morton, 2008: 116), the interventions of the Turkish state in implementing neoliberal reforms can be assumed to express the economic-cooperative interests of fractions of capital. An example which can be mentioned in this context is the Economic Coordination Council (ECC), which played an active role in promoting public-private dialogue, especially after the 2008–09 global financial crises which began in the USA following the bankruptcy of Lehman Brothers. This global crisis is the worst one since the Great Depression in 1929 because most of the countries were badly hit due to the globally integrated economic system (Hanieh, 2009: 61). This crisis caused a dramatic increase in production costs and thereby a decline in global foreign trade volumes in most of the developing countries (Hanieh, 2009: 75). Turkey was not the exception in this case. Turkish state authorities and domestic capital faced a challenge in 2008–9 because of the global financial crisis. 2009 witnessed sharp decreases of 22.6% in Turkish exports and 30.2% in imports (see Figure 4). The ECC brought state authorities and the representatives of the different fractions of capital together to offset the negative consequences of the crisis reflected within Turkish capitalism and the Turkish state. It is important to emphasise that the financial apparatuses of the Turkish state made a significant effort to enhance regulations as part of this process.

7   Conclusion

This chapter provided a conceptual and empirical framework through which to understand the historical development of capitalist relations in Turkey. In terms of the theories outlined in Chapter 1, it shows that the development of capitalism in Turkey is uneven and combined, which means that capitalist development has taken different forms at different times in the context of Turkey as a late-developing capitalist country. The evidence of the uneven and combined development of capitalism in Turkey are: first, state intervention appears as the precondition for the emergence of capitalist relations, and second, the adoption of economic regulations such as five-year plans materialised as a different path of transition to capitalism as opposed to the European countries. Third, the process of primitive accumulation in Turkey happened in the commercial capital cycle rather than benefiting mainly industrial capital, as in advanced capitalist countries. Furthermore, industrialisation did not create a mass proletarian class in the early years of the Republic, in contrast with advanced capitalist countries. The petty-bourgeois character of small merchants and the connections between rural areas and big metropolitan cities remained strong until the early 2000s. Fourth, the specific form of integration of Turkey into the global relations of production has created dependency on imports of intermediate goods in producing industrial products.

In relation to the uneven character of capitalism in Turkey, this chapter has divided the analysis of capitalist development in Turkey into four distinctive but related phases which are: (i) commercial and agrarian capital-based accumulation until the 1950s, (ii) industrial capital-based accumulation based on the ISI model until the 1980s, (iii) export-led capital accumulation in the aftermath of the transition to neoliberalism, (iv) transnationalisation of productive capital in Turkey. This chapter placed special emphasis on the social relations of production, class composition and state-capital relations in each of the phases. This chapter also argued that the transnationalisation of Turkish capital has begun with the initiation of the transition to neoliberalism. It noted that, despite the differences in the patterns of capital accumulation in different phases of integration into global free trade system, there is not a distinctive divergence among each phase. This chapter instead argued that each phase accommodates the internationalisation of different circuits of capital. The distinguishing characteristics of the phases are each defined by one particular section of capital (commercial, money, and productive) which came to prominence in each of these phases. In this regard, this chapter argued that each phase of capital accumulation was determined by intra-state and intra-capital alliances and contradictions within and outside the power bloc.

The concept of capital accumulation has been used to highlight the way in which Turkey has integrated itself into the global system of free trade. Also, the integration of Turkish capital into the global value-production process is also determined by the uneven and combined nature of capitalist development. As the shifting patterns of capital accumulation in advanced capitalist countries have affected the patterns of capital accumulation in late-developing capitalist countries, the emergence and development of the capitalist classes in Turkey and the structure of the Turkish state have also been affected by this universal rule of capitalist development. In this chapter, the analysis of business associations in Turkey and the institutionalisation of class struggle within and outside the power bloc are assumed to operate based on these premises. In addition to this, this chapter also provided a basis for the analysis of the institutionalisation of regulatory reforms imposed by both the IFIs and the state apparatuses in each of the specific phases of capital accumulation.

To situate the emergence of business associations in Turkey, this chapter examined the late Ottoman period and the early years of the Turkish Republic, in which the first forms of business associations were founded by a rising industrial bourgeoisie. The chapter also put a particular emphasis on state policies so as to demonstrate the role of the state in the emergence and rise of business associations and capitalist classes in Turkey. It then focused on the integration of Turkish capital into global free trade relations in the aftermath of the transition to neoliberalism starting in the late 1970s. In the three phases of internationalisation of different circuits of capital (commercial, money, and productive), a new set of the relationships was constructed in both the capital accumulation process and within the state formation. Internationalisation in the commercial capital period involved a departure from an inward-looking capital accumulation model to an outward-looking model based on export promotion, and a liberalised foreign trade regime. When this stage reached its domestic limits, which resulted in the foreign currency crisis in the late 1980s, Turkey shifted to money capital-led internationalisation between 1989 and 2001. In this phase, state control over capital flows was lifted and restrictions on establishing private banks were removed, leading to changes in the class composition of the Turkish capitalist classes. This shift provided a conducive atmosphere for the emergence of MUSIAD. This also helped some fractions of capital to grow faster than others, leading to the emergence of the bigger holding groups among the TUSIAD members. When this pattern of capital accumulation became unsustainable because the appropriation of surplus value was not realised in production, and because of the favouritism towards the finance sector which resulted in the 2001 banking crisis, Turkey shifted its mode of capital accumulation towards a productive capital-based approach.

The transnationalisation coincides with the AKP's coming to power at the beginning of the 2000s, and this occurred in the production sphere whereas the previous forms of internationalisation were realised in the circulation sphere. This was essential since the competitiveness of the Turkish firms developed more slowly than their global counterparts. The AKP has established itself as a hegemonic power which unifies the conflicting interests of the different fractions of Turkish capital. The transnationalisation of productive capital has, therefore, generated pressure to expand into new markets in this period. This period also witnessed the emergence of TUSKON as a different fraction among business associations in Turkey, as is explained in more detail in Chapter 5. As a result of pressure to find investment links, the AKP has developed its foreign economic relations with the neighbouring countries in the Middle East and post-Soviet countries in Central Asia, with the purpose of internalising global free trade relations within the Turkish social formation. This has resulted in a dramatic increase in Turkish foreign trade volume and diversification of foreign trade partners. In addition to this, this period also witnessed a dramatic increase in FDI. The internationalisation of Turkish productive capital gained momentum through FTAS and High-level Strategic Cooperation Council Meetings. In accordance with these developments, the member firms of TUSIAD and MUSIAD have shifted their base of production into low-wage countries and started to specialise in higher value-added sectors in order to extract more relative and abstract surplus value.

This period also witnessed a transformation in the role and the structure of the state. The reforms in the banking sector, and transformation of the executive branches of the state in the late 2000s, aimed at eliminating the contradictions within the state structure and restructuring patterns of capital accumulation so as to put neoliberal policies into practice. These reforms and changes in the AKP era have not only altered the balance of power in the power bloc but have also had a significant impact on the intra-capital relations reflected within the different business associations. The following chapters examine these relationships in detail.

CHAPTER 3

The Formation of TNC, Global Free Trade, TUSIAD and the State

The way Turkey integrated into global free trade created international unevenness as well as internal unevenness, which positioned Turkey somewhere between two extremes: highly transnationalised capital comparable to that of advanced capitalist countries coexisted with areas and sectors which were highly underdeveloped. Internally, this unevenness is expressed in differential interests of capital fractions, with the core-like fractions being the most powerful. As Kiely also explains, internal unevenness arises without any necessary intent on the part of actors (Kiely, 2010: 188), such as the members of TUSIAD in the Turkish case. TUSIAD has a persistent hegemony over other capital groups, which is a direct result of the uneven development of a few giant companies within TUSIAD, such as KOÇ, SABANCI, and ANADOLU holdings. The largest fractions in TUSIAD were able in this period to expand their base of production to encompass other countries in the Global South which have lower wages and costs of production compared to Turkey. In this regard, the main motivation of this chapter is to examine the formation of a transnational capitalist class in Turkey which is a direct result of the integration of Turkey into global relations of free trade and whose material basis involves uneven and combined development. Unevenness refers to international inequalities between countries as well as internal differences within class and institutional relations. If the degree of penetration of foreign capital varies between different countries, the way internal capital interacts with foreign capital also differs. It is not only the power and class relations which are transformed, but also the way nationally based capital integrates into global free trade. The formation of TUSIAD is crucial to the analysis of the expansion of capital in Turkey towards different areas as well as internalisation of global process of capital accumulation in Turkey.

This chapter explores class and power relations in the Turkish social formation to map out the role of TUSIAD affiliates in the social relations of production in Turkey. By doing this, it places an emphasis on the contradictions of the process of capital accumulation, and different forms of integration into the global relations of production which are at the centre of the reproduction of TUSIAD-affiliated firms in different periods. It challenges mainstream categorisations which fail to recognise the significance of the social relations of production in their examinations of TUSIAD. Secondly, the chapter uncovers the dialectical relationship between the state and TUSIAD throughout the different stages of integration of Turkish capital into global free trade relations. It also unravels the complex relationship between the state and TUSIAD during the AKP period. In the same way, it reveals the contradictory nature of power and class relations within the power bloc. Thirdly, the chapter investigates the extent to which TUSIAD integrates into transnational relations of production, and it also examines the position of TUSIAD in global free trade relations. In relation to this, it examines the extent to which TUSIAD internalises the patterns of global free trade relations. The chapter concludes with an argument that the dominant fraction within TUSIAD is a transnational capital fraction which engages in production across borders and has plants outside the country, but TUSIAD also represents internationally oriented capital groups which produce in Turkey for export. This means TUSIAD does not only consist of large companies which operate in different countries, but also companies which only produce in Turkey.

1   The Social Formation in Turkey and the Development of TUSIAD

As highlighted in the previous chapter, the representation of business actors in the state was limited to the Chambers of Commerce and Industry until the first significant business association, TUSIAD, was established in 1971 (Buğra, 1994: 237). Until this time, the interaction between the chambers and government was very limited. The first examples of business associations were established under the initiative of a few big capital groups in the 1970s. Thus, the establishment of TUSIAD coincides with an epoch of rapid social and economic change, and of a large-scale restructuring of modes of capital accumulation at a time when Turkish capital was integrating into global relations of free trade. My analysis of TUSIAD explores the impact of TUSIAD affiliates on the shift in capital accumulation in Turkey, the place of TUSIAD affiliates in global free trade and the association's relationship with the state and with other business associations.

The class relations within both political and civil society prevalent in all domains in the context of the Turkish social formation in the late 1960s paved the way for the establishment of TUSIAD. The primary motivations for establishing TUSIAD were the ineffectiveness of TOBB[1] in terms of representing the

---

1   TOBB (Türkiye Odalar ve Borsalar Birliği, Union of Chambers and Commerce) is one of the largest business organisations in Turkey. This organisation is very significant in terms of its

interests of big family-based holding groups, the class struggle between capital and labour in the late 1960s, and the need for an association with a remit to encourage the government to join the European Union (Gulfidan, 1993: 26–39). TOBB was the largest and the most active association which represented the interests of business prior to 1971, which is a semi-public association of companies in Turkey. However, it was unable to take on the roles required by large capitalists in this period. The primary functions of TOBB are regulating the relations of production and promoting dialogue between the private sector and the governments (Sönmez, 2010: 65). As a result, TOBB lacked the ability to formulate hegemonic projects in contexts of divisions among member companies. It was the arena of class struggle between different fractions of capital until TUSIAD was established (Tuna, 2009: 304).

The need for a new organisation only became apparent once cleavages emerged among different capitalist class fractions. The larger fractions of the Turkish bourgeoisie created their own base for investment in industry in the 1960s. However, they did not establish their hegemony within the organisational structure of TOBB. Consequently, intra-capital conflict within the chambers emerged because of the tensions between big capital and SMEs. The founder members of TUSIAD argued that the decision-making process within TOBB was an obstacle to their development. At the same time, Necmettin Erbakan, who was the founder of the Welfare Party (Refah Partisi) and a prominent figure among the political Islamists, won the Union of Chambers election. His election campaign mobilised SMEs within the chambers which felt alienated by the chamber's leadership by larger fractions of capital (Buğra, 1998:525). More precisely, the clashing interests within TOBB were obstacles to the pursuit of a profound deepening of capital accumulation desired by TUSIAD affiliates. Most of the members of TOBB were commercial bourgeoisie and, in line with their interests, they encouraged the government to give more incentives to exporting companies as well as to encourage industrial policies, in contrast to which was demanded by larger fractions, which were already internationally competitive and no longer needed such support (Akçay, 2007: 56). In other words, the fractions within TOBB based on smaller capitalists were in favour of the maintenance of ISI policies and protectionism in foreign trade, policies which would aid these fractions' further development. On the other hand, larger capitalist fractions in TOBB were against protectionism in international trade and were ready to expand internationally. In this period, TOBB

---

role in the making of the hegemonic project as well as shaping the foreign trade patterns of Turkish companies. However, it is beyond the scope of this thesis. For furher information see Tuna (2009).

supported the commercial bourgeoisie, while larger capitalists specialising in the production of industrial goods were neglected (Öztürk, 2011: 113). In this context, because of the monopolisation and hegemony of finance capital, and the underrepresentation of the interests of big capital within TOBB, TUSIAD was established by big capital in 1971.

TUSIAD was established on 2 April 1971 through a protocol signed by big capital groups operating mostly in Istanbul and Izmir. The founding members of TUSIAD were Vehbi Koç (KOÇ Holding), Selçuk Yaşar (Yaşar Holding), Feyyaz Berker (TEKFEN Corporation), Hikmet Erenyol (Elektrometal Industrial Corporation), Nejat F. Eczacıbaşı (Eczacıbaşı Holding), Raşit Özsaruhan (METAŞ Corporation) Melih Özakat (Otomobilcilik Corporation), Osman Boyner (Altınyıldız Mensucat Company), Sakıp Sabanci (SABANCI Holding), Ahmet Sapmaz (Güney Industry Company), İbrahim Bodur (Çanakkale Seramik Company), and Muzaffer Gazioğlu (Elyaflı Çimento Industry Company). These are the largest companies in Turkey, which have plants elsewhere in the international market, and thus represent the transnational fraction of Turkish capital which engages in trading industrial goods, including companies whose activities in industry range from metallurgy to steel. In 2021, TUSIAD has eight representative offices in Istanbul, Ankara, Washington, Brussels, Berlin, London, Paris and Beijing. It represents 4000 companies which between them account for 50% of the value added in Turkey, 85% of Turkey's total foreign trade, more than 50% of the non-agricultural, non-governmental workforce, and 80% of corporate tax revenue. The dominant groups in TUSIAD are KOÇ, SABANCI, ANADOLU, ECZACIBASI, BOYNER, OYAK, DOGUS, DINCKOK, ENKA and TEKFEN.

It is important to point out that most of the business groups in TUSIAD, such as KOÇ, SABANCI, ECZACIBASI, BORUSAN, YAŞAR, and ANADOLU, gradually increased their economic power and constituted their base for capital accumulation during the inward-oriented accumulation period from the 1950s onwards. Their enthusiasm for free trade came after they had already benefited as much as they could from ISI, and their agenda consisted in effect of pulling up the ladder, at the expense of their weaker competitors. As demonstrated in the previous chapter, the industrial bourgeoisie in Turkey had completed the process of internal accumulation of capital in its different circuits and were ready to expand internationally. Their material presence in industrial production and the finance sector was also solidified in this period. There were two paths available to TUSIAD-affiliated companies in the late 1970s. The first was to maintain an inward-oriented capital accumulation model, and the second was to shift towards export-based internationalisation which would provide them with state protection in infant sectors, but also an opportunity to integrate into the international market. TUSIAD chose the second way as it would ease the fragility of productive capital in the early years of internationalisation (Öztürk, 2011: 124–25).

According to Zafer Yavan, General Secretary of TUSIAD between 2009 and 2016,

> State subsidies through tariffs and import quotas in the ISI period have allowed us to accumulate our capital more rapidly, and to increase the level of specialisation. To be honest, we are always in favour of the free market and competition, but there is this reality that the trade walls established by the state in the 1970s have increased the import of capital goods and investment opportunities for us. When Turkish foreign trade became liberalised in the 1980s, the needs of the international market were satisfied easily.
>
> Interview 1, 18 August 2016

There was another structural obstacle to the expansion and development of larger scale capital in Turkey. Specifically, the regime had a labour problem on its hands, which had to be overcome. To ensure the transition to a new mode of capital accumulation, Vehbi Koç, the owner of KOÇ Holding, penned a letter to the president Kenan Evren after the military coup in 1980. He politely presented his demands and cautions to the new president. According to Koç, the main task which the military government should perform was to create a secure environment for big capital owners by suppressing labour militancy, and as soon as the safe environment is created the military regime should step back and allow free trade (SOL, 16 September 2011). The demand of Vehbi Koç and the way in which the letter was penned, demonstrate the establishment of an alliance between the military government and TUSIAD within the power bloc. As a consequence, the labour movement in Turkey which had its heyday in the 1970s with the increased number of strikes and a high unionisation rate, was defeated by the coalition of the military and the TUSIAD members. The development of TUSIAD as a representative of larger-scale capital groups in Turkey was, therefore, furthered with the 1980 military coup.

Along with other political reasons, the shift in the patterns of capital accumulation provided the material basis for the military intervention. It was essential to create a new hegemonic project. It was now essential for the leading capital groups to move from domestic production to global production. TUSIAD, therefore, welcomed the fresh start after the 1980 military coup because the process of capital accumulation was in crisis. Towards the end of the 1970s, Turkish capital represented by TUSIAD was on the eve of international integration into the global free trade system. This military coup, therefore, provided the ground on which a new power bloc was established. However, there were some contradictions between TUSIAD and ANAP (Anavatan Partisi, Motherland Party), which held power between 1983 and 1991. More precisely, Ozal did not fully satisfy the demands of TUSIAD. For instance, TUSIAD criticised him for not introducing immediate reforms in foreign trade, and for not making substantial changes to state subsidies (Akçay, 2007: 64). As the later chapters will discuss, the emergence of MUSIAD and TUSKON also characterised this period, meaning that TUSIAD lost its exclusive position as representative of large capital.

At this stage, there were class struggles between national units of capital in the process of creating more surplus value. This required expanding production globally. Accordingly, there was a need for cooperation between the state and capital, as class contradictions and compromises arose which are internal to the state. The first priority of the military government after the 1980 military coup was to reassure both global financial circles and the fractions organised within TUSIAD that the government are going to remain loyal to the requirements of the structural adjustment programmes inherited from the civilian government. As the capital fractions are organically linked to the establishment of state policy favouring the bloc in power (Poulantzas [1978]2000: 132), TUSIAD became an active partner in imparting this message to the world, at a time when the military regime banned the activities of all other business associations except TUSIAD. In point of fact, TUSIAD became an active part of the new hegemonic strategy after the 1980 military coup (Yalman, 2002: 39).

As touched upon in previous chapter, Turkey experienced the internationalisation of money capital in the 1990s, which was an era of fragmentation of capital in both national and international spaces. In this period, a lot of social space and many formerly state-controlled sectors were commodified, such as fertiliser production, agricultural pesticides, and agricultural machines. This was a consequence of the expansion of the global free trade agenda to agriculture in the aftermath of the GATT Uruguay Round in the 1990s. At the same time, the living conditions of ordinary people in Turkey underwent a radical shift in the 1980s and 1990s due to urbanisation. This created new demands based on new needs, such as toilet paper, TVs and radios, white goods, and automobiles. The fragmentation of capital also created a new sector of accumulation based on shopping malls and supermarkets. These new areas, along with health, sport, education and art, were captured by the TUSIAD coalition of companies (Öztürk, 2011:167).

The process of expansion, which has been realised to the near-exhaustion of the domestic market by the transnational fraction of capital, focused on the aspiration to penetrate advanced capitalist countries in the 2000s. TUSIAD launched its representative branches in Brussels in 1996, Berlin in 2003, and Paris in 2004. The motivation behind opening a Brussels office was to set up lobbying activities on behalf of Turkish firms which were ready to do business with European companies (Güzelsarı & Aydın, 2010: 63). TUSIAD also did not ignore economic relations with the Americas. The representative office in Washington was opened in 1998, with the aim of improving Turkish-American business relations, and establishing networks with academia, international organisations, and the US government. Sometime later, a representative office in Beijing was activated in 2007 to improve the relationship between private sectors in Turkey and Asia-Pacific countries, during a period in which the Chinese economy was undergoing rapid growth. TUSIAD has also organised annual conferences on China since 2012, which are called "Çin'i Anlamak & Çin ile İş Yapmak" (Understanding China & Doing Business with China). The focus of these conferences is on understanding contemporary developments in China's manufacturing and industry which may provide investment opportunities for Turkish enterprises (TUSIAD, 16 December 2016). With a particular focus and motivation, TUSIAD established 'TUSIAD International' in 2001. The aim of this unit is to improve the competitive power of Turkish firms and contribute to the improvement of bilateral trade and investment relations with foreign countries. To this end, TUSIAD aims at expanding the capital of its members to international markets through increasing their production facilities in these countries and establishing trade relations with the transnational companies at the centre of the world-system.

2   The Class Characteristics of TUSIAD Affiliates

The definition of TUSIAD from a class perspective is crucial since the literature on the capitalist fractions in Turkey is today mostly limited to religious, cultural, and regional explanations. This is also important in terms of examining the class composition of TUSIAD affiliates. This book argues that TUSIAD represents both internationally oriented capital which produces for export and a transnational fraction of Turkish capital which has production networks across national borders. The latter fraction occupies the dynamic centre of the Turkish social formation because it has had a prominent role in the establishment of capitalist relations of production in Turkey, and is the driver of the expansion of capital towards the international market. Despite the differences between the companies within TUSIAD, the dominant group within TUSIAD engages in transnational relations of production in various countries, and their system of production is tightly integrated into global relations of capital accumulation. This fraction of capital represents the specific interests of a particular fraction of the capitalist class in Turkey, which is socio-economically dominant in the current national social formation and is the *hegemonic fraction* of the bourgeoisie in Turkey. This study, therefore, identifies TUSIAD as the core representative of the transnational capitalist class in Turkey.

The patterns and strategies of capital accumulation pursued by TUSIAD members have always changed with regards to the shifting patterns of global capital accumulation. As mentioned in the previous chapter, larger groups within TUSIAD had initially started the process of capital accumulation in the commercial capital cycle and had submitted themselves to the rules of capitalist relations of production before the rest of the capitalist classes. This was followed by the accumulation of industrial capital until the 1980s, supported by ISI, and continued acquisitions of small firms in the years of stagflation in the 1980s. In the period in which capital controls and restrictions on private banking were relaxed, this fraction of industrial capital created and controlled its own banks, which advanced the process of the concentration and centralisation of capital under a single roof. Hence, this fraction of capital dominated both productive and commercial capital (Öztürk, 2011: 139; Ercan, 2002), and thus transformed into finance capital. Also, one cannot forget that the method of capital accumulation also involves arbitrage profits, which are based on borrowing cheap credits from abroad and selling a large amount of government bonds at a profit (Özden & Akça & Bekmen, 2017:191). For instance, KOÇ Holding was the owner of *KOÇBANK* which merged with *YAPI KREDI Bank* when it was purchased in 2005, SABANCI Holding owned *AKBANK*, CUKU-ROVA Holding owned *Pamukbank* which was confiscated by the TMSF (Saving Deposit Insurance Fund of Turkey) in 2002, OYAK Group owned *OYAK Bank* and *Sumerbank*, Doğan Group owned *Alternative Bank* which was sold to ANADOLU Group in 1996, DOGUS Group owned *Imar Bankası* between 1975 and 1985, and Garanti Bankası in 1983, ENKA Group owned *Chemical Mitsui Bank* between 1985 and 1992, TEKFEN Group held the shares of *Arap-Türk Bankası* between 1990 and 2006, and *Bank Express* between 1994 and 1997, ZORLU Group owned *Denizbank* between 1997 and 2006, and ANADOLU group is the owner of *Alternative Bank* since 1996. This shows that big capital, based initially in production, concentrated on the accumulation of money capital in the 1980s-90s. Some fractions of capital organised within TUSIAD have developed unevenly at the expense of others, and this has shifted the power relations among capital fractions. The power of SME fractions with influence in TOBB and in the pre-1980 power bloc was undermined in favour of the larger capital fractions represented by TUSIAD. This newer class fraction was also allied to larger transnational finance capital and the state. The increased amount of state subsidies for internationally active trading firms helped this fraction to grow faster and changed its form of capital accumulation. This demonstrates that the state internally engaged in relations of production through different mechanisms. To this end, export promotions issued by the government exceeded the amount of the tax the firms paid (Öztürk, 2011:139), transferring rents from the state to corporations on condition the latter engage in export-focused activity. This policy resulted in a large increase in the volume of trade in industrial products compared to previous years. The share of industrial goods in Turkish international trade was 36% in 1986, but reached 60% in 1982, 80% in 1990, and 90% in 2000 (Öztürk, 2011:140). This suggests the dominant fraction within TUSIAD accumulated their capital through their international trade linkages and the support provided by the government.

The restructuring of the social relations of production since the 2001 banking crisis led to changes in the composition of capital within the bigger fraction of Turkish capital. This means that, despite the continued centrality of these companies, there have nonetheless been shifts in the way they operate. The holding companies who were allowed to own private banks after the banking reforms in the post-2001 crisis era were also the ones who were able to compete in the global market (Gültekin-karakaş, 2009: 204). The government supported these capital groups at the expense of others which have been eliminated in the post-crisis era. The state policy in this period was a result of the class contradictions between different capital fractions. This means the state has chosen winners among different fractions of capital. In this sense, the post-crisis period is a new era in which the domestic composition of Turkish capital within the bigger fraction has been transformed and restructured. This also changed the inter-class relations within the power bloc, as the weaker and smaller companies in the large-scale fraction of Turkish capital have been eliminated. This helped the larger fractions in TUSIAD to integrate into the global value chain, which even resulted in a monopoly in some sectors.

The monopoly of TUSIAD affiliates on foreign trade was achieved through legal regulations. The first step was taken in 1984 to create a legal environment and organisational basis for firms operating internationally. This was a new company model which was called "Foreign Trade Companies" and aimed at encouraging big capital to engage in free trade. It was expected to increase the volume of foreign trade through providing significant state incentives, such as tax refunds, additional promotions, and a monopoly on trading with the Soviet bloc countries (Erkan, 1994:85–90). These trading companies reached more than 50 in number in the 1980s, and were asked to trade in industrial and mining products. Consequently, more than 50% of Turkish foreign trade were carried out by these firms which not only exported their own products but also exported the products of other Turkish companies. For instance, TEKFEN Foreign Trade Company exported the products of more than 200 companies to more than 50 different countries (Altun, 2006: 182). In short, by creating these trading companies, the government has encouraged the monopolisation of foreign trade in the hands of a few large firms, and these companies have gained a great deal of power to control the economy. Most of these enterprises, in turn, are members of TUSIAD.

The largest trading companies are RAM Foreign Trade (KOÇ Group), EXSA (SABANCI Group), CUKUROVA Foreign Trade (CUKUROVA Group), and IMEKS (DOGUS Group). With their monopoly on foreign trade and domination of the financial sector, the biggest fractions in the TUSIAD have created an ongoing and apparently impermeable hegemony over the rest of the Turkish capitalist classes (See Table 5). In addition to this, TUSIAD members have also launched foreign trade companies in foreign countries. For instance, KOFISA Trading (KOÇ) was started with an Italian partnership, SABANCI started EXSA Handels GmbH in Germany and CUKUROVA group founded Equipment and Parts Export in the US (Öztürk, 2011:142). This trading company system still exists in Turkey, although the original companies no longer have a monopoly or such a high share of exports as in the 2000s. There are 50 companies today with Foreign Trade Capital Company status. KOÇ Group owns five of these businesses, and SABANCI Group owns two of them. These companies controlled 30% of Turkish total exports in 2008 (Öztürk, 2011:153). Based on the lists published by Fortune Turkey, the tables below list the top exporters in Turkey in 2010 and 2016. As indicated in the tables below, TUSIAD has an uncontested hegemony among Turkish exporters, and its members have benefited disproportionately from the exponential growth in Turkish exports.

In relation to their presence in the finance sector, it is also important to note that the bigger fractions in TUSIAD (particularly KOÇ and SABANCI) accumulated capital in the stock market and centralised their existing capital in global capital circuits. The motivation behind investing in the stock market was to establish hegemony in the market. For instance, the biggest shareholders in Istanbul Stock Exchange (IMKB) were KOÇ, SABANCI and ISBANK with 43% of holdings in 1988, 45% in 1991, and 34% in 1997 (Yildiz, 1999: 75–8). In 2001, the top ten shareholders in the IMKB (of whom seven belonged to TUSIAD) had 64% of the total capital. The stock exchange market was also used to provide financial funds to industrial firms within the same holding companies. It would be fair to say that TUSIAD members have dominated both the banking sector and the stock exchange market during the 1990s and 2000s, which have given TUSIAD a near-monopoly on foreign trade. Overall, these mergers, and the resultant concentration and centralisation of capital, increased the interdependence between the larger capital groups as well as the contradictions

TABLE 5   Top exporters in 2018

Rank	Company name	Controlling ownership	Business association affiliation	Export (Billion $)
1.	FORD Automotive	KOÇ Group	TUSIAD	5.6
2.	Toyota Automotive	Toyota Motor Europe/Mitsui & Co.	-	4.5
3.	TOFAS TURK Automotive	KOÇ Group	TUSIAD	2.9
4.	Kibar Foreign Trade Company	Kibar Holding	TUSIAD	2.7
5.	TGS Foreign Trade Company		-	2.5
6.	TUPRAS Oil Company	KOÇ Group	TUSIAD	2.4
7.	VESTEL	ZORLU Group	TUSIAD	2.2
8.	ARÇELIK	KOÇ Group	TUSIAD	1.9
9.	Oyak-Renault		TUSIAD	1.7
10.	HABAS Sınai ve Tıbbi Gazlar		-	1.5

SOURCE: AUTHOR'S COMPILATION BASED ON TIM REPORT, 2019

between them. This means the contradictions between larger capitals were internalised in a power bloc within which these capitals were also mutually enmeshed. Overall, the dominant group within TUSIAD is TNC which also operates in the finance sector and actively engages in foreign trade. This confirms that TUSIAD represents mainly transnational fractions of the Turkish bourgeoisie, which have production networks elsewhere in the international market. These companies mainly operate automotive, energy, finance, and construction sectors.

3   TUSIAD and Power Bloc: The Internal Relations between TUSIAD and the AKP

Poulantzas argues that it is through the mediating capacity of the state that other fractions of capital can overrule the dominant fractions if they attempt to promote their specific interests. This then results in a power struggle within the power bloc (Poulantzas, [1968]1978: 255). In Turkey, this power struggle has taken different forms at different times with regards to the patterns of capital accumulation, and the changing form of the state. It is this which allows us to grasp the essential relationship between the state and TUSIAD, and thus provides an opportunity to interpret the materiality of power. It is also crucial to bear in mind that the capitalist state engages in social relations of production by restructuring the activities of capitalists, at the expense of dominated classes, to ensure better market discipline (Saad-Filho & Fine, 2004: 172). This is to say that the essence and appearance of internal relations within the state structure matter for the systematic analysis of these complex relationships. Mainstream theories studying the relationship between the state and capital, such as liberal and institutionalist theories, fail to recognise the internal contradictions and antagonisms between competing fractions within the power bloc. Contrary to the totalising analysis of theories of liberal-neoclassical and instrumentalist understandings of the state, the complex relations between TUSIAD and the state must be grasped inclusively, as determined by intra-class and inter-class struggles, conflicts, compromises, and contradictions within the power bloc. In this sense, it is explained how a specific policy of the state works in favour of the dominant classes and how the state seeks to resolve or pacify the internal contradictions within the power bloc.

As suggested in previous chapters, one of the main objectives of this study is to analyse the dialectical relationship between the state and business associations. It is important to note that the relationship between the state and TUSIAD is constructed in specific circumstances shaped by the capitalist mode of production. In relation to this, the relations between the AKP and TUSIAD cannot be reduced to the personal ties between individual capitalists and state authorities. Rather, I will place particular emphasis on class struggles between different fractions of capital, which (re)produce hegemony within and outside the power bloc. This will also help to uncover the complex relations within the power bloc, which is represented through internal relations between each of its parts. "Fractions of capital", "hegemony" and "power bloc", are the most appropriate concepts to analyse the relations between the AKP and TUSIAD in a Poulantzasian framework. The mainstream views fail to capture the peculiarity of the relations between TUSIAD and the state as they treat these agencies as separate entities and treat TUSIAD as a monolithic bloc without cracks. Contrary to these analyses, this study argues that there is always a clash of interests between TUSIAD and other business associations and among fractions of capital within TUSIAD. Without disregarding the dialectical relationship between the state and business associations, I will here focus on the power struggle within the power bloc as well as the mechanisms employed to mediate the contradictions within the power bloc.

When we examine power relations since the establishment of TUSIAD in 1971, TUSIAD has been a hegemonic class not only in terms of its organisational capacity but also its structural power in shaping and reconfiguring the social relations of production. TUSIAD's real presence in the power bloc crystallised in the 2000s, during which the transnationalisation of productive capital gained considerable momentum. This period also coincided with the rise of the AKP, which had a transformative impact on the previous power relations in the late 1990s and early 2000s. The AKP's coming to power was a response to the hegemonic crisis within the power bloc. There was a need for a force which would mediate contradictions within the power bloc while also re-establishing hegemony over civil society. In this sense, the complex relationship between the AKP and TUSIAD not only reconfigured power relations in political society but also caused the restructuring of the state in the aftermath of the banking crisis in 2001.

An analysis that suggests the existence of contradictory relations between the AKP and TUSIAD can be formulated on the basis of the formation of the relations within the power bloc, and the changing patterns of the power dynamics between capital fractions. Given the conditions which changed the balance of forces within the power bloc, it is fair to say that TUSIAD employs a variety of tools and strategies to maintain its domination both within state structures and over other capital fractions. These include lobbying for govern-ment policies and direct influence on the capital accumulation processes. For instance, inwardly oriented capital accumulation reached its limits in the late 1970s. TUSIAD, at this stage, wanted the current state authorities to find new markets, or in other words, to integrate the Turkish economy into the global circuit of capital. As the state became internationalised in the aftermath of the transition to neoliberalism in the 1980s, the state was expected to play a new economic role in the reproduction of the world market. TUSIAD's main argument in the late 1970s was that the government did not take the necessary measures to overcome the over-accumulation crisis and did not encourage export firms to integrate into global free trade relations (Güzelsarı & Aydın, 2010: 54).

The intervention of TUSIAD also targets national media channels, and circu-lates through annual reports, statistics, research forums, press conferences, and newspaper advertisements, which are the most well-known mechanisms that TUSIAD uses in its struggle for power. To influence the government, TUSIAD published four full-page manifestos in four national newspapers between May and June 1979. The titles of the memorandums were "The Realistic Way

Out", "The Nation is Waiting", "Sharing Scarcity or Creating Prosperity" and "Inflation: The Enemy of Prosperity and Freedom" (TUSIAD. 1979). In these memorandums, TUSIAD asked the government to encourage free trade, to integrate into the neoliberal market system, to reconfigure tax reforms and to take fiscal measures. These memorandums played a crucial role in Bülent Ecevit's resignation as Prime Minister. This campaign served as the primary public indicator that TUSIAD wanted to change the economic policies of the governments (Oğuz, 2008: 100).

The reflection of the class struggle within the power bloc changed in the 2000s. The construction of every moment of TUSAID's hegemony has been professionalised through the research forums established in partnership with top universities in Turkey. These included TUSIAD Competitiveness Forum with Sabancı University, TUSIAD Foreign Policy Forum with Boğaziçi (Bosporus) University, TUSIAD Information Society Forum with Bilkent University, and TUSIAD Economic Research Forum with Koç University were established for this purpose. In addition to this, TUSIAD organises PARKUR (*Parlamento ve Kamu Kurumları ile İlişkiler,* Relations with the Parliament and Public Institutions) meetings with deputy chairs of political parties in the parliament, and with ministers and senior bureaucrats. In these meetings, TUSIAD proposed its resolutions about many critical things relating to the social relations of production. For instance, in the session held on 22 June 2016, legislative reforms regarding tax payments, labour market regulations, industrial property rights, computerization of manufacturing (Industry 4.0), and relations with the EU were raised (TUSIAD, 22 June 2016). These are the tactics and devices which TUSIAD uses to varying degrees in its struggle for power.

The material basis of these strong relations was the AKP's ability to carry out a series of complex manoeuvres which helped it to maintain its relative autonomy and organise its hegemony in the power bloc. Constructing relative autonomy was necessary for the Turkish state, as it was not supposed to act against the collective interests of the capitalist classes. A report published in 2001 stated that to maintain the sustainability of the Turkish economy, government intervention should remain minimal. However, this does not mean that TUSIAD was in favour of a neo-classical minimalist state. What they call for was a state which regulates the market in favour of global free trade principles (TUSIAD & OECD, 2003: 27). In another report published in 2003, TUSIAD expressed its appreciation to the government since the government took the initiative to accelerate structural reforms of the economy (TUSIAD, 2003: 17). In this sense, TUSIAD supports an institutionalist understanding of the state (Evans, 1995:10). TUSIAD's former president Cansen Basaran Symes stated that:

The political decision process must be in coordination with the principles of market economy, and the rule of law. There must be some rules
regulating a free market system, having a free market does not mean
removing all the regulations. And the decisions relating to market conditions must be participatory.

BAŞARAN-SYMES, 6 June 2016

For TUSIAD, state intervention in the market is a given. Therefore, the central
question is not "how much" but "what kind" and "when" (TUSIAD, 2002: 19).
The reform programmes implemented after the 2001 banking crisis pushed
the Turkish state to become more important and influential, which reproduced and strengthened the space of the state and capital. For their part, the
Ministers of the Economy (such as Ali Babacan, and Mehmet Şimşek) always
represented the interests of big capital on global platforms, and a coalition
between TUSIAD and the government was established in the sense of coop-
erating in the administration of the economy (Akçay, 12 April 2016). Specific
state apparatuses focusing mostly on foreign trade, such as the Ministry of the
Economy and the Ministry of Energy, successfully dealt with the demands of
different capital fractions (Akçay, 12 April 2016).

There was a consensus within the power bloc in AKP's early years in power.
The reforms proposed by the IMF were fully implemented by the AKP government, which therefore, reoriented the role of the state in social relations of
production (Gültekin-karakaş, 2009: 185). Also, the AKP renewed the stand-by
agreement with the IMF between 2005 and 2008, which was encouraged by
TUSIAD whereas the smaller capitalist fractions were against the renewal of
the agreement. This indicates that the changing dynamics of the global circuits
of capital, or in other words, the transnationalisation of capital has changed the
internal relations between the state and capital in Turkey (Ercan & Gültekin-
karakaş & Yilmaz, 2016:141). The AKP has become the hegemonic power within
the power bloc which was expected to manage the contradictory interests of
different capitals and reorganise the social formation around a new hegemonic
project (Yaka, 2011:134). An active state was sought to ensure the mobilisation
of the active consent of the dominated classes, since the short-term and unsta-
ble coalition governments of the 1990s did not manage to establish hegemony
over the dominated classes and/or bring the dominant classes together under
the hegemonic fraction. This type of state, in a Poulantzasian sense, may unite
the power bloc, while dominating the working classes. Being relatively autonomous from the dominant classes, such a state could play an intertwined economic role in the relations of production, and the reproduction of the world
market and capitalist social relations in the Turkish context.

The neoliberal economic reforms suggested after the 2001 banking crisis of Turkey were fully implemented by the AKP government as the state must represent the long-term interests of the whole bourgeoisie. This representation occurs not in a mechanical sense, "but through a relationship of forces that makes of the state a condensed expression of the ongoing class struggle" (Poulantzas [1978]2000: 130). TUSIAD, therefore, suggested some significant reforms in the banking and economic sector of Turkey, which were crucial to establish the unity of the dominant classes as well as to reconfigure the relationship between dominant and dominated classes (TUSIAD & OECD, 2003). In this sense, TUSIAD has become an active supporter of the reforms suggested by Kemal Dervis, who was the architect of the restructuring of the Turkish state in the post-crisis era. This complex relationship was improved in the sense of creating a suitable environment in the aftermath of the 2001 banking crisis, which has, therefore, formed a prevailing consensus among the power bloc. This alliance within the power bloc was reflected in the coverage provided by the largest media channels owned by the most prominent members of TUSIAD (for instance, DOGUS and DOĞAN groups), which was largely sympathetic to the AKP. This demonstrates that the state, contrary to neo-classical arguments, is not an abstract entity external to the market. Rather, as Poulantzas argues, the class struggle within the power bloc is not static, and the state is not a neutral agent (Poulantzas [1978] 2000: 73). Hence, state power is class power, and the state and class cannot be examined separately.

A relational approach to the state is helpful in explaining the alliance between TUSIAD and the AKP, which was anchored in a win-win situation for the AKP and TUSIAD, which are the dominant fractions within the power bloc. Economic figures illustrate that TUSIAD members have experienced remarkable growth during the AKP period. For instance, the total assets of KOÇ Holding rose from $7.3 billion to $51.2 billion in 2007. In the same period, the total assets of SABANCI Holding increased from $21 billion to $43.9 billion. OYAK and its shareholding companies' assets rose from $4.6 billion to $19 billion. Çalık Group's total assets also grew from $1 billion to $3.3 billion; and ENKA Group's total assets (Öztürk, 2011:185). In the relational approach to the state, the intervention of the state in the economy might operate in favour of some fractions, and against others (Poulantzas [1974] 1975:71). The sale of TUPRAS to KOÇ Holdings is worth discussing, to reveal the dialectical relationship between the AKP and TUSIAD, and how the intervention of the state has changed the power relations within the capital bloc, benefiting some fractions of capital over others. In 1983, four oil refineries in Turkey, at Izmit, Izmir, Batman and Kırıkkale, were united under the corporate control of state-owned company TUPRAS. This company controls most of Turkey's refining capacity and is the owner of 59% of the country's total petroleum products storage capacity. The partial privatisation of TUPRAS started in 1991, and in 2005 a consortium of KOÇ Holdings and Shell acquired 51% of the shares in the company for $4.1 billion, a fraction of its true value. This investment has been more than paid back. The annual revenue of TUPRAS was $16 billion in 2004, $20 billion in 2005, and reached $25 billion in 2011. Largely due to this purchase, KOÇ Holdings' annual revenue increased from $18 billion in 2005 to $34.5 billion in 2006. This increased the ranking of KOÇ Holding in the Fortune Global 500 list; it jumped from 358th to 190th in 2006. As of 2021, KOÇ holding exports to more than 145 countries and the rate of its international sales to its total sale is 33%. The state's sale of TUPRAS thus helped KOÇ Holding to obtain hegemony over the other dominant fractions of capital within TUSIAD and expand its activities to the international market.

Notwithstanding the consensus about the general strategy of capital accumulation in the AKP period, there have always been cracks and contradictions between the AKP and some fractions within TUSIAD regarding the laws regulating power relations within the power bloc, and the relations between the working classes and capital. As Poulantzas argues, the state is not a monolithic bloc, and there are always contradictions between competing fractions within the power bloc. The near-monopoly power of TUSIAD placed restrictions on the state's relative autonomy vis-a-vis the other fractions of capital within the power bloc, as it would be costly for the state to defy TUSIAD. However, the balance of power between the AKP and TUSIAD shifted in the AKP's favour in the second half of the 2000s (Mert, 2013). As noted in Chapter 3, hegemony is not reducible to the relations between dominant and dominated classes, but also involves the class struggles within the power bloc (Poulantzas [1978] 2000: 169). In Turkey in the 2000s, the dominant classes united under the hegemony of the AKP, despite their conflicting interests, since the AKP could secure and advance the interests of all fractions. The material framework for the AKP's hegemony was thoroughly grounded in its relationship to the relations of production, which provided the basis for its capacity to organise a power bloc. The issue which initially ruptured the consensus between the AKP and TUSIAD was the amendment of the Public Procurement Law (Milliyet, 15 November 2008). This modification of the law changed the bidding regulations so as to provide the other fractions of Turkish capital with more opportunities to gain revenue from the state tenders. Some members of MUSIAD and TUSKON have been directly favoured by these regulations. This changed the power relations within the power bloc as well as those between the business associations.

Another contradiction surfaced in the late 2000s around the negotiations between the IMF and the AKP held after the 2008–9 global financial crisis.

This world financial crisis deepened the contradictions between capital fractions within Turkey, and the AKP failed to manage the tensions between the different fractions of capital represented by TUSIAD and MUSIAD. This contradiction demonstrates beyond all doubt that the state is a material condensation of classes and class struggles reflected in the political field (Poulantzas [1978] 2000: 73). TUSIAD publicly declared its support for the renewal of the stand-by agreement with the IMF. On the other hand, the SMEs represented by MUSIAD and TUSKON were against renewing the agreement as the reforms proposed by the IMF involved cutting local expenditures, a measure which would be detrimental to the survival of some SMEs (Bekmen, 2014: 65). Consequently, the AKP government refused to sign a new stand-by agreement with the IMF, which created tension between the AKP and TUSIAD, and affected the power relations within the power bloc. The AKP position was viewed as populism by TUSIAD (Bulut, 2008). There was another apparent contradiction between the AKP and TUSIAD on the constitutional referendum in 2010, which demarcated the spheres of activities of different state apparatuses, and thus impacted how they could be used in intra-bloc struggles. This referendum led to a break between the AKP and TUSIAD. TUSIAD was against the proposed reforms and changes in the referendum as they argued that this will increase the power of the executive branch of the state at the expense of judiciary, undermining the rule of law which was part of TUSIAD's vision of a free market. The AKP, in turn, began to question the influence of TUSIAD and the power of large capitalists in Turkey. The Prime Minister Erdoğan threatened TUSIAD, stating that:

> Those who do not take a side will be eliminated ... we will not allow the bourgeoisie to establish hegemony over the country ... you used to treat the previous governments as your pet but be aware that you cannot do the same to this government.
>
> ERDOĞAN, 18 August 2010

In another speech in 2010, Erdoğan explicitly stated that:

> Istanbul capital, somehow, works with us when it comes to making a profit, but they do not do the same when it comes to politics ... the money is changing hands substantially, and the export volumes of Anatolian capital are growing in a serious way ... maybe you began to feel uncomfortable about this, but you should not have this feeling ... whether you like it or not, capital is changing hands in a serious way.
>
> ERDOĞAN, 11 September 2010

As Poulantzas mentions, the state can intervene against the long-term interests of one fraction within the power bloc, when this is seen necessary for the realisation of its own political class interests (Poulantzas, [1968] 1978:285). Applying this analysis to the class struggle within the Turkish power bloc, it becomes possible to analyse the contradictions between the AKP and specific fractions within TUSIAD and theorise the reconfiguration of the relationship of forces within the power-bloc. For instance, the government imposed a $2.5 billion tax fine on DOĞAN Group, one of the largest members of TUSIAD, because of the anti-government attitude expressed in its media channels (OSCE, 16 September 2009). As Poulantzas also argues, the state's economic interventions are also political interventions, which means that the state has an intertwined role in both economics and politics (Poulantzas [1974]1975: 160). This tension between the AKP and DOĞAN Holding, therefore, reflected the contradictions within the power bloc, which were a result of the increased fragmentation among transnational fractions of capital in TUSIAD and internationally oriented fractions within MUSIAD and TUSKON. The AKP aimed at reunifying the power bloc under its hegemony by taming some fractions within the power bloc, and in particular, reducing DOĞAN Group's capacity to universalise its interests (Benlisoy, 26 January 2017).

The contradictions between the AKP and TUSIAD appeared in different ways at different times. The transfer of big media groups like ATV-SABAH is another example related to the fight against the DOĞAN media channels. The sale of these media groups to ÇALIK Holding, whose CEO was Berat Albayrak, the son-in-law of Erdoğan and Minister of Finance and Treasury between 2018 and 2020, led to a dispute between TUSIAD and the AKP. DOĞAN Group, which used to own almost 50% of the media outlets in Turkey, wanted to take over ATV-SABAH as part of its centralisation strategy. Instead, ÇALIK Holding, which at the time was outside the TUSIAD coalition, won the bid for these media groups. However, the struggle never turned into a pure antagonism with TUSIAD. While the government wiped out some big groups in TUSIAD from the market, other fractions were actively supported by the government. This means some capitalist fractions were destroyed in order to strengthen other fractions. This conflict within the power bloc has also created a divergence within TUSIAD. For instance, Arzuhan Doğan Yalçındağ, who is the daughter of Aydın Doğan, and the president of TUSIAD at that time, expressed her disappointment with the group, stating that "TUSIAD gave the impression that we are all silent together". Ali Koç, Vice Chairman of KOÇ Holding, took the podium and said that "we should lend our support to Doğan Holding, we are losing our influence as TUSIAD ... We are started to be perceived as even weaker than MUSIAD" (SOL, 20 January 2011). Ironically, ÇALIK Holding joined TUSIAD in 2014. Another example of the contradictions in the power bloc was the sale of STAR TV and NTV media groups to the DOGUS Group which is one of the biggest fractions in TUSIAD. Hence, the AKP's slight to DOĞAN in 2011 did not reflect a general disposition to keep the media out of the hands of TUSIAD.

In this sense, although there have always been cracks and contradictions between the AKP and TUSIAD, they did not remain permanently active as open antagonisms. After the general elections on 1 November 2015, the Prime Minister Ahmet Davutoğlu gave a speech at a TUSIAD High Advisory Council Meeting. He stated that *"I would like to promise you that we will ensure stability for four years, and we will keep all of our promises"* (CNN TURK, 2 November 2015). Not long after this speech, ARÇELIK, a KOÇ Group company, benefited from a 1 billion 135 million Turkish lira tax reduction and promotion. In particular, the Turkish Ministry of the Economy's Directorate of Incentive Implementation and Foreign Investment has approved industry subsidies, customs duty exemption, VAT exemption, 2-year social security premium support for employer's share and a 55% corporate tax deduction with the Decree No 2012/3305 (ARÇELIK, 01 January 2016).

Overall, the study argues that the contradictions between different fractions of capital and the state can be analysed in relation to the functions of capital since the relations between the state and the current mode of production are determined by these internal relations within the power bloc (Ercan & Gültekinkarakaş & Yilmaz, 2016: 147). The contradictions and conflict between the AKP government and TUSIAD, and those between the so-called Islamist bourgeoisie and TUSIAD are not simply a religious or political problem as mainstream academic circles argue. As Tanyılmaz also argues, this was a struggle between the interests of different class fractions (Tanyılmaz, 2015: 90). The struggle reflects an intra-state and intra-capital conflict within the power bloc. This includes the argument that the material basis of the contradictions between different fractions of capital represented by different business associations can be found in the foreign trade arena which this chapter covers in the next section.

4   The Shift in Global Free Trade and the Uneven Trajectory of TNC in Turkey

As part of the shift in the process of capital accumulation in the peripheries of capitalism in the 2000s, surplus value created in peripheries is once again mostly transferred to core capitalist countries through unequal exchange. This period is also called the age of free trade imperialism. More precisely, as Hart-Landsberg argues, companies tend to produce in different countries because of the need for more labour flexibility and a cheap labour force (2013: 54). With regards to the transformation in the global free trade regime in the 2000s, it was the process of creating cross-border production networks that was vital for the development of TUSIAD members. This strategy required the maintenance of the liberal trade regime and regime of capital movement adopted by the government, and the implementation of the standards and institutions of a competitive market. TUSIAD thus endorsed the neo-classical argument which considers free trade as a win-win situation for all parties engaged in it, but it tends more towards an institutionalist position in its national-scale politics. Rather than wanting to reduce the role of the state, TUSIAD members were in favour of a state which can manage the internal social and political conditions for their operations inside the country. As a goal of state trading policy, TUSIAD affiliates assign a special role for their expansion towards new spaces. This demonstrates that proponents of free trade use different tactics and adopt different strategies to gain and hold their market share, a process which regulates the trade between nations as well as within countries.

In the aftermath of the 2001 Turkish banking crisis, the process of capital accumulation in Turkey also entered a crisis. In this period, TUSIAD has become increasingly concerned about the declining profitability of Turkish capital and the sustainability of the current accumulation model. In order to overcome the negative consequences of declining profitability, TUSIAD members coordinated with the ruling power bloc to advocate the continued adherence of the trade regime in Turkey to the global process of capital accumulation. This also included a strategy to target different countries as foreign trade partners. It was accompanied by a proliferation of foreign trade networks and diversification of partners, which was a direct result of the transnationalisation of productive capital in Turkey. For instance, the share of Middle Eastern countries in Turkish foreign trade increased in the second half of the 2000s while the share of European countries declined in the same period. In this sense, TUSIAD members have expanded their base of production into different countries by increasing foreign trade facilities, or through mergers and acquisitions. This was also typically accompanied by increased mobility of their money capital. The quotation from another large group in TUSIAD, BORUSAN Holding's owner Asim Koçabiyik, is worth considering here:

> The industry in Turkey has come to a certain level, which is not sustainable anymore. Our country must find new ways and areas to invest. We cannot achieve more employment or make a profit unless we produce more sophisticated products.
>
> BAYRAM, 2016: 144

In this period, TUSIAD members have both expanded and diversified their trans-national activities regarding both geographical and sectoral spaces. The regional expansion of TUSIAD appears as a hegemonic project which involves class struggle within the power bloc. It reflects the contradictions between TNC which are represented by TUSIAD and SMEs which are represented by MUSIAD and TUSKON, as well as between the AKP and TUSIAD. In this dynamic relation, TUSIAD advocates the expansion of free trade opportunities in the international market with the goal of creating more surplus value. The statement of Zafer Yavan is worth quoting here:

> If the cost in energy, production, and employment of producing a textile product in Turkey is much higher than in China, Afghanistan, Pakistan or Egypt, [a Turkish producer] cannot survive. As both of us want to sell this product to France, Spain and England, in other words, we are aiming at selling to the same destinations; we are not going to sell this product to Madagascar, are we? We are going to sell these products to ones who have money, and who can buy consumer goods. Then, if the cost of workers is 40% of the total cost of the product in Turkey, and if it is cheaper in China, I would go and launch my factories in China then. Or, one should tell us to whom I can sell this product in Turkey if you want us to settle our facilities in Turkey. If there is not a potential consumer profile for my textile goods in Turkey, I would not say that I grew up here in this country, so my investment should not leave the country. This is insane. If I do this, I will go bankrupt certainly. This means I will commit a higher treason against my homeland. If you produce in China, you will at least transfer your profit to this country. And maybe, you will make another investment here, or maybe you will have a new technical know-how, or maybe you will have a new foreign partner and you two together will make another investment in Niger. This is the new world.
>
> Interview, 18 August 2016

The process of transnationalisation was solidified in the 2000s, during which Turkish capitalism combined with global imperialism through transnationalisation of productive capital. This transnationalisation has shifted the production process of already transnationalised groups which obtained priority in producing intermediate goods in many different sectors, particularly finance, manufacturing, foreign trade and construction. Transnationalisation has also occurred in certain sectors like construction led by ENKA, DOGUS, RONESANS and TEKFEN Groups, software by ZORLU Group, and media by DOĞAN Holdings. Finance and foreign trade have undergone the most rapid transnationalisation.

The largest groups which have completely integrated into the global value production process in the financial sector are İş-BANK, CUKUROVA, KOÇ, DOGUS, and SABANCI. In particular, KOÇ Holding established links in Algeria, Germany, the USA, Iran and France via RAM Foreign Trade Company. It concentrated in some sectors like consumer products, washing machines and dishwashers in foreign countries (Öztürk, 2011:164). The second largest transnational capital group within TUSIAD is SABANCI Holding. SABANCI Group concentrated its capital in certain sectors in the 2000s, such as car tyres, banking, insurance, cement, energy, and retail. SABANCI Holding expanded its cord fabric and synthetic fibre production towards the USA, England, Germany, Iran, France, Indonesia, Thailand, China and South American countries. In parallel with this, most of the members of TUSIAD also engaged in transnational financial activities through owning banks in foreign countries. For instance, CUKUROVA Group owns banking interests in the USA, Germany, Switzerland and Russia, SABANCI Holding in England and Germany, YAŞAR Group in Germany, KOÇ Group in Holland and Azerbaijan, ANADOLU Group in Ireland, and DOGUS Group in Russia, Holland, Cyprus and the Channel Islands (Öztürk, 2011:150). Hence, TUSIAD affiliates expanded internationally in the 1990s and the 2000s through penetration of foreign credit and banking systems. This was a consequence of the expanded free trade regime in relation to finance in the 1990s, which was suggested by the GATT Uruguay Round. This shift helped TUSIAD affiliates to integrate into the international circuit of capital by shifting their mode of capital accumulation from commercial to financial capital.

Although the process of capital accumulation at the global scale was interrupted by the 2008–09 global financial crisis, so-called emerging countries like Turkey have since become a new hub for global financial flows. This included the flow of hot money to Turkey as well as providing new opportunities to Turkish finance capital. Since it benefits from these shifts, TUSIAD did not isolate itself from the new strategy of the Turkish state in the aftermath of the 2008–9 global financial crisis which proposed to expand in Middle Eastern and Central Asian markets and actively engaged in these complex relations (Institut du Bosphore, 2012). Table 6 reveals some significant examples of TUSIAD's presence in non-EU countries.

The process of TUSIAD affiliates' economic development may be captured by examining foreign direct investment (Figure 5), which expanded the productive capacity of TNC in Turkey to different spaces. FDI has been a significant stimulus for the integration of TNC in Turkey into global relations of free trade which in turn has transformed the social relations of production in Turkey. New FDI undertaken in Turkey via cross-border mergers and acquisitions reached $6.1 billion in 2015, concentrated in three sectors,

TABLE 6   The production facilities of TUSIAD in non-EU countries

Business group	Sector	Country
IS BANK-SISECAM	Glass and Glass Products	Georgia, Russia, Ukraine, Bosnia-Herzegovina, Egypt
KOÇ Group	Whiteware, and automobile	Tunisia, Russia, China and Uzbekistan.
ANADOLU Group	Bear and Beverage	Kazakhstan, Azerbaijan, Kirgizstan, Georgia, Russia, Moldovia, Ukraine, Serbia, Jordan, Syria, and Pakistan.
SABANCI Group	Cord fabric and artificial fibre	Argentina, Brazil, Iran, Egypt, Indonesia, Thailand, China, and Egypt.
ECZACIBASI Group	Ceramic and bath furniture	Kazakhstan
ZORLU GROUP	Textile	The USA, South Africa Republic, Turkmenistan, Macedonia, and Iran
	Electronic/white ware	Russia
ÇALIK Holding	Textile	Egypt and UAE.
ENKA	Pipe Profile	Russia
	Steel Tube	China
	Power Plant	Iraq, Russia
	Oil, Gas and Petrochemical	Kazakhstan, Iraq
	Construction	Kosovo, Iraq, Libya, Jordan, Saudi Arabia, Russia, Nepal, Papua New Guinea.
BORUSAN Holding	Steel, Heavy-duty construction, mining etc.	Azerbaijan, Georgia, Kazakhstan, Kyrgyzstan, and Russia

SOURCE: AUTHOR'S COMPILATION BASED ON WEBSITES OF COMPANIES AND ÖZTÜRK, 2014: 245

TABLE 7   The largest home-based transnational companies, 2010

Company name	Industry	Sales (Billion $)	Controlling ownership	Business association affiliation
OVM Petrol Ofisi*	Retail Trade	10.498	OVM Company & DOĞAN Holding	TUSIAD
ENKA Insaat ve Sanayi AS	Construction	5.029	ENKA Holding	TUSIAD
Ereğli Demir ve Çelik Fabrikaları	Metals and Metals Products	4.772	State & Oyak Holding	TUSIAD
ARCELIK AS	Electrical and Electronic Equipment	4.507	KOÇ Holding	TUSIAD
Turkiye Şise ve Cam Fabrikaları AS	Non-Metalic mineral products	2.733	Türkiye İş-Bank	TUSIAD
Anadolu Efes Biracılık & Coca-Cola AS	Food, Beverages and Tobacco	3.898	Anadolu Group	TUSIAD
HABAS Sınai ve Tıbbi Gazlar Istihsal Endüstrisi AS	Chemicals and Chemical Products	1.724	Mehmet Rüştü Başaran	-
DOĞAN yayın Holding AS	Publishing and Printing	1.703	Aydın Doğan	TUSIAD
TEKFEN Holding AS	Construction	1.470	TEKFEN Holding	TUSIAD
AKSA Akkirik Kimya Sanayi AS	Chemicals and Chemical Products	0.929	AKKOK Holding	TUSIAD
Vestel Beyaz Esya	Electrical and Electronic Equipment	0.925	ZORLU Holding	TUSIAD
KORDSa Sanayi AS	Textile, Clothing and Leather	0.821	Sabancı Holding	TUSIAD

TABLE 7   The largest home-based transnational companies, 2010 (cont.)

Company name	Industry	Sales (Billion $)	Controlling ownership	Business association affiliation
HAYAT Kimya Sanayi AS	Chemicals and Chemical Products	0.578	HAYAT Holding	TUSKON
Kastamonu Entegre Agac Sanayii ve Ticaret AS	Wood and Wood Products	0.519	HAYAT Holding	TUSKON
ARZUM Elektrikli Ev Aletleri AS	Wholesale Trade	0.1	Mediterra Capital & Kolbaşı Family	TUSIAD

* The shares of this company were sold to VITOL Group on 13 July 2017

SOURCE: AUTHOR'S COMPILATION BASED ON UNCTAD 2012, RETRIEVED FROM HTTP://
UNCTAD.ORG/EN/PUBLICATIONSLIBRARY/WEBDIAEIA2012D6_EN.PDF

namely manufacturing ($4.1 billion), finance and insurance ($3.5 billion), and transport and storage ($1.5 billion). FDI outflows mostly targeted EU countries in 2014 and 2015. The amount of FDI flow to these countries was almost $10 billion, which was achieved via mergers and acquisitions in manufacturing, retail, trade companies and infrastructure (DEIK & DELOITTE, 2016: 24). According to World Bank statistics, Turkey's outward FDI stock has increased from $5 billion in 2001 to $22 billion in 2010 (UNCTAD, 2012:1). There has also been diversification in the sources of FDI to Turkey. More precisely, the share of the EU countries in FDI to Turkey has decreased while the share of Asian, Middle East and North African countries increased. For instance, the share of the EU countries in FDI coming to Turkey decreased from 70% to 58% between 2012 and 2015 (Ministry of Economy, 2016:5). Notwithstanding the drop in the share of EU countries in Turkey's FDI, TUSIAD continued to benefit from diversification thanks to its transnational investments and sales in different spaces. For instance, FDI by Qatar accounted for a significant share of cross-border sales, as Mayhoola bought a 31% stake in Boyner Perakende for $330 million, and Banco Bilbao Vizcaya, a Spanish company, made a

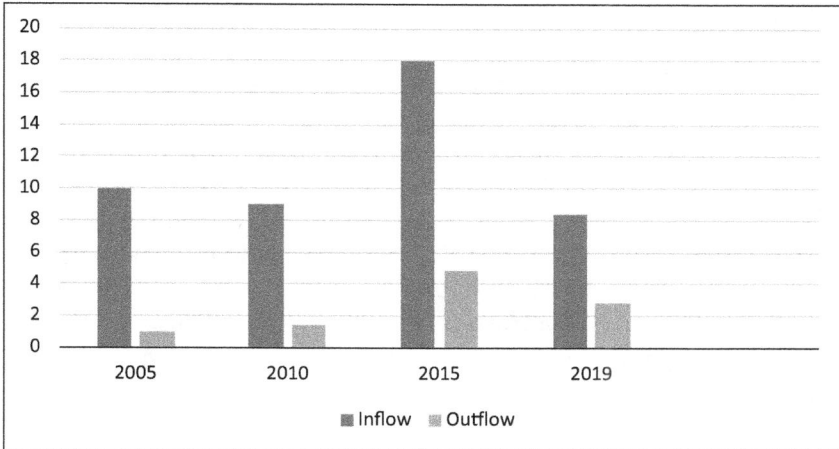

FIGURE 5   FDI and financial resources
SOURCE: AUTHOR'S COMPILATION BASED ON TUIK DATA (2021)

$2.5 billion acquisition of Türkiye Garanti Bankası A.S. (UNCTAD, 2016: 47). In addition to this, Malaysia Airports has taken over the shares of Limak Investment Energy Company for $316 million. China Merchant Holdings also purchased a 64.5% stake in Fina Holdings for $940 million in 2015 (Ministry of the Economy, 2016: 18).

Also, FDI in Turkey exceeds FDI by Turkish companies abroad, Turkish companies also invested around $1 billion in Peru and Chile through mergers and acquisitions in 2014 and 2015 (DEIK & DELOITTE, 2016: 13). The FDI of Turkish companies in the Middle East and Africa also increased to $1 billion in 2014 and 2015 (ibid, 2016:16). The top sectors for Turkish outward FDI in these countries are manufacturing, logistics and retail. The level of FDI in Asian countries has also increased. FDI outflows to China in 2014 and 2015 were around $1.24 billion, and the largest investments made by TUSIAD members were in Thailand (by ARÇELIK, a KOÇ Holdings brand) and India (by Kale Industry Holding) (ibid., 2016:19). The investments of Turkish companies in Eurasian countries were almost $3 billion in 2014 and 2015. The top invested sector was manufacturing, and the top investors were TUSIAD members. For instance, BORUSAN made the largest investment in 2015 through mergers and acquisition in Russia (Ibid, 2016:21). Also, Gedik Holding has shifted its interests towards destinations in Africa (HT Ekonomi, 01 August 2016). In total, Turkish companies have made almost $23 billion in investments between 2010 and 2015 (UNCTAD, 2016: 198). Their outward FDI stock was $3.6 billion in 2000, while this increased to $22.5 billion in 2010, and $44.6 billion in 2015 (UNCTAD, 2016: 202).

As the member firms of TUSIAD have integrated into the global market, any change in the international structure of capital relations might affect the total circuit of their capital. This is because their domestic investment is heavily dependent on capital inflows or in other words, Turkish production is dependent on the import of low-value-added intermediate goods, a type of dependency which has become a characteristic feature of the Turkish economy. This suggests that the dominant fractions in TUSIAD have shifted their mode of capital accumulation in response to the necessities of the global value production process, and this shift has also transformed the internal social relations of production in Turkey. For instance, from the 1990s onwards, KOÇ Holding has expanded its base of production and financial activities towards different countries, and this paved the way for the uneven development of KOÇ group along with a few other companies. Historically, KOÇ Holding engaged in its first exports in Bulgaria and Pakistan in 1967 and launched its first international service station in Iraq in 1979. It started producing commercial vehicles in Uzbekistan in the 1990s, and white goods in Tunisia a little later. The primary means of KOÇ Group's integration into the global free trade system were franchising, licence agreements, and joint ventures with foreign companies. It entered into deals with US companies such as Standard Oil, General Electric and Ford Motor, and made contracts with several foreign companies like Uniroyal and Pirelli. As KOÇ Holding was one of the first capital fractions which engaged in joint ventures and licence agreements with foreign corporations, it dominates most of the sectors in Turkey. This has created internal unevenness among capital fractions in Turkey.

Free trade also (re)produces intra-regional and intra-societal unevenness, which results in the monopoly dominance of some fractions within their domestic sector, and which is also reflected in the global exploitation of labour. The first mover advantage provided these capital groups with a competitive advantage in the total circuit of capital. For instance, During the ISI period from the late 1950s to the 1980s, KOÇ Holding shifted its means of capital accumulation towards domestic production. In this time, KOÇ Holding started to produce automobiles, trucks, tractors, refrigerators, washing machines and other white goods. This was the period in which KOÇ Group became dominant in those sectors with their international partners. For instance, they made contracts with Siemens for producing consumer goods, with FIAT for producing tractors (TURK Traktor), and produced the first locally manufactured automobiles. TOFAS Company, which was established as a joint venture with FIAT, produced 445,000 cars between 1971 and 1988 (Öztürk, 2011: 222). Within the transnationalisation of productive capital, KOÇ group shifted its manufacturing strategy, and moved its production from producing private cars to commercial vehicles. This was also reflected in its foreign trade policy. For instance, whereas TOFAS exported 3% of the 445,000 cars which it produced until 1988, this figure had increased to 69% by 2007 (Öztürk, 2011: 223). In 2014, TOFAS achieved 19% of total production in Turkey and exported around 142,000 vehicles (KOÇ, 2017).

The domination of KOÇ Holding and a few others have increased through mergers as well as acquisitions. In this endeavour, KOÇ Holding has taken over the Bloomberg Company which produces washing machine in Germany, and Elektra Bregenz Company which markets white goods in Australia. In the same year, the Leisure and Fragel brands, and Arctic Company which produces white goods in Romania were taken over (Öztürk, 2011:227). BEKO, a brand of KOÇ Holding, has taken over the Grundig brand and has increased its share in the consumer electronics market in Germany from 5% to 19% in 2007 (ARÇELIK, 2015: 32). In the same year, KOÇ Holding has started electronic goods production and white goods production in Russia. BEKO Company is ranked the second biggest producer of television sets in Europe in 2007; the first firm in the list was another TUSIAD member, Vestel, which is a ZORLU Group brand (Öztürk, 2011:228). KOÇ Group has also purchased 40% of shares of OPET, which is the second biggest petrol retailer in Turkey, took over YAPI Kredi Bankası from CUKUROVA group in 2005, and acquired TUPRAS in 2004. In the same manner as KOÇ Holding, a few others like SABANCI, ANADOLU, TEKFEN, ECZACIBASI and CUKUROVA groups became the most dominant fractions within Turkish capitalist classes. Acquisition of foreign companies was also a means of integration into global free trade relations for these companies. For instance, ECZACIBASI Holding has taken over Villeroy & Boch ceramic tile department, ÜLKER has taken over the global chocolate firm Godiva, ANADOLU Group has taken over Krasny Vastok Beer in Russia and Lomisi Beer in Georgia, and SABANCI has taken over DuSa. SABANCI Holding is the second largest group within TUSIAD, which operates in 16 different countries, and engages in global circuits of capital across Europe, the Middle East, North Africa, and North and South America. The total revenue of SABANCI Holding was $17.6 billion in 2015 (SABANCI, 2017). Another significant group is ENKA, which has completed 121 projects in Turkey amounting to a contract value of $7 billion, and another 371 projects with a contract value of $34 billion have been awarded to ENKA in foreign countries (ENKA, 2017). ANADOLU Group operates 25 plants in 10 different countries including Iraq, Syria, Jordan, Kazakhstan, Kyrgyzstan, Turkmenistan and Tajikistan (ANADOLU, 2017. CUKUROVA Holdings has operated in the Northern Iraq Kurdish Federal Region since 2002. This group invests in the energy sector, and its subsidiary which is called Genel Energy is the largest oil and petroleum producer in the area (CUKUROVA, 2017).

Integrating into free trade expanded the sphere of social relations of production for these few Turkish companies. In this sphere, TUSIAD members adopted different strategies to broaden their base of production on a global scale. First of all, some capital fractions have become sales representatives of transnational capital in the aftermath of the collapse of the USSR. For instance, BORUSAN has become the sales representative of Massey Ferguson and Caterpillar in some Central Asian countries. In a similar way, ANADOLU group has become the sales and marketing representative of Coca-Cola in many different countries. Secondly, some fractions of bigger capital have introduced sales and marketing branches in foreign countries. For instance, KOÇ Holding launched sales and aftersale services in Eurasian and European countries. In addition to this, these capital groups have launched giant shopping malls and retail stores in Russia, Azerbaijan and elsewhere. For instance, Romenka established with KOÇ-ENKA a major pioneering partnership. These partners ran 543 stores in more than 78 countries in 2005.

This expansion of large firms was accompanied by the transnationalisation of production together with global integration into free trade relations. In this era, Turkish companies' base of production expanded into different countries through new international trade and investment networks, while the relationship between big and small capital and the relationship between different regions of Turkey have taken a new direction. The local firms in industrial estates in smaller cities in Anatolia like Denizli, Gaziantep, Kayseri, and Konya have established both international trade links and internal trade ties with the bigger capitalists in Istanbul and Izmir (Öztürk, 2011:183). TUSIAD has continued to open new branches in different countries and played a leading role in establishing TURKONFED in 2004. TURKONFED was established with the help of TUSIAD to correct the negative image of TUSIAD (which is regarded as the big businesses' club with no room for the smaller players). More precisely, TURKONFED was intended to form networks between SMEs (Buğra & Savaşkan, 2014:126). At the time of writing, TURKONFED had become a competitor to TUSKON, which the following chapters discuss in detail. TURKONFED brought smaller companies together in a confederation linked to TUSIAD. The establishment of TURKONFED is an attempt to create hegemony on the part of TUSIAD over the internationally oriented capitalist fractions organised within MUSIAD and TUSKON. As Chapter 6 and 7 discuss in detail, SMEs operating in Anatolia mainly produce in Turkey for export. Having dominated these SMEs, the main purposes of TUSIAD are to expand its base of production in sectors in which transnational companies do not directly operate, and to prevent companies in these sectors from becoming members of MUSIAD or TUSKON. In a similar vein, another federation created under the guidance of TUSIAD is SEDEFED (Sektorel Dernekler Federasyonu, the Platform of Industrial Associations) (Buğra & Savaşkan, 2014:124). Through these initiatives, TUSIAD aimed at encouraging regional SMEs to integrate into the total circuit of capital both inside and outside the country. Overall, around 60.5% of the international companies, 28,782 in total, are based in Istanbul. Antalya is the second with 4715 companies, Ankara is 3rd with 2683 companies, and İzmir is the 4th with 2237 companies. In terms of the TUSIAD presence in the east and southeast regions of Turkey, we shall look at the activities of TURKONFED and later also the BORGIP (The Project of Developing Cooperation between Regions) project arising from collaboration between TUSIAD and TURKONFED (BORGIP, 2017). The aim of this project is to give assistance to new entrepreneurs who would like to set up a business in the East and Southeast regions.

5   Conclusion

This chapter examined the class characteristics of TUSIAD affiliates in order to scrutinise the material basis of the contradictions between different fractions of capital represented by TUSIAD and other social forces in the power bloc which is reflected in the foreign trade arena. To this end, the chapter examined TUSIAD which is the largest and most effective business association in terms of its members' sales, production, trade volume and transnational networks. This chapter suggested that the capacity of TUSIAD to promote its interests within and outside the power bloc does not result from its organisational capacity. It results from the structural power of capital in the class struggle and the social relations of production. TUSIAD was established to protect and advance the interests of the bigger fractions of Turkish capital. The chapter argued that many of TUSIAD's affiliates have further integrated into global relations of free trade since its establishment in 1971. It also pointed out that TUSIAD members had generally completed the inward-oriented accumulation process before the 1980 military coup. The adjustment policies after the military coup paved the way for these companies to integrate into the world economy. The change in the mode of integration, as noted in the previous section, is visible in international investments, joint ventures and licencing agreements between TUSIAD members and foreign firms.

TUSIAD is the hegemonic fraction amongst business associations in Turkey. The hegemonic position of TUSIAD suffered some decline in the late 1990s but gained renewed upward momentum in the 2000s. This chapter also contended that there is a distinction between capital fractions in TUSIAD. The largest companies, such as KOÇ, SABANCI, ANADOLU, ECZACIBASI, DOGUS Holdings and a few others, dominated the total circuit of capital, which resulted in a hegemony of these groups in Turkish foreign trade. Their domination deepened and concentrated in manufacturing, banking, the stock market, retail and international trade in the 2000s. The chapter also argued that bigger fractions in TUSIAD shifted their pattern of capital accumulation based on the extraction of relative surplus value through higher technology and increasing labour productivity in the 2000s. This hegemony of TUSIAD has been challenged by the new generation of capital represented by MUSIAD and TUSKON, a process which will be explained in the next chapters.

The chapter revealed the extent to which members of TUSIAD engage in transnational relations of production and global relations of free trade. Specific holding companies, such as KOÇ, SABANCI, ENKA, and ANADOLU, were examined to provide a comprehensive analysis of the transnationalisation of TUSIAD's social base. These large members of TUSIAD increased their rate of surplus value extraction by lowering the value of their constant capital. The ways in which TUSIAD, as an agent of international free trade relations, internalises the interests of transnational companies was also revealed. For instance, giant transnational firms like Ford Motor, FIAT, ISUZU, TOYOTA, HONDA RENAULT, LG Electronics, Uni Credit Group, Faber-Castell, Philip Morris and many others operate in Turkey through joint ventures and licence agreements signed with TUSIAD members.

The chapter also mentioned the class struggles within the power bloc in each phase of capital accumulation, which were represented among TUSIAD members and the AKP in different ways at different times. Following Poulantzas, this chapter argued that the class struggle within the power bloc (re)produces the social relations of production. Thus, the compromise between the AKP and some fractions within TUSIAD demonstrates the way in which the state is thoroughly grounded in capitalist relations of production, and the peculiar materiality of the state, which helped the AKP to place itself above civil society. Accordingly, the chapter argued that the contradictions within the power bloc reflect the short-term struggles between different fractions of capital, and is not a relationship between equals. However, when it comes to the maintenance and reproduction of the social relations of production, consensus within the power bloc becomes necessary. This also demonstrates that the state is a material condensation of the class struggle. This is evident in the specific configuration of the power bloc and the struggle for hegemony between TUSIAD and the AKP in the late 2000s. In this regard, this chapter argued that the determinants of the relationship between TUSIAD and the AKP are not only religious, cultural or ethical dimensions, in contrast to what mainstream analysis contends, but also the extent to which the reproduction of the social relations of production is secured. TUSIAD has always taken a determined stand in support of the AKP-led power bloc as long as the AKP has implemented anti-labour policies and enhanced the global integration of Turkish capitalism. On the other hand, the relationship is weakened when the class struggle becomes deepened due to their clashing interests, for instance if the AKP is restricting liberalisation or favouring SMEs.

In the next two chapters, the place of other business associations in the social relations of production and global free trade relations will be examined to provide a better analysis of the class struggle within the power bloc, as well as to reveal the internal unevenness which was created in the process of integration into transnational relations of production.

CHAPTER 4

MUSIAD, the State and Global Integration

The emergence of MUSIAD (Müstakil Sanayici ve İşadamları Derneği, the Independent Industrialists and Businessman Association) coincides with the transition of the industrial bourgeoisie into finance capital in the 1990s. The main change which can be gleaned from the emergence and rise of MUSIAD is the shifting pattern of capital accumulation, which resulted from the international mobility of Turkish productive capital in the last three decades. Although this process was initiated by TUSIAD affiliates, it created new bourgeois class fractions with distinct interests. In this sense, the chapter argues that the rise of MUSIAD is not simply an outcome of the conflict between the *secular* and *Islamist* bourgeoisie, defined in superstructural terms in isolation from the social relations of production. Rather, the rise of MUSIAD is part of a process of transformation in the patterns of global capital accumulation and uneven development of capitalism in Turkey. This means that the uneven and combined character of Turkish capitalism is much more visible when it comes to analysing MUSIAD.

This chapter examines how MUSIAD engages in social relations of production. It also sketches out how MUSIAD mediates the consolidation and survival of the capitalist class, and explores the class characteristics of MUSIAD-affiliated firms. The chapter outlines the dominant sectors in which member firms of MUSIAD operate and lays out the differences and similarities between MUSIAD-affiliated companies and other companies affiliated with TUSIAD and TUSKON. Secondly, this chapter investigates the role of MUSIAD in the power bloc, and explores the dialectical relationship between MUSIAD and the state. As highlighted in Chapter 2, this study examines the role of agency in global free trade relations and argues that the state is a material condensation of class struggles (Poulantzas [1974]1975:26). Following these conceptualisations, the chapter examines the role of specific state apparatuses and, in particular, AKP municipalities in increasing MUSIAD's ability to accumulate capital, and to engage in relations of power and class struggle. This chapter argues that municipal governments in provincial cities materialise state power in their interaction with the member firms of MUSIAD. Contrary to mainstream arguments, this chapter argues that the patterns of internationalisation of capital accumulation shape the way in which this business association engages in the global relations of free trade. To this end, this chapter uncovers the ways in which the member firms of MUSIAD engage in the relations of production, exchange and revalorization. Furthermore, it uncovers how free trade creates unevenness between different fractions of capital represented by MUSIAD. Finally, the chapter concludes with an assessment of these complex relations.

1   The Emergence of MUSIAD and the Social Formation in Turkey

To grasp the emergence of MUSIAD and the dialectical relationship between MUSIAD and the state, there is a need to address the fragmentation of political Islam in Turkey in the late 1990s, as well as the relationship between neoliberalism and political Islam in Turkey. The legal-political Islamist party which was supported by some significant fractions within MUSIAD was initially the Welfare Party (Refah Partisi, RP). The RP was closed after the 28 February 1997 *postmodern coup*,[1] and re-surfaced five times with different names: National Order Party (Milli Nizam Partisi), National Salvation Party (Milli Selamet Partisi), Welfare Party (Refah Partisi), Virtue Party (Fazilet Partisi), and currently Felicity Party (Saadet Partisi). After the closure of the Virtue Party, there appeared two different Islamist political parties in Turkish politics. One is the Felicity Party, which was founded by the *traditionalist* wing within the RP, and the other one is the AKP founded by the *reformist* wing within the RP.

The trajectory of political Islamist parties in Turkey, such as the RP, represents the ups and downs of power relations within the social formation in Turkey. The 1980s involved a break within capitalism, leading to the emergence of MUSIAD, because the export orientation policy created an environment conducive to SMEs entering in the circuit of capital. As a result, the small-capital fraction of the bourgeoisie started to operate in sectors which were abandoned or neglected by the big-capital groups. As mentioned in Chapter 2, the military coup in 1980 was an attempt to put an end to class-based politics. It was led by the military junta which united the power groups and defused the crisis of hegemony in the power bloc. MUSIAD, therefore, views this military coup favourably. The ex-president of MUSIAD, Ömer Cihad Vardan, argued that 12 September 1980 military coup saved the country from a situation of anarchy which brought the country to the brink of disaster (Vardan, 2012:26). As smaller fractions of capital knew that integration into the world economy

---

1   The National Security Council of Turkey issued some decisions on 28 February 1997, which were based on the views of generals regarding the threat to secularism. The Prime Minister, Necmettin Erbakan, was forced to sign this memorandum, and the coalition government was ended by this process. This military intervention is called a "postmodern coup" because the constitution was not suspended, nor the parliament dissolved.

was vital for their survival, they supported the neoliberal economic policies of the Ozal government in the 1980s even when most small companies only produced for the national market. MUSIAD initially represented nationally oriented capital.

Apart from the economic transformation of Turkey from the 1980s onwards, religion and culture also played an important role in the emergence of MUSIAD. Member companies mostly established business networks with the help of their religious networks, especially in Konya and Kayseri. New legal regulations also paved the way for operations of *cemaats/tariqats*[2] which constituted the organisational base for the capital accumulation of MUSIAD-affiliated capital. For instance, the Foundations Law implemented by the government in the 1990s provided legal spaces for MUSIAD to reach a broader audience (Doğan, 2006: 53). The Ozal period is the period in which MUSIAD flourished and was strengthened in both public and private spaces. Hence, the policies of this period not only changed the radical vision of Islamists in Turkey but also transformed the way in which they engage in business activities (Yavuz, 2009: 56). This is not only seen in civil society, as mainstream theories contend, as emerging capital fractions also found spaces in political society. After the victory of the RP in municipal elections in 1994, the relationship between the state apparatuses and the so-called Islamist bourgeoisie was also transformed. For instance, the latter benefited from public funds through bids and local business networks in big cities in Turkey like Ankara and Istanbul (Yavuz, 2009: 59). Also in this period, new financial networks were formed in foreign countries, which played a crucial role in transformations in the manner of accumulation of capital by MUSIAD affiliates. Moreover, Turkish citizens living in EU countries were integrated into the process of capital accumulation through donations and charity organisations led by Islamist NGOs.

In the 1990s, the discourses of MUSIAD representatives in opposition to the state and Western institutions, global free trade relations and capitalism became more radical. The goals of MUSIAD were mainly: (i) to make more profit from the privatisation processes as they thought the big bourgeoisie organised under TUSIAD had a domination over state contracts; (ii) to enter into sectors, such as automotive and finance, which were dominated by TUSIAD members; (iii) to follow an alternative model of integration into the world economy based on the idea of an "Islamic Common Market" rather than integration with the EU or the USA; and (iv) to follow a different path of

---

2   Tariqat/Tariqa/Tariqah means 'cult' in English, and refers to a school or order directed towards a particular person or a school of thought.

money-capital accumulation and stop the IMF-backed strategy which favours a small number of big capital groups, while dominating small-scale capital groups (Özden & Akça & Bekmen, 2017: 191). Despite the radicalism of aspects of the rhetoric of this period, it is clear that MUSIAD in the 1990s was neither against the idea of internationalisation of capital nor against global free trade *per se*. Their criticism was focused on opposing the dominant view of which markets that Turkey should target. In short, the main strategy of MUSIAD was to challenge the domination of TUSIAD in all sectors.

The close relationship between the RP and MUSIAD reconstructed the relations of power and class within the state structure. As mentioned in Chapter 3, TUSIAD was the hegemonic fraction in Turkish capital in the 1980s-90s, and the rise of MUSIAD in the late 1990s created contradictions among different capital fractions. The rapid and uncontrolled growth of MUSIAD members could jeopardise TUSIAD's position as the centre of traditional finance capital. For instance, the firms affiliated with MUSIAD have accumulated almost $50 billion through the Islamic banking system, which was to some extent outside of the legal control of the government (Doğan, 2006: 60). Another contradiction emerged between MUSIAD and TUSIAD in the privatisation of state's electricity provider (TEDAS) in 1997. To outbid a TUSIAD member firm in the privatisation process, over 3000 MUSIAD members made financial contributions to launch a new firm which is called Investment Partnership Inc. (Gürakar, 2016: 15). This is a good example of why TUSIAD attempted to reduce the power of SMEs affiliated with MUSIAD.

The military intervention in 1997, which resulted in the resignation of the Prime Minister Necmettin Erbakan who was the leader of the RP government, brought a change in the discourse of MUSIAD representatives (Buğra & Savaşkan, 2014: 130). MUSIAD publicly declared that capital had no colour or religion. It also became much less vocal in its criticism of the EU and of integration into the global political economy (MUSIAD, 1999: 46). This demonstrates that SMEs who had close ties with the RP government realised that they would not be able to realise their goals in the current circumstances (Akça & Özden, 09 November 2015), as the RP and MUSIAD were not strong enough to confront the dominant power bloc. The Constitutional Court opened a court case against MUSIAD just after the 28 February 1997 coup (Yankaya, 2012: 2). As a result, the leaders of MUSIAD recommended its members not to use religious references in their commercial and promotional activities. While this was partly a strategic move in response to repression, the fraction of capital within MUSIAD was also unsympathetic to traditional Muslim attitudes towards market principles. For instance, they were in favour of competition in the free market and contended that Islam was compatible with capitalism.

Therefore, MUSIAD reorganised its relations with political and civil society after the military intervention on 28 February 1997. They supported the establishment of the AKP whose leaders represented the reformist fraction within the RP (Göl, 2009: 803). Integration into the world economy provided smaller companies with new areas in which to produce, especially through sub-contracting (Ercan, 2002). It is this period which accelerated the transformation of some of the nationally oriented fractions within MUSIAD into larger fractions which invest in foreign countries and engage in subcontracting relations, such as Kombassan, Jetpa, Yimpaş, Ittıfak, Endüstri, Çalık, Albayrak and Boydak Holding (Öztürk, 2015: 120).

2   A Class Based Analysis of MUSIAD

It is widely argued by mainstream scholars that the members of MUSIAD are distinct from the members of TUSIAD primarily in terms of their religious and conservative orientations. This is also upheld by the founders of MUSIAD in the claim that they are *homo Islamicus* (Islamic men or people). They claim that, unlike the Western *homo oeconomicus*, who is selfish, egoistic and profit-seeking, *homo Islamicus* is collectivist, moral and honest (traits associated with paternalistic, trust-based business networks). The revenue of *homo Islamicus* should come from productive activities conducted in a free market, not from hoarding, speculation, gambling, or destructive competition. This is not an anti-capitalist orientation; it can be considered a different version of Max Weber's idea of the Protestant (Calvinist) ethic as a central factor in the making of European and hence global capitalism.

In order to define the relationship between capital and labour in the context of "homo Islamicus," however, Weberian explanations seem insufficient. While MUSIAD may try to differentiate itself ideologically from capitalist values, the relations of production in the factories and in other aspects of in the circuit of capital owned by "Islamic capital" are still determined by the rules of capitalism. The main distinctive feature in the case of "Islamic capital" is the role of religion in getting the active consent of the working classes. For instance, the workers are told that they will get their wages before their sweat is dried, which is a general principle recommended by Islam (Durak, 2011: 68). In the 1990s, the dominant discourse of MUSIAD-affiliated firms was based on mutual trust between the "Islamist bourgeoisie" and workers who are expected to be hard-working and respectful to their employers (Buğra, 2002: 136). More precisely, labour strikes and any kind of collective action by workers are harshly criticised because they allegedly lead workers to terrorism or strife which is banned in

Islam and reduces the feeling of solidarity between capital and labour. Also based on religious and moral appeals, Islamic preachers and schoolteachers encouraged their followers and students to buy the products of these companies rather than buying from secular or non-Muslim transnational companies. This was recommended for the sake of the common good. While such appeals differ little in substance from those of "secularist" companies (who also oppose labour militancy and seek to expand sales), they represent a particular type of hegemonic appeal which is attractive to some workers, giving MUSIAD a political edge at the popular level.

The transformation of wider patterns of capital accumulation in the late 1990s affected the way in which the member companies of MUSIAD engaged in capital accumulation. Most of the smaller firms in MUSIAD entered into the process of capital accumulation through donations, charity organisations led by Islamist NGOs, and the remittances of Turkish citizens living in European countries (Demir, Acar & Toprak, 2004: 170). The largest companies established with the help of foreign remittances are Kombassan Company, Yimpaş Holding, Büyük Anadolu Holding, Jet-pa Holding, and İttifak Holding (Demir & Acar & Toprak, 2004: 170). Some companies became more conventionally powerful and hence became capable of winning government bids. For example, Kombassan Holding won the bid for PETLAS in 1997 when the political Islamist RP was in power. This was a potential challenge to the constructed relations of power and class within and outside the power bloc. Islamic banking (interest-free banking) has also been a significant mechanism to accumulate capital, and is often also connected to communal linkages. Islamic banks in Turkey were initially established through cooperation between Saudi and Turkish capital. At a later stage, the Arabic share in banks in Turkey decreased and Turkish capital established its own Islamic banking system in the 1990s. The main Islamic financial institutions formed in this period were Anadolu Finance owned by Istikbal Group, a leading furniture manufacturer in Kayseri, Ihlas Finance House, an Islamic financial institution which was closed in 2001 because of liquidity problems, and Asia Finance House which started its operations in 1996 (Syed Ali, 2007: 40). Islamic banking capital provided credit opportunities for SMEs, which helped them to mobilise and concentrate their capital. This allowed them to adopt new strategies because they were excluded at the time from the credit system regulated by the government. These banks provided a solid amount of capital for MUSIAD affiliates to further expand in the 2000s. In this way, smaller fractions of Turkish capital operating mainly in the textile, construction and service sectors got a chance to connect with transnational companies and integrate into global free trade relations. The institutional responses to the Islamic prohibition on using the interest-based banking system made it easier for the member firms of MUSIAD to make sub-contracting and licence agreements with international capital to operate in Turkey as *Islamic* capital. This pattern of capital accumulation is maintained through personal relationships, and different forms of networking through religious organisations like *cemaats* and *tariqats*, which also have close relationships with political parties (Hoşgör, 2011: 344). Islamic *cemaats/tariqats* have played a crucial role in the development of MUSIAD as they provided network facilities to the companies and created a base for reaching a wide range of customers. The network relations between conservative businesspeople led to the opening-up of new channels for capital accumulation. However, the differences between informal network-based systems and formal capitalism are not simply superstructural questions of religious belief. Rather, networked accumulation involved a different style of bourgeois class formation.

Additionally, the members of religious communities undertook joint investments, got loans and credit from each other, and established mutual assistance networks to buy and sell inputs, such as raw material, machinery and intermediate goods, which helped them to reduce the costs of transportation and transactions. Another form of capital accumulation that some member firms of MUSIAD have adopted is collecting money from religious entrepreneurs, a practice which is not subject to regulations by capital market authorities. Instead, it is run on a trust-based system, which *precludes the sins of interest income* (a doctrinal justification for the network-based nature of small-scale capital accumulation). This fund-raising system was eventually subject to intervention by the Capital Market Board as it escaped from legal supervision, and hence, was viewed as an attempt to change the basis of the market economy (Buğra & Savaşkan: 2014: 58).

Regarding the categorisation of MUSIAD from a class perspective, this study draws on Poulantzas who states that the relations of production have the determinant role in the social formation, but the ideological and the political also occupy a very significant space (Poulantzas [1974]1975:14). As Ollman additionally argues, viewing these elements separately may lead to ignorance of the contradictions that appear in the process of reproduction of the social relations of production (Ollman, 1993: 18). When examining the place of ideology in the process of capital accumulation, this section argues that the process of capital accumulation of MUSIAD affiliates is primarily shaped by class and power relations, not politics or ideology. This means that the analysis of MUSIAD is not only based on the personal or institutional attachments of businesspeople to the state but, more precisely, through its relationship with production relations, productive forces and class fractions.

3   Different Capital Fractions within MUSIAD

Without ignoring the importance of the religious and ideological attachments of businesspeople to MUSIAD, this study argues that it is the material conditions which shape their class positions. Accordingly, the main features which distinguish MUSIAD from TUSIAD are the scale of business, the patterns of capital accumulation, the formation of the relationship between the state and MUSIAD, and the specific forms of integration into global relations of free trade. Regarding these differences, there are today three different fractions within MUSIAD which are respectively national, internationally oriented, and transnational in organisation. The internationally oriented fraction is the dominant one in MUSIAD, and is mostly composed of SMEs which produce in Turkey for export. These export-oriented companies have adapted their pattern of capital accumulation to the global circuit of capital with regard to the necessities of global relations of free trade. As smaller fractions of capital knew that integration into the world economy was vital to their survival in the 1990s, they integrated into the global relations of free trade in their own specific ways. More importantly, the uneven development of this fraction is a direct consequence of the timing of its process of beginning to accumulate capital and integrating into the international relations of production. Whereas TUSIAD members internationalised early, and were seeking to transnationalise by the 1980s, most of the MUSIAD members were still nationally oriented companies in the late 1980s and 1990s, and have transformed into internationally oriented capital which produce for export in the 2000s. This transformation coincides with the rise of the AKP in the early 2000s.

The internationally oriented fraction within MUSIAD concentrated on extracting absolute surplus value until the 2000s and is only now in the process of appropriation of relative surplus value through technology transfer. This means that the majority of MUSIAD members produce mainly in low-value-added sectors which are labour-intensive. According to the reports and working papers published by MUSIAD, the majority of its members operate in the construction, logistics, furniture, services, transportation, and textiles sectors (Atiyas & Bakis, 2013:12). Importantly, these sectors all require low-tech production facilities and a cheap labour force.

The largest example of an internationally oriented company within MUSIAD is IÇDAŞ Holding, which is one of the five companies in MUSIAD which export products worth more than $100 million in a year. This company is the second largest steel producer in Turkey and exports its products to more than 70 different countries (IÇDAŞ, 2017). Another internationally oriented company is Çınar Boru Company which produces pipes, tube fields, and steel products in

Turkey, and exports them mainly to Georgia and Azerbaijan (Çınar Boru, 2018). HABAS Group is another example of an internationally oriented member of MUSIAD which produces in Turkey for export. This company produces industrial and medical gauze, steel, electrical energy, and heavy machinery, and also operates seaports (HABAS, 2021). There are other companies which also produce in Turkey for export, such as Arbel Group which produces grain products, AK Gida which produces dairy products, and Elita Gida which produces liquid oil. It is clear from these examples that there is a strong bias towards low-technology, low-skill, labour-intensive production among internationally oriented MUSIAD members.

Internationally oriented fractions of MUSIAD were encouraged to shift their mode of production towards a model which is compatible with the transnationalisation of production. In this period, member firms used different network channels to find international partners in foreign countries (Interview 2, 01 August 2016). For instance, the MUSIAD branch in Sivas organised a business trip to Dubai in 2015. This trip brought together construction companies from both countries. The costs of this trip were covered by the Small and Medium Enterprises Development Organisation (KOSGEB) which is an official institution of the Ministry of Science, Industry, and Technology. Another member company of MUSIAD, *Nitrocare Sivas,* which produces hospital furniture and medical equipment, attended a business trip to Egypt in 2009. This company established networks thanks to this trip and exports to more than 60 different destinations across the world (Interview 3, 04 August 2016). The growth of MUSIAD's role in global trade is also associated with the changing patterns of Turkish foreign trade policy after the 2008–9 global financial crisis. As detailed in Chapter 4, the share of Middle Eastern and African countries in Turkish foreign trade increased after the crisis due to declining market opportunities in the EU and US (Figure 6). This meant that the member firms of MUSIAD, who were already partly oriented towards Middle Eastern trade partners, were able to play a significant role in the diversification of Turkish foreign trade (Atiyas & Bakis, 2013: 11).

On the other hand, MUSIAD also represents some larger, transnationally operating firms. As stated in Chapter 4, TUSIAD represents the fraction of Turkish capitalists which became transnationalised in different forms of capital, such as commercial, money and productive, by the 1980s. In contrast, MUSIAD represents the latecomers to the transnationalisation process who were marginalised by the hegemony of the larger holding companies affiliated to TUSIAD. MUSIAD had more than twenty member firms among the top 500 biggest companies on the list compiled by the Istanbul Chambers of Industry in 2020. The mentioned companies are the larger ones within MUSIAD, and

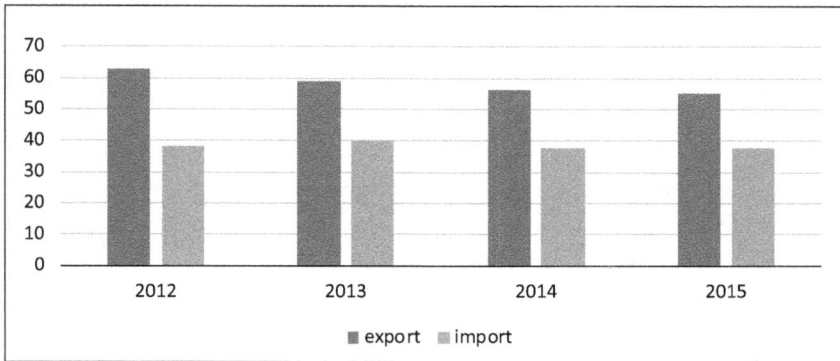

FIGURE 6   The share of SMEs in foreign trade 2012–2016
SOURCE: AUTHOR'S COMPILATION BASED ON TUIK STATISTICS ON SMES,
RETRIEVED FROM HTTP://WWW.TUIK.GOV.TR/PREHABERBULTENLERI
.DO?ID=21540

mainly operate in the metals, construction, food and beverages industries (again generally low-valued-added, labour-intensive and low-technology sectors). Some of these companies operate production facilities in different countries. For instance, Tosyalı Holding has wire rod and steel producing facilities in Algeria (Tosyalı, 2021), and Ülker Holding has production facilities in six different countries, some of which are subcontracted to transnationally operating capital (ÜLKER Holding, 2021). Another significant example of a transnationally operating company within MUSIAD is AGT Agac San ve Tic As. This company operates in the wood industry, and produces MDF, MDF-LAM panels, and profiles in the city of Antalya in Turkey. It also exports to more than sixty different countries. It also has a production facility in Tehran, Iran and engages in transnational production (AGT, 2021). Another example of this fraction is AYTAC company which produces meat and meat products. This company has a production facility in Belgium and exports to different countries in Europe, the Middle East and Central Asia (AYTAC, 2021). This means that some MUSIAD affiliates (Table 8) are in a way part of transnational capital, though this is generally combined with production in Turkey for export.

The peculiar materiality of transnational capital within MUSIAD stems from internal relations which shape these companies' systems of production and their engagement in the circulation of capital. Though starting in similar conditions to other MUSIAD members, some fractions within MUSIAD rapidly transformed into larger capital. To expand the influence of this integration to the small-scale capitalists among their members, MUSIAD launched branches in many provincial cities, such as Kayseri, Gaziantep, Konya, Denizli, and Bursa.

TABLE 8   The list of MUSIAD affiliated companies in the ISO top 500 list in 2019

Company name	Area of operation	Ranking 2019	Export 2019 (Million $)
IÇDAŞ Çelik Enerji Tersane ve Ulasim San. AS	Main Metal Industry	16	857
Tosçelik Profil ve Sac Endüstrisi AS	Main Metal Industry	24	-
Konya Şeker San. Ve Tic. A.Ş.	Food and Beverages	31	69
IÇDAŞ Elektrik Enerjisi Üretim ve Yatırım A.Ş.	Energy	63	-
Tat Metal Çelik A.Ş.	Steel Industry	81	
ÜLKER Çikolata San. AS	Food Beverages and Tobacco	90	59
Yeşilyurt Demirçelik End. ve Liman Isl. Ltd. Sti.	Main Metal Industry	113	120
Safa Tarım A.Ş.	Chemical Products	132	-
Panagro Tarım Gıdacılık Gıda San. Ve Tic. A.Ş.	Food Products	134	-
Limak Çimento San. Ve Tic. AS	Construction Industry	140	35
Tosyali Demir Celik San. AS	Main Metal Industry	176	-
AGT Agac San. Ve Tic. As	Wooden Products and Furniture	198	79
HEMA Endüstri AS	Automotive Industry	221	130
Yayla Agro Gıda San ve Nakliyat AS	Food Beverages and Tobacco	233	21
Besler Gida ve Kimya San. Ve Tic. AS	Food Beverages and Tobacco	265	113
Elita Gida San ve Tic. Ltd.Sti	Food Beverages and Tobacco	272	
Durmazlar Makina San ve Tic AS	Metallic Products, Machine and Equipment	279	114
Cinar Boru Profil San. Ve Tic. AS.	Main Metal Industry	297	-
Boycelik Metal San. Ve Tic. AS	Main Metal Industry	317	31

TABLE 8   The list of MUSIAD affiliated companies in the ISO top 500 list in 2019 (*cont.*)

Company name	Area of operation	Ranking 2019	Export 2019 (Million $)
Pamukkale Kablo San ve Tic As	Metallic Products, Machine and Equipment	357	77
ENKA Süt ve Gıda Mamülleri San ve Tic. A.Ş.	Food Products	411	8
Kangal Termik Santral Üretim A.Ş.	Electricity, gas and ventilation systems	484	-

SOURCE: AUTHOR'S COMPILATION BASED ON; ISO, 2020; MUSIAD, 2017A

However, the share of MUSIAD companies in industrial value added is slightly lower than that of TUSIAD-affiliated companies. This is associated with a new regime which came into force during the 2000s, which divided the country into six different, hierarchically organised zones based on each region's development level (Hosgor, 2016: 125). With the implementation of regional development policies, the southern and eastern regions of Turkey were encouraged to focus on labour-intensive sectors, while western regions were encouraged to focus on high value-added sectors (Ercan & Oğuz, 2015: 121). According to my interviewee in MUSIAD Sivas Branch, this new regime is disadvantageous to the provincial cities in lower-ranked zones since they are less able to benefit from incentives such as reduced corporation taxes, interest and investment support, and social security premium contributions (Interview 2, 04 August 2016). This, therefore, constitutes an intra-capital contradiction among MUSIAD-affiliated firms based in different regions, and between MUSIAD and TUSIAD. As stated in previous chapter, having assisted the establishment of TURKONFED, TUSIAD wants to challenge the hegemony of MUSIAD over the SMEs operating in low value-added sectors.

It is fair to say that the process of capital-formation of different fractions organised within MUSAID is expressed in patrimonial relations between capital owners and workers, longer working hours and lower wages (leading to competitiveness in labour-intensive, low-value-added sectors). The significance of MUSIAD-affiliated firms in contributing value-added in Turkey also stems from their ability to integrate a low-skilled labour force into the production process. Since the growing labour force cannot be absorbed by capital-intensive sectors, MUSIAD-affiliated firms have emerged as a spin-off (Hosgor, 2016: 123). This also constitutes another distinction between MUSIAD-affiliated firms and TUSIAD-affiliated ones, which is the way they appropriate surplus value. MUSIAD members employ the labour power of 1.6 million workers in Turkey (MUSIAD, 2017b). This represents a remarkable growth of firms represented by MUSIAD, but these firms have relied to a large extent on the hyper-exploitation of their workers. According to the figures published by TUIK in 2016, 59.7% of SMEs operate in low value-added sectors (TUIK, 2016). In general, the form of surplus value appropriation by these SMEs is more brutal than that of larger-scale sectors, and paternalistic relations have become a deterministic feature in terms of regulating the social relations of production in which MUSIAD-affiliated firms engage. For instance, workers in MUSIAD-affiliated firms were less likely to sign up to collective bargaining, and these firms discouraged their workers from forming trade unions (Doğan, 2006: 54). The corrosion of labour rights is also encouraged by some firms represented by MUSIAD on the basis that there is no need for a secular labour code if working conditions are characterised by the functioning of Islamic principles (in practice, paternalism). MUSIAD also encouraged the government to make reforms which would modify capital-labour relations in ways which encourage flexible working hours and contracts (MUSIAD, 2011: 125). Overall, although MUSIAD encourages its members to focus on producing high-tech products and to create more added value (MUSIAD Ankara, 2017; MUSIAD, 2012: 112), a deeper look at the production structure of the firms represented by MUSIAD demonstrates that most of the MUSIAD members still operate in low value-added sectors like furniture, construction and services.

4   Configurations of Relations in the Power Bloc

The relationship between the state and MUSIAD can be analysed in terms of the dialectical nature of the relationship constructed in the power bloc, and this section explores the relationship between the state and MUSIAD and between MUSIAD and other business associations. There are different factors that constrain the impact of MUSIAD in the power-bloc, which helped MUSIAD to enter into a new set of relations with the ruling class. This reflects the class struggle between capital represented by MUSIAD and labour as well as between different class fractions which compete in MUSIAD and the ruling class. There was a crisis of hegemony within the power bloc when the AKP came to power in 2002. The AKP was a candidate for hegemonic leadership which was able to mediate the clashing interests of different fractions of power and capital within the power bloc so as to reunite them. The AKP can be seen as a hegemonic power which can work for the benefit of the dominant capital fractions and which is able to provide a mechanism to obtain the active consent of the working classes including conservative Muslim sections of society and the urban secular middle-classes (Özden & Beymen, 2017: 31). The AKP encouraged the big business circles represented by TUSIAD to incorporate SMEs in Anatolian cities, which, in addition to helping to resolve the hegemonic crisis, was necessary since productive capital in Turkey was on the eve of transnationalisation. As argued in Chapter 4, the dominant fractions in TUSIAD supported the AKP's hegemonic project since there was a need for a hegemonic power which can mediate the contradictory interests of different fractions of capital. The tactical alliances and compromises between TUSIAD and MUSIAD, which were mediated by the AKP government, facilitated an increased pace of internationalisation associated with the increase in the volume of foreign trade. This section argues that the state played a relatively autonomous role in this process. For different purposes, the various fractions organised in MUSIAD also supported this hegemonic project.

The class struggle in which different fractions of capital within MUSIAD are involved reproduces the social relations of production, including those which occur within the state. This includes the decentralisation of significant mechanisms that shape the power relations between capital fractions, and which became highly important in the 1990s and 2000s. The class struggle that occurs in the case of DEIK (Dış İlişkiler Ekonomik Kurulu, Foreign Economic Relations Board) is a case in point. DEIK was established in 1987 to strengthen the foreign economic relations of Turkish companies. This platform was initially established under the remit of TOBB. However, it was switched to the Ministry of the Economy as part of an omnibus bill in 2014, which assigned the Minister of the Economy the power to assign and dismiss the president of DEIK (Hürriyet, 29 July 2017). Consequently, the ex-president of MUSIAD, Ömer Cihad Vardan, was appointed as the president of DEIK in 2014 (Hürriyet, 30 September 2014). This reconfiguration of power was associated with the integration of MUSIAD at a more fundamental level of the structured relations of power, which led to hegemonic dislocations in the power bloc.

As long as the MUSIAD-affiliated fractions were closely involved in the class struggle, the AKP had to play a mediator role between TUSIAD and the fractions of capital organised in MUSIAD. The main agencies appeared as the mediator of the interests of small capital within the power bloc are the Ministry of the Economy and the Ministry of Energy. These apparatuses of the state are characterised by their function of mediating the economic-corporate interests of the internationally oriented smaller fractions of capital which produce for export. In line with the concrete economic policies of these ministries, MUSIAD adapted to the process of capital accumulation and contributed to sustaining its existence and reproduction. For instance, these ministries were urged by MUSIAD to take on the following tasks: implementing tight monetary policies, reducing the public debt, increasing the non-interest surplus, encouraging FDI to Turkey, promoting export-oriented growth in the manufacturing industry by increasing the entrance of cheap foreign resources and credit, providing a cheap labour force, shifting the process of decision-making away from existing models based on centralisation and technocracy, and promoting the privatization of state enterprises (Akça & Özden, 09 November 2015). In accordance with these policies of specific state apparatuses, MUSIAD also urged the government to foster and espouse investment-friendly policies which might attract foreign capital to Turkey (MUSIAD, 2011: 111). In this sense, the political and economic relations which MUSIAD expresses are materialised and embodied in these state apparatuses.

The relationship between the AKP governments and MUSIAD differs from the relationship between the AKP and TUSIAD because of the genesis and specificity of each association's particular class fraction. Different areas engage in capital accumulation based on different cultural, religious and traditional factors, and this leads to noticeable internal contradictions within the state structure. In accordance with this argument, this chapter contends that the rise of MUSIAD as a political agent transformed class and power relations within the power bloc. In its dialectical relationship with the state apparatuses, MUSIAD establishes and maintains its power in the process of capital accumulation. Confirming the mediating role of the state, this study argues that the relationship between MUSIAD and the AKP government has shifted the relations of power and class in the power bloc. The preferential treatment of MUSIAD by the AKP government has created contradictions between different business organisations since there were also some tensions between the demands of some business associations such as TOBB and the AKP. This provided an opportunity for MUSIAD to replace TOBB. For instance, the AKP government, as a result of various conflicts, transferred some of the semi-public functions of TOBB to other business associations, like MUSIAD, because MUSIAD are politically closer to the AKP government (Buğra & Savaşkan, 2014: 159).

5 Reorganising the Power Bloc through Public Administration

The political and economic agenda of Turkey at the beginning of the 2000s required a new restructuring of both relations between labour and capital and intra-capital relations within and outside the power bloc. The dominant fractions within the power bloc had to make compromises with different power groups in order to reproduce the relations of production. The compromise within the power bloc was basically constructed around issues which regulated labour-capital relations and the ways in which the companies in Turkey integrate into the global relations of free trade (Hoşgör, 2011: 354). However, the AKP's favourable treatment of certain fractions of the bourgeoisie created a significant crisis of hegemony since the share of some fractions in extracting surplus value was higher than others, which created tensions between transnational fractions within TUSIAD and export-oriented fractions within MUSIAD. As mentioned in the previous chapter, some members of TUSIAD became alienated from the government, and were wiped out of the market, while some fractions within MUSIAD, such as Ülker Group, Kalyoncu Group, and IÇDAŞ Holding were supported.

Regarding the new set of relations within the power bloc, MUSIAD urged the government to carry out immediate reform in the education system. For MUSIAD, vocational training in high schools is poor in quality which reduces the skill levels of the labour force. These reforms were taken to require a new constitution (Vardan, 2012: 135). According to a report published by MUSIAD, the education system should transform science to technology, technology to industry, and industry to trade (MUSIAD, 2017a: 118). Vocational training courses conducted in partnership between the state and MUSIAD aimed to increase labour productivity and competitiveness. The aim is to promote business-state cooperation to increase the appropriation of relative surplus value by increasing the number of skilled workers (Ercan & Oğuz, 2015: 121). As predicted by Poulantzas, the state thus entered into the process of determining classes and the reproduction of ideological and economic relations through organising education (Poulantzas [1974]1975:29), in such a way as to materialise the existence and reproduction of MUSIAD-affiliated capital. In other words, the state reproduces the relations of production by reproducing the social division of labour.

Along with the education, another moment of the contestation is the paternalistic relations which were constructed in the workplace. This paternalism reproduces social relations of production by getting the active consent of the popular masses and reduces ruptural instances of resistance. According to Yasin Durak, the workers in MUSIAD-affiliated companies in Konya city do not see their bosses as capitalists but as a "father" or a "big brother", who pays them what they deserve and looks after them (Durak, 2011:79). In short, religion and patrimonialism are used to get the active consent of workers and to soften the historical contradiction between bourgeoisie and proletariat. The compromise

between the AKP and MUSIAD in the power bloc also facilitated the rise of the
AKP in the political realm, and MUSIAD in the economic realm (See Table 8).
This, as mentioned in Chapter 3, helped the AKP to win the cultural and economic consent of the subordinate classes, which was also necessary to maintain the unity of the dominant classes.

It is in this context that the sectoral or local domination of MUSIAD affiliates is achieved through municipal councils or party provincial organisations.
Most of the municipalities in metropolitan cities like Istanbul, Ankara, Kayseri
and Bursa were governed by the AKP in recent years, and played significant
economic roles (Gürakar, 2016: 20), in a manner peculiar to a specific type
of state. This was one mechanism used by MUSIAD in creating a space that
accommodates it inside state structures. To this end, there have been various
legislative changes in the structure and organisation of municipalities in the
last decade. These reforms were partially conditioned by the aim of providing public procurement contracts at the local level (Gürakar, 2016:20), which
MUSIAD affiliates are well-positioned to win in provincial areas. A study conducted by Gürakar (2016) demonstrates that legal amendments to the Public
Procurement Law changed the power relations between different fractions
of capital through rent creation and distribution mechanisms. Specifically,
contracts in the construction and service sectors have usually been won by
business associations which have close ties with the government and municipalities in provincial cities (and not necessarily those which are most influential at the national scale). As a result, 20% of the companies awarded with
public procurement contracts during the AKP era are MUSIAD members
(Gürakar, 2016: 79).

This reorganisation of the relations of power within the power bloc provided a space for MUSIAD members which may shake the hegemonic domination of TUSIAD. The shifts in the organisation of different state institutions
in the AKP era created a space for the newly emerging SMEs to capture state
subsidies and public procurement contracts. The case of 'ENSAR Vakfı' provides a very remarkable example. This foundation has almost 160 branches
in 80 different provinces. Its founding members are Ömer Dinçer, who was a
former AKP minister, Kadir Topbaş who was the mayor of Istanbul, Feyzullah
Kıyıklık who is the former AKP mayor of Bağcılar district of Istanbul, Mustafa
Açıkalın who is a former AKP MP and worked for General Secretary of Istanbul
Metropolitan Municipality when Erdoğan was the mayor of Istanbul, and
Ismail Bacacı who is a managing consultant for Yıldız Holding (Birgün, 19
April 2016). These people also have close relations with MUSIAD. There are
other foundations which work with ENSAR VAKFI and the AKP government,
such as TURGEV (Türkiye Gençlik ve Eğitime Hizmet Vakfı, the Foundation

for Youth and Education), ÖNDER Imam Hatipliler Dernegi (the Association of Imam Hatip Students), İlim Yayma Vakfı (the Foundation for Disseminating Knowledge), and TÜGVA (Turkiye Genclik Vakfi, the Foundation of Turkish Youth). When the concept of hegemony is applied to the relationship between the state and MUSIAD, it could be said that the dialectical relationship between MUSIAD, ENSAR Vakfı, TURGEV, İlim Yayma Vakfı, ÖNDER, TÜGVA, and the municipalities demonstrates how the ideological functionaries of the state have succeeded in constructing the active consent of the people, and thereby reproducing the social relations of production (Milliyet, 29 April 2014). On the one hand, the interests of different fractions of power and capital converge in supporting the foundations and grassroots organisations which are the main mechanism for manufacturing consent (Yaşlı, 21 April 2016). On the other hand, the hegemony of the regime is also constructed through these concrete relations between the municipalities, grassroots organisations and MUSIAD (ENSAR Vakfı, 31 March 2017).

Another useful way to demonstrate the significance of municipalities in distributing public procurements at a local level is by looking at the connections between local governments and firms affiliated with MUSIAD in provincial cities in Anatolia. For instance, the firms that were directly and indirectly affiliated with the AKP municipalities in Gaziantep, Denizli, Konya, Malatya and Kayseri get the lion's share of the procurement contracts which, in these areas, are mainly in the construction and infrastructure sectors (Gürakar, 2016: 101). MUSIAD-affiliated firms have played a significant role in getting the active consent of the popular masses since the public procurement contracts have given them an opportunity to provide employment for workers in these provincial cities. To this end, MUSIAD also works with IŞKUR (Turkish Employment Agency), which is the official employment agency of the state. In addition, there are many different state apparatuses working in collaboration with MUSIAD in order to get the active consent of the people. For instance, chambers of commerce and industry in municipal cities provide a safer space for the members of MUSIAD to integrate into the reproduction of the relations of production than the national-scale chambers dominated by TUSIAD. As these mechanisms of distribution have created new job opportunities for workers in provincial cities, this has helped the AKP to improve its electoral performance. Universities are also important in creating employment opportunities for MUSIAD. Thus, the firms affiliated with MUSIAD are given a special role to sustain the active consent of the popular masses that was not granted to them by the previous governments. The objective of the state in creating more spaces for SMEs is to encourage them to absorb the cheap labour which is created by neoliberal adjustment policies.

6   Contradictions at the State Level

The Turkish state is central to the reproduction of the social relations of production, as is clearly seen in the case of the relationship between the AKP
municipalities and MUSIAD-affiliated firms. The role that the state plays in
shaping the relations of production and mediating the contradictions between
different fractions of capital can be seen in these mechanisms which redistrib-
ute wealth and create rents for particular companies. This also supports the
argument that the state is not a separate entity and is not constructed externally in relation to the different fractions of power within both political and
civil society (Bieler & Morton, 2008: 116). As Poulantzas argues, ideological
relations are at the heart of the reproduction of the social relations of production (Poulantzas [1978] 2000: 28). This means the state is also involved 'in
the process of extended production of capital as a social relation' (Poulantzas
[1974] 1975:100). In Turkey, municipal governments also perform a mediating
role between workers and capital through grassroots and charity organisations
(Buğra & Savaşkan: 2014: 166). The fundamental peculiarity of this relationship is also shown in the case of religious communities which are directly
supported by the government for this purpose. As argued by Poulantzas, these
foundations are the 'particular configuration of the terrain of class domination' (Poulantzas [1974]1975:27).

In the aftermath of the 2001 banking crisis, the structure and the legal status of the Central Bank was the most contradictory issue within the power
bloc. MUSIAD was against the tight monetary policy implemented by the
Central Bank and urged the government to abandon the independent Central
Bank policy. MUSIAD stated that the underlying reason for the 2001 banking
crisis was the country's weak foreign trade performance over the last decade
(MUSIAD, 2003: 61). It also stated that the deflationary policies of the government generated greater pressures on SMEs, as a result of which they called
for the resignation of the head of Central Bank (Hürriyet, 05 June 2003). On
the other hand, TUSIAD was in favour of the continuation of the reform programme and the maintenance of tight monetary policies. It was also claimed
by TUSIAD that the independence of the Central Bank (a central element of the
IFI-led internationalisation of finance) was the sine qua non for the recovery
of the Turkish economy. In its final decision, the AKP's choice between these
different demands of different fractions of Turkish capital was made in favour
of TUSIAD. It was stated by the AKP that the monetary policy will be continued
and normal relations with the IMF will be maintained (Akçay, 2009: 260–261).
TUSIAD was sympathetic to deflationary policies and tight monetary policies,
which might increase the level of FDI to Turkey, because TUSIAD members

had already completed its process of inward capital accumulation and were ready for the internationalisation of productive capital. This, in turn, would increase the level of absolute as well as relative surplus value appropriation. On the other hand, as MUSIAD members were not yet ready for international expansion to the same extent as TUSIAD's, and operated mainly in low value-added sectors, they urged the government to abandon these monetary policies (Akçay, 2009: 263). Currency devaluation would benefit exporters as lower currency values translate into their own products being cheaper internationally. As a reflection of the monetary policy implemented in the early 2000s, the Turkish lira has increased in value. This appreciation of Turkish lira favoured those businesses which employ more labour and engage in more foreign trade and disfavoured those who employ less labour. As the appreciation of the Turkish lira was expected to decrease the cost of constant and variable capital (e.g. imports), this policy was enthusiastically supported by TUSIAD (Ozilhan, 2003).

The State Planning Organisation and the Ministry of Treasury and Finance held a meeting with the chairmen of TOBB, MUSIAD, Turkish Exporters Assembly (TIM), the Central Bank, the Union of Participation Banks, the Chairmen of the Capital Markets Board, and the Banking Regulation and Supervision Agency just after the 2008 crisis. This meeting formed a consensus among the different capital fractions (Hürriyet, 06 November 2009). To conciliate the contradictions between capital fractions, the state has played a mediator role. The role that the state played in this period was vital because the global financial crisis had created a crisis of hegemony within the power bloc. There was finally an agreement between TUSIAD and MUSIAD, in favour of structural adjustment reforms.

The class contradictions and power struggles between TUSIAD and MUSIAD also crystallised in the organisational structure of the Istanbul Chamber of Commerce and Istanbul Chamber of Industry. These two chambers have always been a site of struggle as more than 400,000 companies are registered with the Istanbul Chamber of Commerce, which is the largest chamber in Europe, and almost 18,000 companies are registered with the Istanbul Chambers of Industry (ITO, İstanbul Ticaret Odası). The share of these companies in Turkish foreign trade was 21.3% in 2015 (ISO, 2017). These two largest chambers are also important in terms of influencing the government as they are important tools for business groups to attract state support. In this sense, the elections for positions within the chambers often reflect a clash of interests between business associations. MUSIAD and TUSKON have gained a considerable influence within the organisational structure of the Istanbul Chamber of Commerce. In 2009, Murat Yalcintas, who is a charter member of the AKP and vice-president of the AKP Istanbul organisation, was elected as the President of the Istanbul Chamber of Commerce with a narrow majority of 133 votes out of 254. As a result of the negotiations between business associations, Murat Sungurlu, who was perceived as the candidate of TUSKON, was transferred to Yalcintas' list and stepped down from his candidacy. There were also 7 MUSIAD members on Yalcintas' electoral list for the executive board (Sönmez, 2010: 59). As a result, the executive board of the chamber became a coalition between MUSIAD, TUSKON and the government. In the same year, Tanil Kucuk, who was known to be close to the TUSIAD circles, was elected as the president of Istanbul Chambers of Industry (Sönmez, 2010: 59). As a result of the different strategies of different business associations in relation to free trade, there was also a contradiction within the power bloc among different capital fractions in terms of the renewal of the standby agreement with the IMF in the aftermath of the 2008–9 global financial crisis. On this issue, MUSIAD encouraged the government not to renew the agreement but to have a flexible credit position and abandon tight monetary controls to finance increased spending, which would allow it to increase foreign trade subsidies, reduce the costs of social security spending, and finance a tax reduction for industrialists. The president of MUSIAD, Omer Cihad Vardan, stated that the government should not retreat from investments which could potentially provide new opportunities for SMEs (Vardan, 2012: 129). Vardan also stated that if MUSIAD had not taken a critical stance against the renewal of the IMF standby agreement, the government would have signed it. Another proposal of MUSIAD was to keep interest rates low. The group also encouraged the government to implement incentives in export-oriented sectors like energy and technology (Ergüder, 2016: 23). On the other hand, there was a strong argument made by Ali Babacan, Mehmet Simsek and TUSIAD circles that Turkey needed to adapt its economy in accordance with the IMF suggestions. While TUSIAD adopted an institutionalist position, MUSIAD lobbied for a greater degree of institutional intervention than TUSIAD recommended. Also, to increase its market share and differentiate its foreign trade destinations, MUSIAD launched 21 different branches in many European countries including France, Germany, Netherlands, Ukraine, Belarus, Denmark, Hungary, Romania, North Macedonia and the UK (MUSIAD. 2017d).

Considering the structural contradictions between capitalist companies, different fractions of capital had both common and differentiated demands in terms of capital accumulation after the 2008–9 global financial crisis (Ergüder, 2016: 20). The contradictions between TUSIAD and MUSIAD after the 2008–9 global financial crisis were based on the ways in which they accumulate capital. As a result of the crisis, the differences between the levels of internationalisation and the ways in which the two class fractions internalise the interests of transnational capital, in other words, their variable accumulation capacities, became more visible. In this period, TUSIAD was more transnational than MUSIAD, and TUSIAD moved from extracting absolute surplus value towards relative surplus value.

Relating to this contradiction at the production level, another contradiction came to the surface over the educational reform proposed by the AKP in 2012. The proposal of the government was basically to increase the length of compulsory education to twelve years, and divide it into three four-year periods (Bekmen, 2014: 66). TUSIAD's main counterargument to this proposition was that this reform would increase the rate of dropouts, especially among girls. This, as TUSIAD argues, would decrease the level of well-qualified and high-skilled human resources. On the other hand, MUSIAD's main argument was that this reform would allow students to attend vocational high schools after the first four years of education. It is notable in this context that most of the firms in MUSIAD are based on appropriating surplus value from assembly production (MUSIAD, 2009: 177), which makes Turkey a regional hub for assembly production. MUSIAD, therefore, wanted to ensure the reproduction of labour power and the means of labour. Through this lens, the long-term interests of the bourgeoisie in general are always ensured and mediated by the state. As long as the hegemonic fraction (the AKP) manages to represent the general common interest of the dominant classes by using the institutional power of the state, the contradictory interests of the different fractions do not erode the continuity of the hegemonic project.

7   The Defining Role of Uneven and Combined Development

Unevenness is not only created between countries and regions but also within national industries and companies (Kiely, 2010: 168). In the early 2000s, Turkey has experienced transnationalisation of productive capital which necessitated the integration of different spaces and sectors into the global process of realisation of capital. This shift in the patterns of the relations of production, or in other words, the trans-nationalisation of production, forced transnational companies to divide the process of production into segments in countries like Turkey (Hart-Landsberg, 2013: 83). Some fractions within MUSIAD integrated themselves into this global process as subcontractors to transnational capital, while others were eliminated because of their scales and patterns of capital accumulation. This, therefore, created a process of fragmentation within MUSIAD. On the one hand, there was the traditional petty bourgeoisie, such as artisans and craftsmen, who flourished with the help of incentive policies implemented by the governments. As suggested in Chapter 3, the monopoly position of big capital slowed down the process of development of smaller fractions of capital. This has led to dependency of these fractions on financial capital to speed up the process of development. In these circumstances, MUSIAD members integrated themselves into the changing dynamics of the global relations of free trade. As they could produce at lower wages than western companies, they became easily adapted to the situation. Most of the firms represented by MUSIAD have a higher share in producing relatively low-tech products, and in industries in which labour productivity depends on lower wages and long working hours (Atiyas & Bakis, 2013: 9). This demonstrates how free trade increases the value of variable capital (Marx & Engels, 1894: 237), by increasing the appropriation of absolute surplus value. On the other hand, MUSIAD also contained construction companies which worked with the municipal governments ruled by political Islamist parties, and relied heavily on government contracts. These SMEs were mainly located in organised industrial zones in Anatolian provinces (Demir & Acar & Toprak, 2004: 169). These clusters were differentiated from the smaller fractions within MUSIAD, as they were willing to integrate into the global relations of free trade, cooperate with the national and international big bourgeoisie in order to grow faster, and ready to enter into sectors from which the government retreated through privatization policies (Doğan, 2006: 59). This relatively bigger fraction in MUSIAD stated that the smaller companies within MUSIAD should be removed from membership as they were not able to play in the bigger leagues (Özdemir, 2006:157).

The uneven integration of Turkey into global relations of free trade also affected the way Turkey combines with global capitalism. The combination of Turkey with global imperialism necessitated the transformation of the organic composition of capital. The fractions within MUSIAD became concentrated in labour-intensive sectors, and they also became subcontractors for the bigger fractions of Turkish and transnational capital (Hoşgör, 2011: 345). For instance, construction companies engaged in free trade by exporting construction materials to foreign countries. These companies also engaged in transnational relations of production through foreign direct investments in various countries. However, as part of the integration strategy of Turkey in the process of transnationalisation of capital it was necessary for capital fractions organised within MUSIAD to increase their appropriation of relative surplus value as well as absolute surplus value. As a result, these fractions which have previously concentrated on extracting absolute surplus value will have to reorient their process of production towards the appropriation of relative surplus value through technology transfer. To this end, MUSIAD affiliates concentrated in the Organised Industrial Districts in most of the bigger Anatolian provinces have benefited from changed power dynamics within the power bloc, which provided an opportunity for these capital fractions to grow and increase their ability to accumulate more capital and engage in the total circuit of capital (Özden & Beymen, 2017: 190). This demonstrates that uneven integration into global free trade not only creates new mechanisms for creating surplus value but also changes the internal dynamics in each national social formation.

As a result of these shifts, there has been an increase in the share of provincial cities in total exports from Turkey. For instance, the share of exports from Konya, Denizli, Kayseri, Kahramanmaras and Denizli (in which MUSIAD and TUSKON have been increasingly active and have increased their membership) increased from 3.40% in 1996 to 7.84% in 2012 (Buğra & Savaşkan, 2014: 155). Although the export-oriented strategy was not designed to favour the SMEs organised in MUSIAD, they have supported this process of export-oriented internationalisation due to the effects it has in terms of reduction of real wages, social security reforms and legislation promoting sub-contracting (Akça, 2014:31). As detailed in Chapter 2, during the process of internationalisation of Turkish capital in the 1980s, the state adopted more export-oriented policies to integrate into the global economy. At the core of this integration was the insistent TUSIAD demand for deeper integration into global free trade relations so as to promote the interests in its own members in scaling-up their participation in value production. The largest TUSIAD-linked holding companies were also the major winners from this shift in the process of capital accumulation. However, the process also created various opportunities for the capital fraction organised in MUSIAD (Hoşgör, 2011: 344). Since this is not a unidirectional relationship, the reproduction of the SMEs also depended on the class struggle in the social formation (Poulantzas [1974]1975:30). Confirming Poulantzas' theory, the activities and reproduction of MUSIAD members are not constructed exclusively in relation to the activities of TUSIAD. Rather, their accumulation process reflects the class struggle between different capital fractions. This demonstrates how the AKP managed to unite the different interests of different fractions of capital. The integration of MUSIAD-affiliated companies into the global relations of free trade required them to internalise these relations into the domestic structure of production and its forms of surplus value extraction. Despite the increase in the engagement of provincial cities in the relations of production and global free trade relations, these provincial cities have not grown at the expense of metropolitan cities like Istanbul, Bursa and Izmir. It is still the case that the main winners from global integration were big capital groups in metropolitan cities. However, the profits of SMEs in provincial cities also significantly increased (Hosgor, 2016: 121). This means that the provincial cities in which MUSIAD is primarily active are becoming relatively more significant, while metropolitan cities are becoming more integrated. Among other things, metropolitan cities like Istanbul have become the centres of financial activities while the base of production has shifted towards provincial cities. It should also be remembered that most of the bigger companies in TUSIAD expanded their base of production towards countries in the Middle East and China since the cost of production is much cheaper than in Turkey.

In order to provide institutional and financial support for the companies which are on the path of integration into global free trade, MUSIAD established the Foreign Relations Board which deals with the international activities of MUSIAD members (MUSIAD, 2017a). The purpose of this board, according to Vardan, is firstly to educate entrepreneurs on how to get a visa, and secondly to encourage businesspeople to invest in foreign countries. These businesspeople are then expected to transfer technology to the home country. In other words, they learn how to engage in international free trade. Another mechanism that provided opportunities for MUSIAD members to operate in global free trade system is through FTAS and international business forums. This mechanism is also used by TUSKON, as will be discussed in the next chapter. For this purpose, MUSIAD organises regional business forums with members of the Organisation of Islamic Countries (OIC) (MUSIAD, 2011: 120). The first attempt to form such links was made in 2011 in Jordan, which brought 100 firms together. In this business forum, representatives of SMEs from Turkey met their counterparts from Jordan, Saudi Arabia, Pakistan, Egypt, Palestine and other countries in the region. During these trips, MUSIAD also organises meetings with government authorities in foreign countries, and among businesspeople, and the Turkish Minister of Foreign Trade sometimes attends as a speaker and honorary guest. As part of its integration strategy into the global relations of production, MUSIAD also launched International Business Forums in this period and organised business trips to the USA, Germany, the UK, South Africa, Malaysia, Sudan, Russia and many other countries (Vardan, 2012: 59). Additionally, MUSIAD organises international trade fairs, conferences and trips; encourages Turkish citizens living abroad to work with their member firms; and establishes global networks with Muslim merchants which generate joint venture investment opportunities for the smaller firms on both sides. Thus, MUSIAD helps its members to expand towards new markets and integrate into relations of global free trade. This demonstrates how MUSIAD, as representative of different fractions of class, mediates the consolidation and survival of different class fractions.

8   Conclusion

This chapter examined the dialectical relationship between MUSIAD and the state, and the ways in which it is reflected in the Turkish social formation. The chapter showed the limits of the hegemonic framework which reduces the contradictions and tensions between MUSIAD and TUSIAD to conflicts among sects and cultures and ignores the class-based nature of the conflict. In other words, neither the institutionalists nor the neoclassical-liberal approaches take sufficient account of class-based socio-political relations of production. In their examinations of MUSIAD, the focus on religious and cultural elements takes place at the expense of understanding its capitalist institutionalisation, and these hegemonic approaches refuse to take notice of the class-based activities of SMEs organised in MUSIAD and the connections between these social relations of production and the state. They also treat business associations and the state as engaged in purely external relations, which leads them to ignore the dialectical relationships within the state and between the capital fractions in the dominant power bloc.

Although MUSIAD occupies a very significant place in the ideological and political structure, this chapter suggested that the main distinction between TUSIAD and MUSIAD is more material than ideological. What differentiates this Marxist approach from mainstream approaches is the analytical priority accorded to class as a relation and process, and additionally, the understanding of ideology as a constituent part of the process of reproduction of the social relations of production, which is important to mediate class relations, rather than as a simple matter of religious or political belief. This chapter also examined the activities of MUSIAD within and outside the power bloc. It argued that most of the firms represented by MUSIAD are SMEs which are mainly based in local provinces and were not ready for integration into global relations of free trade until the end of the 1990s. It was also suggested that there are three different fractions within MUSIAD. The first is nationally oriented capital which produce in Turkey for the domestic market. The second fraction, which is the dominant one, is the internationally oriented fraction which produce in Turkey for export. The third fraction is the transnationally operating grouping, which produces in different countries.

The chapter further showed that mainstream approaches explain the role of the state and the contradictions among capital fractions through the institutional power of the state or the power of state elites. In contrast to such mainstream approaches, this chapter suggested that neither the institutional approach, which cannot go beyond merely focusing on the rise of political

Islam and the development of peripheral spaces, nor the liberal-neoclassical approaches inspired by the dualism between capital and the state, provide adequate explanations for the emergence and development of MUSIAD. Following the methodological and theoretical premises mentioned in the previous chapters, this chapter reconsidered the class characteristics of MUSIAD as a capital fraction, its role in the social relations of production, and the shifting patterns of relations between the state and MUSIAD. It argued that the capital groups within MUSIAD meet the requirements of capital accumulation and expansion with its structural power stemming from its nature as capital, rather than its ideological positioning.

As mentioned in the previous chapters, the transnational expansion of capital and the shift in the base of production increased the extent to which SMEs integrate into global relations of capital accumulation, a situation which has led to the emergence of new structural and institutional forces governing the relations between capital and the state apparatuses. In this regard, dividing the process of production into different sub-processes and places became essential for the reproduction of capitalist relations. As a result, the base of production was shifted towards provincial cities where MUSIAD-affiliated firms are able to exploit flexible working conditions and lower wages. This means that smaller fractions of capital had the chance to use labour power more efficiently because of the lower costs and patronage relations in the provincial cities. This was supported by vocational training courses provided by the AKP government and cooperation between religious foundations and MUSIAD. This chapter, therefore, argued that the rise of MUSIAD changed capital-labour relations in Turkey.

The chapter argued that, in line with Poulantzas' predictions, the AKP is a hegemonic power which works for the benefit of the dominant capital fractions and is also able to provide a mechanism to win the active consent of the working classes including Muslim-conservative sections of society and the urban secular middle-classes. As part of this hegemonic strategy, MUSIAD is given a special role to sustain the active consent of the popular masses that was not granted to them by the previous governments. In the same period, the state regulated capital-labour relations by implementing policy reforms encouraged by TUSIAD, MUSIAD, and the international financial institutions in the post-2001 period. However, TUSIAD and MUSIAD favoured different strategies which reflected their different positions within unevenly developed capitalism, with MUSIAD supporting a more interventionist approach and greater deviance from neoliberal orthodoxies compared to TUSIAD. This was seen in the struggle to influence of the state apparatuses in various policy areas such as the independence of the Central Bank, the relationship to the IMF, and education reform. While TUSIAD dominated the political decision-making process with its influence on ministries, bureaucrats and MPs, MUSIAD sought means to challenge this hegemony of TUSIAD. The specific state apparatuses, such as the Ministry of the Economy and Foreign Trade, became a field of contestation in this sense, which helped MUSIAD affiliates to get tax expansions, import-export permissions and investment incentives.

To conclude, as mentioned in the first chapter, unevenly developed states are brought into global relations of free trade in different ways. The last two chapters have analysed how the Turkish state responded to the developments in the global capitalist system, and in which ways the largest fractions of Turkish capital, TUSIAD and MUSIAD, have internalised these relations. The next chapter, which is the last empirical chapter, explores how TUSKON, as a representative of certain class fractions, engages in global relations of free trade. Further to that, the next chapter will also examine the role of TUSKON in examining the tensions and contradictions within the power bloc, which changed the power relations among business associations engaging in global free trade relations, and how it changed the class relations within the structures of the state.

CHAPTER 5

TUSKON, the State and Free Trade

This chapter examines the formation of Gulenist capital organised within TUSKON (the Turkish Confederation of Businessmen and Industrialists, Turk Sanayici ve Is Adamlari Konfederasyonu). The analysis encompasses the place of TUSKON in the social relations of production in Turkey, the role of TUSKON in the state structure, and the role of its affiliates in international free trade relations. It draws lines of demarcations and cleavages between TUSKON, MUSIAD and TUSIAD, which also involved contradictions among fractions of capital. It argues that the contradictions among different business associations cannot only be grasped in terms of the religious and cultural cleavages. As outlined in the introduction to this book, and contrary to mainstream approaches, the theoretical priority of this chapter is to show the dialectical relationship between business associations and the state, and the relationship between global free trade relations and the firms affiliated with TUSKON. Rather than reducing the particular positions of different class forces to their religious and cultural positions, this chapter examines such positions through an empirical analysis based on the relations of production, exchange and reproduction.

Following the framework set out in the early chapters of this book, the purpose of this chapter is to provide a historical materialist perspective on the development and rise of TUSKON-affiliated capital through three levels of analysis. This is important to relate the formation of capitalist classes in TUSKON to the global process of capital accumulation and the international state system. The first section focuses on the social relations of production to map out and define the class characteristics of TUSKON-affiliated companies. This will help locate different fractions of capital organised within TUSKON. This is crucial to understand the internal relations embedded in TUSKON, which is connected to the uneven and combined development of the state system. In relation to this, the section outlines the historical development of TUSKON, and the ways in which the companies affiliated with TUSKON engage in the processes of production, exchange and reproduction. Following the theoretical arguments of the U&CD approach, the section examines the sectoral and regional unevenness between TUSKON and the larger capital fractions represented by TUSIAD. With reference to the previous chapters, this analysis attempts to grasp the differences between TUSKON and other business associations in terms of the way they engage in capital accumulation process and the relation of this process to different social classes and state apparatuses. Accordingly, the following section examines the role of TUSKON-affiliated companies which are affiliated with the Gülenist movement (GM) in the power bloc. It investigates the class struggle between the different fractions of capital represented by different business associations. It also uncovers the dialectical relations between the state apparatuses and TUSKON-affiliated capital. The final section mostly focuses on the ways in which TUSKON-affiliated capital integrates into global relations of free trade. The section also examines the functions of schools funded by TUSKON-affiliated companies and the effectiveness of the trade bridges and conferences organised by TUSKON. It concludes with a final analysis in the last section.

1   The Material Basis of TUSKON

This section examines the material basis of the relationship between the state and TUSKON and explores what makes TUSKON distinctive in comparison with the other, larger associations explored in the previous chapters. According to Buğra & Savaşkan, what differentiates TUSKON from MUSIAD and TUSIAD is "the nature of the role they play in shaping, rather than merely representing, the interest of their members" (2014: 110). Along similar lines, mainstream scholars argue that the main motivation behind the rise of TUSKON is spirituality rather than any material factor (Kurt et al., 2016: 696). However, this approach underestimates the importance of the class-based character of TUSKON and does not explicitly delineate the real differences between the three business associations. These differences can hardly be reduced to ideological and religious dynamics. The institutional materiality of the relations between the state and capital are based on the political, economic and ideological dimensions of capitalist social relations (Poulantzas, [1974] 1975: 201). These business associations should, therefore, be characterised in terms of the nature of their relationship with the state apparatus, and by their ability to use their networks of resources to establish connections between different sizes of companies operating in different sectors and engaging in global relations of free trade. This demonstrates that the distinct class fractions organised within TUSKON did not exist externally to the other social classes in different social formations; the different fractions only existed in relation to their struggle for power and activities in foreign countries. In this sense, this fraction of capital within TUSKON is defined by its place in the social division of labour which also includes political and ideological relations.

TUSKON, in the same way as MUSIAD, emerged and developed in parallel with the rise of political Islam in Turkey, and its development cannot be grasped without examining the GM (currently referred to by the government as FETO – the Fethullah Gülen Terror Organisation). The GM emerged in the 1970s, flourished after the military intervention in the 1980s, and became very influential in the 1990s. After many trade unions and leftist organisations had been crushed, the GM found a conducive environment to grow faster and to get strategic positions in the state structures in the post-1980 period (Buğra & Savaşkan, 2014: 112). This period coincides with the transition to neoliberalism, whose dominant characteristic is the dominance of export-oriented foreign trade policy. Although the roots of TUSKON date to the 1990s, its effectiveness was then quite limited in terms of representation of its members' interests. It was officially established in 2005 with a very specific focus on foreign trade. In fact, the emergence of TUSKON represented the establishment of new contacts between SMEs in Anatolian provinces and international entrepreneurs (Bacik, 2011:156).

Although the exact comparative and associational statistics are impossible to find, the sizes of members affiliated with TUSKON were diverse. Although there were larger members or various members with different scales and scopes in TUSKON, like Orkide, Boydak, Ipek-Koza and Ülker Group, most of the firms were SMEs operating in textiles, construction, and services. There were three different fractions of capital represented within TUSKON. The first fraction consisted of nationally oriented companies which invested mainly in the education, media, health and construction sectors. For instance, Feza Publications Inc. was a media conglomerate which was the owner of the Cihan News Agency, the daily newspaper Zaman, Samanyolu TV channel and many other media concerns. The education sector was also a strategic field for the GM and TUSKON as it was very influential in private teaching in Turkey (Gürel, 2015:36). The organisation owned 210 private schools, 460 private teaching houses, 13 universities and tens of thousands of university preparatory courses. To illustrate the scale of penetration of the education sector, 967 out of 3667 private teaching institutions were owned by the Gülenists in 2013, which is equivalent to 25% of private teaching institutions in Turkey (ODA TV, 18 December 2013). Another section within the nationally oriented fraction consisted of trading and construction companies which were directly supported by the municipalities in their process of capital accumulation, relying mainly on government contracts in the same manner as MUSIAD-affiliated construction firms. This section was dependent on cheap labour and intended to invest in the international market at a later stage. Aydinli İnsaat, Dumankaya Insaat, Eroglu Gayrimenkul, Inanlar Company, Cikrikcioglu Company, Paralel Yapi Insaat, Durmazlar Insaat, and Fi Yapı were the largest companies in TUSKON which mostly operated in the construction and real estate sectors (Karar, 12 March 2018).

The second fraction is internationally operating capital groups which mostly produced in Turkey for export. This fraction of capital already aimed to internationalise their relations of production through free trade by the 2000s. They mainly operated in the iron and steel, copper mining, wooden products, sugar refinery, furniture, textiles, goods, tobacco and beverages sectors. NAKSAN Holding, Orkide Group, Akfel Holding, Abalıoğlu, and Ekinciler Holding were the most important TUSKON affiliates (Table 9) in terms of their integration into global free trade. This fraction has affected the position of Turkey in global capitalism in a specific manner. In particular, NAKSAN Holding,[1] which is a company from Gaziantep, a southern province of Turkey, operates in different sectors such as energy, plastic packaging, logistics, textiles and technology. This company exports to more than 140 countries and has over 7000 employees. It owns two companies in the 500 biggest companies list in Turkey which are Naksan Plastik and Royal Hali. This company has also purchased some global brands such as Pierre Cardin Carpets in 2007. Also, it became a local distributor for global companies. For instance, *Elmasepeti.com* which is a company under the roof of Naksan is the biggest distributor of Apple products in Turkey (NAKSAN, 2021). In the late 2000s, some companies captured new investment areas and became international players. For instance, Akfel Holding is the largest non-governmental natural gas importer in Turkey, which imports 55% of Russian natural gas to Turkey, and 14% of the natural gas that Turkey needs (Akfel Commodities, 2021). There is another capital group mainly operating in liquid cooking oil and margarine production, which is called ORKIDE Group.[2] This company exports 25% of its products to 102 countries (Orkide, 2014: 1). At the same time, Orkide Company is an official supplier of the charity organisations of the World Bank, such as UNRWA (United Nations Relief and Works Agency) and WFP (World Food Programme) (Orkide, 2014:7). This company supplies 35% of Turkey's oil production requirement and is also ranked 133rd in the 500 biggest company list compiled by Istanbul Chambers of Industry in 2011 (Orkide, 2013a: 4). Orkide Company often attended trade fairs and trips organised by TUSKON and joined the 19th World-Turkey Trade Bridge Conference. One of the CEOs of Orkide Company stated that 'this conference

---

1   43 different firms under the roof of Naksan company were taken over by the TMSF (Savings, Deposits and Insurance Fund of Turkey, a regulatory body) in 2016 because of its alleged ties with the FETO.

2   The owner of the company, Ahmet Kucukbay, is a founding member of ESIDEF and TUSKON. He cancelled his membership of TUSKON in 2015 and is currently in jail.

is important since they could find new networks and partners to engage in global trade relations' (Orkide, 2014: 12). In 2013, Orkide attended the EXPOCO-MER Trade Fair organised by TUSKON in Panama in 2013. This company also joined the Afghanistan Trade Fair organised by TUSKON in 2013 and used this fair to diversify its foreign trade partners (Orkide, 2013a: 20). Orkide Group has also financially contributed to the Turkish Olympics, which is another mechanism that TUSKON used to expand its network with international firms, by sponsoring the Japanese stand in 2013 (Orkide, 2013a: 21). In 2011, It received an award as the company which attracted the largest amount of foreign currency to Turkey (Orkide 2013b: 4). This company was still ranked 240th among the 500 biggest company list published by Capital Business Magazine in 2015 and still exists at the time of writing.

The third fraction is transnationally operating capital which engages in production relations in different countries. This fraction allows more precise analysis of TUSKON-affiliated capital as it is the purest representative of the capital organised within TUSKON: it is the fraction which entails a particular position at the global level, and it has a relatively transformative role in the ideological and political structure of the Turkish social formation. This means, it does not exist in isolation from other social classes and class fractions in different social formations, whereas the other fractions within TUSKON only aspire to transnationalisation. For instance, BOYDAK Holding,[3] which was the largest member of TUSKON, started its activities in 1957 in Kayseri, operating mainly in furniture, textiles, marketing, chemistry, logistics, iron and steel, informatics and energy. It operates in seven different sectors with seven different brands namely Istikbal, Mondi, Bellona, Form Sunger, Boycelik, Serko and Moyteks. This company has more than 12,000 employees and exports to more than 140 countries. 342 of its distributors have opened abroad. This is one example of the extended reproduction of the TNC in TUSKON in different countries. TUSKON also had 7 firms in the list of the 500 biggest companies in Turkey (Hes Hacilar and Boytas Mobilya are included in Table 9). Although the company's head office is in Kayseri, it has branches or affiliates in Adapazari, Sakarya, Eskisehir, Zonguldak and Istanbul. This holding company also has brands and manufacturing facilities abroad, such as ALFA MOBEL Trade Co. in Dortmund established in 1997 (Boydak Holding, 2017a), and Sunset International Trade L.L.C. in the USA, established in 2002. These manufacturing firms have links with international manufacturing companies through

---

3   This company's shares and assets were transferred to the TMSF (Tasarruf Mevduati Sigorta Fonu, Saving Deposit Insurance Fund), in 2016 because of its affiliation with TUSKON (Capital, 06 September 2016).

TABLE 9   The list of TUSKON-affiliated companies in the ISO top 500 list in 2010

Name of the company	Area of operation	Rank in the top 100	Total output (Billion TL)
Sarkuysan Elektronik Bakir San ve Ticaret AS.	Copper Mining	26	1.4
Toscelik Profil ve Sac Endüstrisi AS	Iron and Steel	28	1.4
Kastamonu Entegre Agac Sanayii ve Ticaret AS	Wooden Products	49	0.96
Kayseri Seker Fabrikasi AS	Sugar Refinery	95	0.58
Ekinciler Demir ve Celik Sanayi	Iron and Steel	85	0.6
Boytas Mobilya Sanayi ve Ticaret AS	Furniture	82	0.63
Abalioglu Yem Soya ve Tekstil AS	Goods, Tobacco and Beverages	70	0.74
HES Hacilar Elektrik San ve Ticaret AS	Metallic Products	69	0.71
Besler Gida ve Kimya Sanayi ve Tic. AS.	Goods, Tobacco and Beverages	92	0.58
Naksan Plastik ve Enerji Sanayi ve Tic. AS	Plastic and Energy Products	129	0.54
Kucukbay Yag ve Deterjan AS	Goods, Tobacco and Beverages	133	0.43

SOURCE: AUTHOR'S COMPILATION BASED ON ISO, 2011

subcontracting and joint ventures which provide them with opportunities to increase their technological investments. Another example of transnationally operating companies is AKFA Holding, which operates in health, construction and information technologies. Seven out of twenty-two companies affiliated with AKFA Holding operate in multiple countries through export and production chains ranging from Russia to Qatar (Dunya, 02 April 2013). Sarkuysan Company is another example of this fraction, which produces electrolytic copper products. Although its main production facility is in Gebze in Turkey, it launched a production facility in Albany in the USA in 2009 (Sarkuysan, 2018). Kastamonu Entegre Company is another significant example of this fraction, which operates in the wooden panel industry, and the retail and construction sectors. This company engages in production relations in seven different countries, operating eighteen factories and exporting its products to almost 100 countries (Kastamonu Entegre, 2018). Tosçelik company also has production facilities in Algeria and Montenegro.

Among the relations of TUSKON with other class fractions and the state apparatuses in the power bloc, the financial activities of TUSKON-affiliated transnational firms are another decisive factor shaping the class characteristics of this fraction. In the secure political and economic conditions after the 1980 military coup, TUSKON members found opportunities to evolve as part of finance capital (Tanyilmaz, 2015:98). TUSKON-affiliated companies organised their financial activities under the Bank Asya which was initially established in 1996 under the name of Asia Finance. This bank is founded and operated by the GM. The opening ceremony brought important figures together including Fethullah Gülen, Abdullah Gul, Tansu Çiller and Recep Tayyip Erdoğan (Apaydin, 2015:454). This Bank enhanced the power of the firms affiliated with TUSKON vis-à-vis the rival companies operating in similar sectors and markets. This demonstrates the level that the capital owned by TUSKON-affiliated companies reached, their relationships within the power bloc, and their support for the activities of TUSKON. The Bank Asya was the largest participation bank in Turkey in 2006, with assets totalling $4 billion. (Hendrick, 2009:358). With the help of TUSKON-affiliated firms, it increased its market share in Turkey. It made investments in the Middle East, North Africa, Russia and Ukraine in 2007. Thus, the transnational fraction within TUSKON operated across borders by the late 2000s. In a Poulantzasian framework, this meant that the interests of different fractions of capital (transnationally or nationally based) were transferred to the various fractions of capital affiliated with TUSKON. These companies also extensively invested in Central Asia, and were involved in transferring money from Turkey to companies in Central Asia (Balci, 2003:158). Some companies within TUSKON also had their own banks. For instance, BOYDAK Holding also owned a finance capital concern called Turkiye Finans Participation Bank in alliance with Ülker Group. This bank was established through the merger of Family Finance and Anadolu Finance Institutions in 2005 (Boydak Holding, 2017b). The National Commercial Bank holds 67% of its shares (Turkiye Finans, 2017), and Boydak Holding has withdrawn its shares from the bank in 2016. Overall, the increase in the level of production and the promotion of foreign trade facilities transformed some of the larger capital groups in TUSKON from commercial capital to finance capital which operates across borders through transnational production chains in the late 2000s.

2   The Formation of the Relationship between the State and TUSKON

To understand the political class struggle embedded in the Turkish social formation, it is important to grasp the establishment of the relationship between
the AKP and TUSKON. This relationship includes inter-class and intra-class
contradictions at the state level which has constructed the existence and
reproduction of the power bloc in different ways. In this regard, the most
important issue is the consolidation of power bloc as a 'unity of politically
dominant classes and fractions under the protection of the hegemonic fraction' (Poulantzas, 1978: 239). In this light, the crystallization of the alliance
between the AKP and what were later TUSKON-affiliated fractions of capital
started in the early 2000s. The construction of this alliance is a hegemonic
project which also included different fractions of capital, the military, bureaucracy, liberal democrats and the Kurdish movement. After political Islamists
split from the centre-right mainstream in the 1970s, the AKP eventually managed to establish an alliance between the transnationalised capital groups
organised under TUSIAD and the economically developing but politically subordinated fraction of the bourgeoisie which consisted of companies that have
much greater diversity in their size and geographical location, often MUSIAD
and TUSKON members. To a considerable extent, the AKP's coming to power
represents the integration of what later became TUSKON (as well as fractions
belonging to MUSIAD) into the power bloc (Bekmen, 2014: 62). This means
the AKP integrated different fractions of capital in the same process of capital
accumulation in different ways (Benlisoy, 26 January 2017). The AKP organised
the relations of power and softened the contradictions between different fractions of capital to consolidate the unity of the power bloc in its early years in
power. It managed to convince the large-scale capital represented by TUSIAD
to upgrade their manufacturing facilities. On the other hand, it also advanced
the interests of SMEs organised within TUSKON, as the previous chapter
already demonstrated in the case of MUSIAD. The needs of SMEs were met
through privatization and public tenders in this period, which created rents
for SMEs and prepared them to become ready to expand in the global market
(Bekmen, 2014: 64).

    This hegemonic project had a two-fold tendency: to establish an alliance
with different fractions of capital, and to convince different power groups to
maintain this alliance. In fact, the hegemonic project could only exist by subor-
dinating other power groups or establishing alliances with them to overthrow
the current power bloc. Politically, the most significant ally of the AKP government in this project was the GM. This alliance was important in terms of

occupying strategic positions within state apparatuses, gaining control over media organs, and fighting against the old state elites and the secular groups within the Turkish Army (Hendrick, 2009: 351). Consequently, the presence of Gülenists in state positions increased in this period. In practice, students who graduated from Gülenist schools in Turkey have occupied strategic positions within the ministries, bureaucracy, and media in Turkey. Moreover, the AKP government appointed Gülenists to critical positions in the state apparatuses as a response to the secularists' attack against the AKP when it came to power in 2002 (Yavuz & Koç, 2016:136).

The government's selective empowerment of particular SMEs in this period was a crucial feature of the Turkish social formation, in which the class and power relations between business associations became institutionalised. In addition, the mechanisms that TUSKON adopted to interact with the state included large-scale international business events, and participation in state officials' visits to other countries (Atli, 2011: 117). As large-scale business events bring together the executives of the biggest associations with state officials, this is a very effective way of interacting with the state. What is more important here is that the relationship between the state and TUSKON is not merely external. In this dialectical relationship, TUSKON influenced the government through the chambers of trade and commerce in the provincial cities, the local branches of the central administration; universities funded by the Gülenists; and supranational institutions which sought to shape local governance structures (Buğra, 04 March 2013). More precisely, the Prime Ministry, the Ministry of Foreign Affairs, The Ministry of Industry and Trade, the Undersecretariat of Foreign Trade, and TIKA (Turk Isbirligi ve Koordinasyon Ajansi Baskanligi, Turkish Cooperation and Coordination Agency) are some of the state apparatuses which crystallised the power class struggle between the state and TUSKON. Incorporation ogf TUSKON was achieved through financial support sponsoring its in foreign countries and providing it with bureaucratic and technical support (Alkan & Mercan, 2013: 35). Importantly, the general assemblies of TUSKON have always been attended by ministries and official AKP delegates (Buğra & Savaşkan, 2014:133). For instance, the AKP MPs and the ex-President Abdullah Gul, always praised TUSKON for their contribution to the national economy (The Economist, 25 March 2010). The AKP's former economy minister, Ali Babacan, attended the opening ceremony of TUSKON's Brussels office and a conference organised by TUSKON with South East Asian nations in 2007 (Ministry for EU Affairs, 04 July 2007). The AKP's head and parliamentary speaker also sent letters praising the great achievements of TUSKON. Between 2002 and 2009, the AKP's Foreign Trade Minister, Kursat Tuzmen, attended every summit organised by TUSKON (Hendrick, 2013:166). Moreover, various consultation platforms incorporated with TUSKON, such as the Development Agencies (Kalkinma Ajanslari), were invited to take part in policy-making processes. This involved a mutual interaction between the government and TUSKON, which resulted in TUSKON's support for government policies.

As part of the political class struggle, the status and functions of the Turkish judiciary have always been a contested field between power groups in the state structure. The political class struggle over the juridical system is a specific reflection of the alliances and contradictions within the power bloc. As Poulantzas argues, the judiciary is a significant part of the state apparatus, and the struggle over the judiciary is crucial in establishing the political domination of the hegemonic class (Poulantzas [1974] 1975: 25). The 2010 constitutional referendum dramatically changed the relations of power within and outside the power bloc and reconfigured the institutional assemblies of the judiciary. The changes resulting from the referendum package have been controversial, and consist of amendments to twenty-four articles of the constitution. These changes were proposed by an alliance consisting of Gülenists (TUSKON), liberals, MUSIAD and the AKP government. Gülen himself campaigned in favour of a Yes vote (Strauss, 28 April 2011). At the centre of the class struggle was the composition and powers of the HSYK (Hakimler ve Savcilar Yuksek Kurulu, Constitutional Courts of the High Council Judges and Public Prosecutors). There had been a radical change in the composition and structure of the HSYK in the 2010 referendum (Ozbudun, 2015: 45). This referendum also increased the power of the executive branch of the state over the judiciary, which shifted the power struggle in the field of the judiciary (Yildirim, 11 December 2017). This new system led the Gülenists to increase their presence in the organisational structure of the juridical apparatuses. They filled the judiciary and other key institutions of the state with their own advocates (Bekmen, 2014:68). This resulted in the recentralisation of the state through a series of court cases like the Ergenekon, Balyoz, and Izmir Espionage Affair cases (Sönmez, 2014: 254). Government officials supported these trials in which top military officials and judges were accused of plotting a coup against the government and seeking to overthrow it (Yavuz & Koç, 2016: 136). These trials were a result of the alliance between the AKP and the GM to wipe old state elites out of the power bloc and reflects the establishment of the new hegemonic project.

On the part of the relations of production, what is unique to the AKP period is the shift in the way that the state is involved in the process of capital accumulation towards not only encouraging larger capital but the SMEs (Buğra, 04 March 2013), in contrast with the 1980s-90s when internationalisation occurred largely at the expense of, or at least bypassed, SMEs. This process also transformed the role that the state played in managing the unity of the power bloc. In its application, the state might favour and delimit some certain fractions of classes at the expense of others (Martin, 2008: 319). The previous chapters suggested that the state is the material condensation of class struggle (Poulantzas [1978] 2000: 73), so the contradictions within the power bloc are not exclusively constructed by the state. Rather, the selective policies of the government created tensions between business associations. As Buğra states, in the Anatolian provinces especially, there was considerable unrest among the established bourgeoisie stemming from the rise of the Gülen-affiliated business circles. These contradictions were reflected in the chambers of trade and industry especially in provincial cities like Kayseri (Buğra, 04 March 2013). This also led to contradictions between the big capital represented by TUSIAD and the government, which were reflected inside state structures. For instance, a member of High Advisory Council of TUSIAD, Ayça Dinçkök, stated in an interview that:

> Unfortunately, I see that there is a polarization within the business associations in Turkey ... Sometimes we are not invited to some meetings, but others are ... how is such discrimination possible? I feel uncomfortable as an entrepreneur. They have created a polarization between us and them. I assumed we were all the same. How can you separate us as "us" and "them"?
>
> DINÇKÖK, 03 March 2010

The state mediated the tensions in favour of TUSKON by distributing public resources and giving privileged incentives (such as government contracts). This means the state actively engaged in the alteration of power relations between different fractions of capital. Various agencies and platforms give privileges to particular business associations in terms of taking part in the decision-making process. As Özel also states, the composition of the board of the *Development Agencies* is a good indicator of the balance of power among associations. Under the AKP, four out of five slots were given to TUSKON and MUSIAD. As also stated in chapter 4, TUSIAD and TURKONFED reacted fiercely against this allocation of seats to other business associations which are close allies of the AKP (Özel, 2015:140). However, this does not mean that the state overruled the dominant fraction of capital organised under TUSIAD. On the other hand, the state consolidated the power bloc and maintained its hegemony through maintaining its relative autonomy in the organizational matrix of the state structure. TUSIAD's participation in global value chains continued to be supported by AKP governments, which performed a balancing act between the interests of different fractions of capital so as to hold together the hegemonic power bloc. However, the 2008–9 global financial crisis became a turning point in terms of the hegemonic project of the AKP and its ability to satisfy all three associations at the same time. Since then, the organic relations between the AKP and MUSIAD and TUSKON were deepened at the expense of the TUSIAD fraction. In its role as mediator of the conflicting interests of different fractions, the AKP had to take a different stance in intra-capital contradictions (Akça & Özden, 2015). For instance, as mentioned in the previous sections, the AKP did not sign the IMF-standby agreement, a decision which benefited MUSIAD and TUSKON at the expense of TUSIAD. Umit Akçay also argues that reduction of the AKP's capacity to unify the different fractions of different classes stems from the slowdown of economic growth after the 2008–9 global financial crisis (Akçay, 14 December 2013). This also made contradictions in the power bloc more visible (Benlisoy, 26 January 2017). Thus, on the one hand, the increasing contradictions between the AKP and TUSIAD were a watershed in the sharpening of polarization in the power bloc. On the other hand, the tensions between the AKP and Gülenists led to a later crisis in the hegemony that the AKP has managed to establish.

3 The Collapse of the Relationship and 15 July Failed Coup Attempt

The relationship inside the power bloc between the AKP and TUSKON has been characterised by different moments in which the alliance was realised or collapsed. The internal contradictions between the AKP and the GM came out first in the foreign policy arena after the Mavi Marmara incident in 2010 (Hendrick, 2013:190). The Mavi Marmara was a ship sent to the Gaza Strip on 31 May 2010, with the aim of breaking the Israeli government's blockade (The Guardian, 02 June 2010). The flotilla was organised by the IHH (Insan Hak ve Hürriyetleri Insani Yardim Vakfi, Foundation for Human Rights and Freedoms and Humanitarian Relief) and the Free Gaza Movement. Nine activists on this ship were murdered by Israeli naval forces (Balci, 20 October 2013). This resulted in a deterioration of relations between Turkey and Israel (CBCNEWS, 02 June 2010). A few days later, Gülen criticised the flotilla for not getting the permission of the Israeli government (Cop & Zihinlioglu, 2017: 34). This was the moment in which the collapse of the relationship between the AKP and the GM began to materialise. The incident coincides with the revolutionary processes in the Arab World which has started in 2011. In this regard, it was a great chance for Turkey to implement its neo-Ottomanist foreign policy which seeks to rebuild the Ottoman Empire's historical legacy in the Arab world (Cengiz, 2020, 216).

The second contradiction appeared after the wiretapping scandal in 2011, which involved the discovery of wiretaps in Erdoğan's home and office. After this scandal, contradictions became apparent, and this was followed by disputes on the status of dershanes (private university preparatory courses) (Hamsici, 4 December 2013). As a response, a Gülenist prosecutor in Istanbul, Sadrettin Sarikaya, summoned Hakan Fidan, who is the chief of the National Intelligence Services, one of the closest colleagues of Erdoğan and known as Erdoğan's right hand (Thicke, 28 April 2017). The prosecutor accused Hakan Fidan of holding secret meetings with PKK (Kurdistan Workers' Party) officials in Oslo (Yavuz & Koç, 2016: 139). Erdoğan declared that Hakan Fidan was not going to give a statement in court (T24, 21 February 2014). After this dispute, the law to shield State Intelligence Service officials from political prosecution was amended (Cumhuriyet, 17 April 2014). The response of the Gülenists peaked on 17 and 25 December 2013 (Sönmez, 2014:11). The Istanbul Police Department's Financial and Anti-Corruption Unit detained 47 people, including the sons of the Minister of the Economy, the Minister of the Interior, and the Minister of Environment and Urban Development, many high ranking people including the Mayor of Fatih district of Istanbul, high ranking officials of TOKI (The Housing Development Administration), the general director of the state-owned Halk Bank, and an Iranian-Turkish businessman, Reza Zerrab (Yavuz & Koç, 2016:140). As a counterattack, the government reacted to this corruption probe by retiring, purging and suspending almost 70 percent of the police forces and halting education programmes in police academies (Yavuz & Koç, 2016:141).

The restructuring of the juridical system in 2010 created further tensions after the events of 17–25 December 2013. Erdoğan stated that the government made a mistake in 2010 by weakening the role of the Minister of Justice in the HSYK, while strengthening the autonomous role of the HSYK (Hürriyet, 29 December 2013). The AKP government thus amended the constitutional article 5c, which allowed "the government to be informed immediately of ongoing secret investigations and to take necessary measures, such as changing police officers involved accordingly" (Ozbudun, 2015: 46). In 2014, a law came into force enabling the Minister of Justice to appoint the membership of one of the three chambers which belong to the Plenary of the Council (Ozbudun, 2015: 47). This was followed by substantial transfer operations which replaced the judges and prosecutors who were involved in corruption trials with pro-government replacements. Another provision which came into force enabled the Minister of Justice to totally reorganise the members and structure of the HSYK. After the new elections for the HSYK in September and October 2014, the government obtained the power to control the judiciary. Thus, the new

HSYK suspended some prosecutors involved in the 17–25 December corruption investigations (Ozbudun, 2015:51). Behind these amendments and replacements, there was a power struggle between the AKP and the GM over control of the state apparatuses.

Before the 17–25 Events, TUSKON was the most influential business association in Turkey in terms of its relationship with the state apparatus. One of the representatives of TURKONFED mentioned that several of their members became members of TUSKON since they thought TUSKON had a closer relationship with the government (Buğra & Savaşkan, 2014:125). In addition to this, businessmen in provincial cities felt joining TUSKON was the best way to prosper, and especially, to get a share of municipal tenders (Strauss, 28 April 2011). This also coincided with capital consolidation in the energy market in the late 2000s which took place through patronage relations. Therefore, most of the SMEs resorted to joining MUSIAD or TUSKON to develop new patronage relations (Özcan, 2015: 1731). At the international level, the relationship between the AKP and TUSKON was more intense. There was a class struggle between transnationally operating fractions within TOBB and TUSKON. This created a conflict between the AKP and the Gülen Movement on the issue of the international mobility of Turkish capital. The conflict arose mainly on the issue of the specific markets to be targeted. The AKP government had improved economic relations with the Northern Iraqi (Kurdish) Regional Government, and the region had become the second largest export destination of Turkish exporters by 2010. This economic relationship with the Iraqi government and its implications for the Kurdish question became another conflicting field for the AKP and the GM (Sönmez, 2014: 256). Since the SMEs affiliated with TUSKON were by this stage deprived of profits from construction and highway bids and government spending, TUSKON took a critical stance against this international target of the government (Sönmez, 2010: 254). This has resulted in class struggle between TUSKON-affiliated capital and power groups and the AKP. This can be grasped in the debates on the legislation concerning TIM (Turkiye Ihracatcilar Meclisi, the Assembly of Turkish Exporters). According to this legislation, some prerogatives of DEIK and TOBB were transferred to TIM, in which TUSKON was more powerful (Buğra & Savskan, 2014 133). DEIK had been the most effective business organisation in the fields of organising business trips to foreign countries, establishing business networks, and promoting trade agreements with foreign countries during the 2000s. Ambassador Ender Arat states that "DEIK does its job perfectly, but if it fails to do so someone else can do it in its stead" (Atli, 2011:124). Unlike MUSIAD, TUSKON's main strategy was to take part in TIM and be influential in its organisational structure rather than participating in DEIK (Buğra & Savskan, 2014:137). The struggle did not only take place in the political field but also in the economic field. The rise of TUSKON in state structures and economic activities created tensions between MUSIAD and the AKP. In particular, after 2007, MUSIAD complained that they were unappreciative of the allocation of resources in favour of TUSKON-affiliated companies (Cavdar, 2014: 11).

The share of TUSKON-affiliated firms in Turkey's foreign trade was almost double the share of MUSIAD-affiliated companies in 2010. This led to an intensification of contradictions between the interests of companies affiliated with MUSIAD and TUSKON. In this dispute, the most contested issue was control of export-oriented sectors. In 2010, Russian President Medvedev visited Turkey to join a meeting which aimed to establish a Russian-Turkish trade volume of $100 billion in five years. Behind the scene, there was an organisational battle between representatives of different internationally oriented fraction of capital. There were three organisations hosting this meeting: TOBB, TIM and TUSKON (Özkan, 14 May 2010). Up until then, DEIK was the only organisation hosting foreign delegations. However, DEIK's logo was not displayed in the meeting room, and TUSKON replaced DEIK in the role of organising the meeting. In this case, the Ministry of Foreign Trade, Zafer Caglayan, aimed to create more space for TUSKON to act freely (Tanyilmaz, 2015:92). The 17–25 December 2013 events were, therefore, a reflection of the conflicts between fragmented groups within the power bloc, which changed the class relations among business associations. Following Poulantzas' model, the state acted against the interests of TUSKON-affiliated businesses in order to impose the long-term economic interest of the dominant classes and to secure its hegemony (Jessop, 1985:56; Poulantzas, [1978] 2000: 184). This process was associated with the relocation of industry and rescaling of the state. As a strategy, the government implemented a new plan based on inward-oriented development, based especially on a capital accumulation strategy in the construction sector. After the collapse of the relationship between the AKP government and the GM, the tensions between the two led to further rifts within the power bloc, which also resulted in a new balance of power among business associations. The strategic positions which TUSKON used to hold in official meetings and business trips were redistributed to TOBB and MUSIAD (Özdemir, 27 January 2014). Most of the members of TUSKON resigned from membership and became members of MUSIAD (Ozgenturk, 10 January 2016).

However, it is important to qualify that these fractions of the bourgeoisie, which have been critical of the government after the 17–25 December 2013 events, were previously situated within the power bloc as an element in the construction of a hegemonic coalition of power groups, and that they have lost their critical position in a class struggle among fractions. It is difficult to conceal, however, that the state apparatuses reacted to this conflict in a way which influenced the process of capital accumulation by changing the distribution of groups operating in the economy. Each business association attempted in its own way to promote its own interests within the power bloc. For instance, MUSIAD did not take a critical stance towards the AKP after the corruption probe. However, the president of MUSIAD stated that "our common wish is to investigate corruption probes whatever and whoever claims it. This must be based on freedom of judges" (Haberturk, 21 December 2013). TUSKON, on the contrary, publicly declared that corruption in the state is like cancer in the human body, if not taken seriously it can spread all the body and corrupts the country (Cumhuriyet, 23 December 2013). TUSIAD, on the other hand, stated that the corruption probe is a desperate situation, and we should stay loyal to the independence and freedom of the judiciary whatever happens (Sönmez, 2014:205). It is in this circumstance that the power relations were thus recrystallized after the collapse of the alliance within the power bloc. As a result, the AKP retained its capacity to organise its hegemony effectively through the reorganisation of the state apparatuses and by playing an active role in the restructuring of the power bloc.

The class struggle between the AKP and the GM after the 17–25 Events resulted in the failed coup attempt on 15 July 2016. The parliament was bombed by fighter jets, and the General Secretary of the Turkish Army was kidnapped on that night. People gathered on the streets and squares to oppose the coup against the government. In the confrontation, 241 people were killed and 2194 were wounded. The government declared that Fethullah Gülen was behind the coup attempt, and Gülenists within the army, police and many different groups from different circles were implicated. The failed coup attempt of July 2016 created a situation of political turmoil, and the government declared a state of emergency which lasted around two years. Under the state of emergency, decrees issued by the President and cabinet entered into law without parliamentary debate. This vastly empowered the executive branch against the rest of the state apparatuses and power bloc, and thus allowed the government to regulate the organisational matrix of the state, capital-labour relations, and even traffic rules without consultation within the parliament. Five general strikes were banned during this period[17], and almost 150,000 people were dismissed from public institutions. This provided a pretext to disorganise the working-class and strengthen the power of capital to operate export industries based on cheap, docile labour.

It is crucial to remember that political and economic relations are both part of hegemonic project of the ruling/hegemonic class. This project has taken a new form after the 15 July failed coup attempt and the AKP has established new alliances with different power groups. In this endeavour, the AKP used the state of emergency to get the active consent of the dominant classes, especially those most important to its hegemonic project. This was crucial if the AKP was to reproduce its hegemony through its symbolic and material power, and it was crucial to maintain its structural and material determination in the power bloc. In particular, the AKP has established legal architecture of the presidential system after the coup attempt. The necessary political and economic conditions were also embodied in this period. Accordingly, the AKP and its new allies in the power bloc brought forward a new referendum which was held on 2017. Consequently, the Turkish electorates have voted for the yes vote with 51.41%. With this referendum, the class power of the new social formation in Turkey has been crystallised. The transition to a presidential system corresponds to a significant growth of the AKP's non-political functions, which are not exterior to the rising control of the president over the relations of production. This increased the ability of the AKP government to mobilise different power groups in the power bloc, which lead it to the position of hegemonic class in the Turkish social formation.

On the part of the capitalist classes, the exclusion of TUSKON affiliates from the market after the failed coup attempt has changed the power relations between different fractions of capital. Although capitalist classes in Turkey, represented by different business associations, constitute an integrated whole, one needs to speak about the internalisation of contradictions among them, and the resultant struggle in the post-coup period. As stated earlier, TUSKON has constituted a specific field in the Turkish social formation with its affiliation with the GM and its transnational networks, especially in Africa. It is for this reason that the exclusion of TUSKON has created a gap in the power bloc. This has also created a power struggle between different business associations for the replacement of TUSKON in the state structure as well as the international market. For instance, MUSIAD has replaced TUSKON's activities in the Middle East and Africa. MUSIAD has announced 2018 as the "Year of Africa". This has given rise to distinct moments which have reproduced the presence of Turkey in Africa. For instance, former members of TUSKON became members of MUSIAD, and the AKP has favoured MUSIAD members through different state apparatuses and financial incentives in Africa. However, MUSIAD's presence in state institutions, such as DEIK, business councils, and the ministry of foreign trade, has also created unrest among the TUSIAD and TOBB circles. This complex interplay in the relationship between the AKP and MUSIAD provided an insight to help unravel the transformation of power relations between the BAs in the post-coup period.

As far as political struggles are concerned, the AKP has managed to establish hegemony over the various class fractions and power groups. Although the president was fully equipped with the power to regulate and correct the political issues (a kind of Bonapartism) after the transition to a presidential system, the contradictions between different capital fractions have made it difficult for the Turkish state to internalise its interests in the Turkish social formation. This was both because of the contradictions among TUSIAD, MUSIAD and TOBB after TUSKON's exclusion, and the economic crisis which started in 2018 and intensified with the COVID-19 pandemic in 2020. This economic crisis resulted in further concentration and centralisation of capital, as almost 15,000 SMEs have gone bankrupt since the outbreak of COVID-19 in Turkey. This means relations of production in the context of the Turkish social formation, are under severe strain amid the coronavirus pandemic. Additionally, larger members within TUSIAD which have production facilities in different social formations such as KOC Holding, SABANCI Holding, ANADOLU Group and a few others, may capture the smaller fractions if they go bankrupt. On the other hand, SMEs which are hugely dependent on state tenders and financial credits to reproduce their relations of production will be eliminated if they do not get direct assistance from the state. As a response to COVID-19 measures and to combat its impact on SMEs, the state has played a role through the public banks of Turkey (Ziraat Bank, Halkbank, Vakıfbank, and Eximbank) which have provided credits to SMEs to reproduce themselves.

4   The Combination of TUSKON Affiliated Companies with Global Free Trade

To grasp the power relations between different fractions of capital represented by different BAs it is also important to unravel the integration of TUSKON affiliates into global free trade. The operations of TUSKON affiliates were characterised by a two-fold strategy: to reproduce their relations of production in the Turkish social formation, and to expand outside the national borders. In particular, TUSKON provided spaces for SMEs at a time in which Turkish capitalism became increasingly integrated into global relations of free trade. The motto used by TUSKON was to help transform 'petty merchants to businessmen, businessmen to industrialists, industrialists to exporters, exporters to multinationals' (Özel, 2013:1096). This is the cornerstone of the transformation of companies from a national bourgeoisie to an international bourgeoisie.

The expansion of TUSKON affiliates' relations of production depended on two mechanisms. The first was the Gülenist private schools which were financially supported by the member firms of TUSKON, and which helped them to expand their base of production towards countries in the Middle East, Central Asia, North Africa, and beyond (Yavuz, 2013: 90). In Turkey, the Gülenist schools were initially perceived as an instrument to expand the Turkish influence in these countries (Cakir, 10 August 2016). The ex-president of Turkey, Abdullah Gul, stated that Turkish schools provide an opportunity which gives Turkish businessmen a competitive edge in finding new markets in Sudan, Egypt, Libya, Algeria and many African countries (Alkan & Mercan, 2013:34; The Economist, 25 March 2010). These schools were also used to export the political agenda of the AKP government and its neo-Ottomanist policy. For example, the opening of a complex called Nizam al-Mulk, which was the largest religious educational centre in South Africa (Al Arabiya News, 04 October 2012), was attended by South Africa's president Jacob Zuma and high-ranking state officials from Turkey (Dreher, 2015: 828). Chad's trade minister's statement at the 2006 Turkey-Africa Summit organised by TUSKON shows how transnationally TUSKON was active:

> Westerners came here to take from us, but they brought nothing. The only thing we want now is a real partnership. For Chad, the Turkish schools are the most important doors to the outside world. They also form a bridge between Turkey and us.
>
> HENDRICK, 2013:168

On the part of the relations of production the schools are important in explaining the specific way in which the national fraction of capital within TUSKON engages in the process of capital accumulation and the global relations of free trade. In comparison to the strategies of capital accumulation adopted by MUSIAD and TUSIAD, TUSKON/GM's schools involve an overarching difference which transcends the forms of capital accumulation for TUSKON-associated companies. Most of the national fraction of capital involved in these ventures invested in Central Asia before the collapse of the Soviet Union. This was followed by the Balkan countries, and later almost every single country in the world (Cakir, 31 January 2014). The number of schools reached 2000 in almost 160 countries (Aljazeera, 16 November 2016). In the 2000s, Turkish schools funded by the Gülenists expanded into 100 countries (Hendrick, 2009:357). Additionally, these schools have played an important role in promoting economic relations between SMEs from different provinces of Turkey and foreign companies (Balci, 20 October 2013). For instance, the stationary chain NIL and chocolate and biscuit manufacturer ÜLKER are among the transnational chains affiliated with GM.

The second mechanism that TUSKON members use to integrate into global free trade relations is the creation of trade bridges organised by TUSKON. Since its establishment, TUSKON organised several trade conferences with foreign companies, namely, Turkey-Central Asia in 2006, Turkey-Pacific Asia in 2007 and 2008, Turkey-Middle and Eastern European Countries in 2008 and 2009, Turkey-African countries in 2006, 2007 and 2008, and a Turkey-World Trade Conference in 2011 (Hendrick, 2013:165). The first Turkey-Africa Foreign Trade Bridge was held in 2006. Almost 1000 businessmen from Turkey, 450 businessmen from African countries, and 45 bureaucrats and state officials from different countries attended this forum. More than 16,000 bilateral meetings took place in the forum, with costs totalling $250 million. In the second forum in 2008, 100 Turkish companies, 805 businessmen from African countries and 1515 from Turkey attended. In addition to this, 65 bureaucrats and state officials from different countries attended. 30,000 bilateral meetings took place, and several trade agreements were signed totalling $2 billion, which accounted for one-third of the Turkey's trade volume with African countries in the same year. In the third conference in 2008, more trade agreements were made totalling more than $3 billion. Two years later, Turkey and Kenya signed a $500 million trade agreement with the help of TUSKON. These conferences are important to promote interaction between global free trade and the Turkish social formation since intergovernmental agreements were also signed during these events.

The increase in trade was achieved through Foreign Trade Bridge Forums through which African companies were invited to invest in Turkey and Turkish SMEs to invest in and import from African countries. These attempts were also supported by the state through financial credits provided by the Exim Bank for those would like to invest in African countries (Özkan, 2013: 144). At the initiative of the members of TUSKON, Turkey announced 2005 as the year of Africa and hosted the first Turkey-Africa Cooperation Summit in 2008 in Istanbul with the participation of many companies from 50 different African countries (Özkan, 2012: 113). The primary purpose of these bilateral meetings between businessmen was to sign a trade agreement. The businessmen from African countries are provided with a table and schedule for bilateral meetings. Each participant must stay at their allocated desk, and Turkish SME owners visit these stands. A translator who can speak the mother tongue of the businessmen in that stand is also provided for each desk to enable each participant to communicate easily (Alkan & Mercan, 2013: 37). After the meetings, TUSKON made extra efforts to make the agreements secure and stable. For instance, after the meetings, TUSKON staff organised business trips to African countries with the participation of businessmen and state officials. For instance, 60 businessmen affiliated with TUSKON participated in the official trip of the Minister of Industry and Trade, Nihat Ergun, in 2009. In 2010, a lot of businessmen affiliated with TUSKON took part in President Abdullah Gul's official trip to Niger (Alkan & Mercan, 2013:37). Secondly, TUSKON also organises business trips to Anatolian provinces for the African businessmen who attended the Trade Bridge Forums. During the trips, TUSKON organises business meetings between the firms. For instance, after the second Turkish African Trade Bridge Meeting, TUSKON organised business trips to 43 different Anatolian provinces (Alkan & Mercan, 2013: 38).

The functions of the Gülenist schools and trade bridges in relation to Turkey's expansion towards Africa are not only about the movement of capital as a functional thing, rather, they are about the expansion of capital as a social relation. This indicates that TUSKON played an important role in pursuing AKP's sub-imperialist foreign policy in Africa (Uysal, 2021). Historically, Turkey's political relations with Africa were reshaped in 1998. In this year, an Action Plan was proposed to establish trade and protection of investment agreements with African countries. This plan also suggested providing funds and special technical assistance to companies which were willing to invest in Africa. Accordingly, Turkey's accession to the African Development Bank and the African Export and Import Bank was encouraged. However, this plan could not be implemented until the AKP came to power in 2002. The first official visit by a Turkish prime minister to an African country was held in 2005. TUSKON played a very significant role in promoting economic relations between African countries and Turkey. The trade volume between Turkey and African countries was $2.5 billion in 2005 when TUSKON was established. This figure reached $9 billion in 2010. TUSKON also initiated diplomatic relations with Myanmar, Cambodia, Laos, Vietnam, Papua New Guinea, and New Zealand. In addition to this, TUSKON made an agreement with the Russian Union of Industrialists and Entrepreneurs in 2010 (Altintop, 18 January 2010).

Overall, the expansion of Turkey's national SMEs towards the African market was both a result of the AKP's foreign policy and the power struggle between different business associations which required TUSKON members to find new markets to invest in. The targets of the different fractions of Turkish capital have been diverse in the 2000s. The EU market was largely occupied by members of TUSIAD, and the Middle Eastern and Central Asian countries were occupied by MUSIAD. This meant that TUSKON primarily targeted East Asian and African countries (Gürakar & Esfahani, 2013:377). This does not mean that the African market was solely targeted by TUSKON members because it was not occupied by TUSIAD and MUSIAD members, but on the other hand, to highlight that these fractions of capital focused on producing and investing in these countries.

5   Conclusion

This chapter argued that the fragmentation of the bourgeoisie in Turkey is complex. This occurs not only because of the existence of different fractions of capital - commercial, money and productive – which operate in similar sectors, but also because of the interconnectedness between different levels of capital. Accordingly, this chapter argued that there are three main fractions affiliated with TUSKON. The first fraction is nationally oriented capital which produces in Turkey for the domestic market. These companies mainly operate in the construction, health and education sectors. The second fraction is an internationally oriented one which produces in Turkey for export. These companies mostly operate in the iron and steel, copper mining, wooden products, sugar refining, furniture, textile, goods, tobacco and beverages sectors. The final fraction is a transnationally oriented fraction which produces in sectors such as furniture, textiles, marketing, chemistry, logistics, iron and steel, informatics and energy. This fraction is also involved in finance capital. Overall, this chapter argued that most of the firms affiliated with TUSKON are export-oriented SMEs.

In the following sections, this chapter analysed the power struggle between different power and capital groups and TUSKON-affiliated companies. Following the conceptualisations of Poulantzas, this chapter argued that there was a need for a hegemonic power which can unite the different fractions of power and capital. The AKP, therefore, established an alliance with the GM and the companies affiliated with TUSKON. The analysis also revealed that TUSKON-affiliated companies and Gülenists benefited from the crisis of hegemony in the state structure in the early 2000s. This chapter, further, discussed the inter-class and intra-class contradictions and compromises at different levels of the social relations of production, particularly the state level and the level of global relations of free trade. In terms of grasping the relationship between MUSIAD and TUSKON, the chapter argued that there was a collaboration between these two associations before the 17–25 December 2013 events. Both groups occupied strategic positions, acquired power in different organisations and cooperated to mutually benefit from government incentives. However, there have always been tensions and contradictions between these two fractions as the places and positions they occupied were different and they also had a different kind of influence on state apparatuses. Accordingly, this chapter argued that the conflict between TUSKON and MUSIAD resulted from the struggle over market shares in overlapping sectors (such as government contracts).

The following section on the relationship between the state and TUSKON argued that the AKP's coming to power led to the integration of TUSKON into the power bloc. This meant the AKP integrated different fractions of capital in the same process of capital accumulation in different ways. Therefore, the relationship between the state and TUSKON is not purely external. Rather, these power groups in the power bloc were in a dialectical relationship with each other. Accordingly, the chapter addressed how the contradictions between the GM and the AKP became apparent at the level of different state apparatuses. This chapter argued that the AKP reconstructed the state. In this new state form, the executive branches of the state are strengthened vis-à-vis the administrative branches of the state. This has led to greater capacity for state intervention and involves an increase in the state's relative autonomy within the power bloc. While strengthening some fractions of capital, including MUSIAD and TUSIAD members, at different levels, the state eventually drove TUSKON members out of the market. This was an attempt to discipline the fragments of the bourgeoisie. Accordingly, this chapter argued that the collapse of the relationship between the government and TUSKON changed the relations of power between business associations. MUSIAD started to replace TUSKON in African countries. It has launched branches in Nigeria, Sudan, South Africa, Niger, the Ivory Coast, Senegal, and Benin. In order to do this, MUSIAD is supported by Turkish state officials to organise official meetings with state officials and SMEs in African countries. The final section on the international relations of free trade argued that TUSKON, in the same way as MUSIAD, provided networking opportunities for its members, and helped them to invest elsewhere in the international market, and also to source raw materials from different countries. The emergence of TUSKON coincided with the internationalisation of productive capital in the 2000s. The way TUSKON integrated into global relations of free trade is mainly through subcontracting and exporting. The mechanisms used by TUSKON in order to integrate into global relations of free trade were Turkish schools funded by TUSKON-affiliated companies and trade bridges and conferences organised by TUSKON. This chapter thus revealed the extent to which members of TUSKON engage in transnational relations of production and global relations of free trade.

In conclusion, this chapter argued that the internationalisation of Turkish productive capital in the global free trade system in the 2000s transformed some fractions within TUSKON from commercial capital to productive capital, and from national capital to a more international kind of capital. This transformation process was not based on an external relationship between the state and TUSKON and was characterised by specific power relations within the power bloc, which secured the hegemony of the AKP within the power bloc. After the collapse of the alliance between the AKP and TUSKON, the power relations between different business associations and power groups within the state structure were reshaped. What is most important here is that the state still plays its Poulantzasian role in securing the long-term interests of the different fractions of capital and its hegemony within the power bloc by various means, even when this entails choices among or struggle against particular fractions of capital.

CHAPTER 6

Conclusions to the Theoretical Arguments of the Book

This book established modest connections between abstract concepts (class and value), and their concrete effects (wages, prices, and profits) to analyse how reproduction of capital occurs on a global scale. This analysis was based on an analysis of the global capitalist system as well as the social formation in Turkey, which included an examination of the dialectical relationship between business associations in Turkey and global relations of production. In this regard, free trade is explained as the generalisation of commodity production on a world scale. Contrary to mainstream approaches, the book additionally argued that free trade is not just an exchange relation between different parties, and it cannot be considered simply as inter-state or international exchange relations. On the contrary, it is a process of realisation and reproduction of social relations of production, and more precisely, it is not only realised or reproduced between nations or states but also within states, regions, and sectors.

To understand the process of capital accumulation in the countries of the Global South, this book argues that free trade is the way to extract surplus value from different countries and transfer it from technologically backward countries to core capitalist countries. This occurs by lowering the value of constant capital and increasing the value of variable capital. Additionally, market expansion also creates a capitalist world market, which leads to the generalisation of production on a world scale. The book, therefore, argued that free trade has led to transnationalisation of production which deindustrialised the countries at the Global South and increased their dependency on the social formations in core capitalist countries, while also producing dependent forms of industrial production. The motivations of capital in the core capitalist countries to expand in the countries in the Global South are, (i) the costs of production are lower in less advanced countries because of the availability of cheap labour and raw materials, (ii) working conditions are more flexible in the host countries, and (iii) the absence or weakness of trade unions, and the low rate of taxes provided by national governments, allowing capital to capture a larger portion of surplus value.

To grasp where Turkey sits in this picture, this book followed the model provided by Ray Kiely who argued that the generalisation of commodity production is a new phase of imperialism which can be called free trade imperialism.

In its classical usage, the term "imperialism" means a new phase of capitalism based on the centralisation of capital and the fusion of industrial and financial capital. This led to a new phase of finance capital which included a greater increase in the export of capital because of the accumulation crises in the core countries. In accordance with the arguments put forward by Rosa Luxemburg and to detail how Turkey integrated into global process of production, the book argued that it was necessary to integrate countries in the Global South into the global relations of free trade to ensure an increase in the exploitation of labour and generalise the process of capital accumulation on a world scale through expanding the process of appropriation of surplus value. Contrary to mainstream approaches, the book also argued that core capitalist countries protected their borders with high rates of tariffs and quotas while applying free trade policies in their early stages of development. When the process of inward-oriented capital accumulation was completed, capitalists in the core countries started to expand globally and encouraged or coerced the countries in the Global South to abandon protectionism in their foreign trade policies. At this point, the book benefits from the arguments made by Ray Kiely who argues that trade between core capitalist countries is also significant as well as trade between core capitalist countries and countries in the Global South.

Finally, to explain more recent events, this book engaged with the uneven and combined development approach which argues that, during the global expansion of capital, every country has integrated into the global relations of free trade in different ways at different times. This integration is explained through the lens of the UCD book throughout the book. The uniqueness of the UCD approach is that it sheds light on one of the main arguments of the book, which is that there are differences between classes engaging in the relations of free trade, and, therefore, the condition of unevenness arises out of free trade between states, regions, and sectors. Following Samir Amin, the book argued that the uneven expansion of capitalism is based on unequal exchange which is based on the exchange of products at an unequal cost. This unequal exchange, as the book argued, is based on unevenness in sectoral productivity. Contrary to arguments made by classical and neoclassical approaches, the companies which started to accumulate capital prior to other companies have supremacy in producing high value-added products, and therefore have a competitive advantage against latecomers. At this point, the book applied the arguments put forward by John Weeks who argued that the unevenness between countries, companies, and sectors arises not only because of differences in sectoral productivity, but also as a direct result of differences in the progressive development of the productive forces. Accordingly, this book argued that it is more important to pay attention to the mechanisms which produce surplus value at the global scale rather than focusing on the redistribution of surplus value through free trade relations.

This book argued that free trade does not refer to a borderless global market, it is not a win-win situation for all parties engaged in trade, and it creates neither an economic nor a social convergence among states, societies, or sectors. On the contrary, it creates asymmetrical interdependence as integration is not based on a relationship between equals. In accordance with the arguments made by the UCD approach, the kernel of the argument of the book is that every country in the world (and even each different region or fraction of capital within each country) has integrated into the global relations of free trade in different ways at different times. This global integration was uneven as the countries which integrated into free trade later than the advanced capitalist countries had some significant weaknesses and they suffered from technological underdevelopment. This was a result of the uneven expansion of capitalist relations of production. Accordingly, the book argued that the current phase of free trade is associated with the generalisation of commodity production on a world scale, which included the division of production process into segments carried out in different spaces. This means the global expansion of capital after the GATT Uruguay Round between 1986 and 1994, has expanded the global free trade regime beyond the trade in goods and towards areas such as services, finance, agriculture and public procurements.

As this book analyses the role of agency in explaining the shifting patterns of the global expansion of capital through expansion of the free trade system, it paid attention to the state and capital as agents. It argued that states are the key actors which enter into global relations of free trade. Contrary to mainstream approaches, the book argued that the state is both an economic and a political agency operating in market relations. In other words, the state is neither an abstract entity nor a night-watchman. The texture of the state is not, therefore, based on state versus market or state versus society dichotomies. Instead, the book argued that the capitalist state has always been intrinsic to the social relations of production, and it always comes to rescue the market from collapse in times of economic crises.

The book concluded that the relationship between the state and capital is not an external relationship between separate actors. The state mediates and organises the interests of the different fractions of capital and multiple actions within the power bloc. In fact, this book approached the state from the philosophy of internal relations which means the relationship between the state and business associations is not external. It also critically engaged with Ralph Miliband who argues that the state is a tool in the hands of the capitalist class, as this approach fails to recognise the contradictory relations between different power and capital groups in the hegemonic power bloc.

This book, instead, applied the arguments made by Poulantzas against the instrumentalist idea of the state. It argued that the usefulness of a Poulantzasian understanding of the state is its focus on the institutional materiality of the state. In this endeavour, it provided a theoretical basis to understand how the organisational matrix of the Turkish state has changed since 2002. Secondly, Poulantzas argues that the state is the material condensation of class struggles between different power and capital groups which directly engages in the reproduction of the social relations of production. To challenge the instrumentalist understanding of the state, he argues that the relationship between the state and different class fractions is not static or unidirectional. Rather, there are always contradictions and a dialectical relationship between capital and the state. This means class struggle is not exclusively constructed outside or inside the state. At this point, the book applied the concept of relative autonomy to characterise the relationship between the state and capital. The state plays an intertwined economic role in the social relations of production and also a political role in the class struggle. The role of the state is to manage the contradictions within the power bloc and secure the unity of the dominant classes while disorganising or obtaining hegemony over the dominated classes. The state's functioning might therefore benefit some fractions of capital over others.

The role of the state is not restricted to managing the contradictions between the dominant classes, but also shapes the relationship between the dominant and dominated classes. This book focused on contradictions arising from the process of state restructuring. In this context, it applied the concept of hegemony, which was initially articulated by Gramsci and reappeared in a different sense in Poulantzas. This is understood not just as an ideological phenomenon but also a political practice which brings together the dominant and dominated classes. Hegemony is applied to the relations between dominant classes as well as the relationship between dominated and dominant classes. Since the dominant classes are divided into fractions, they must be organised under the hegemony of one fraction which is able to secure the overall interest of the dominant classes. The hegemonic class within the power bloc also disorganises the dominated classes by getting their active consent.

In accordance with the UCD approach, the book argued that every state has intervened in the economy in different ways. Specifically, in the transition from the ISI model, many states were encouraged to readjust their economies in accordance with Washington Consensus or post-Washington Consensus principles. In general, the book sketched out the role of the state as the agency that appropriates and disburses surplus value through taxation and expenditure, regulates the operations of capitalists, and manipulates exchange rates through macroeconomic policies. Accordingly, the book explained the shifting role of the state in the process of internationalisation of capital. Contrary to mainstream approaches which argue that the role of the state is downgraded in the era of neoliberal globalisation, the kernel of the argument of this book is that the process of internationalisation of capital did not surpass or bypass national states or spawn a transnational state. On the contrary, nation-states have taken on different roles in this process. Neither the space of the state nor the space of transnational capital is superior to the other. This means that the internationalisation of capital has influenced the internal structures of the various forms taken by states. However, the role of the state in this period is to formulate new regulations in accordance with shifting patterns of capital accumulation and to mediate the contradictions between different fractions of capital. The state, therefore, exercises its capabilities within national borders as well as at a global scale. The book, therefore, argued that the functions of the state were also internationalised in a sense that contributes to managing the international capitalist order in different ways. This is essential as nation-states in this period were responsible for creating the necessary internal conditions to maintain the global expansion of transnational capitalist relations of production, and at the same time, to translate the interests of transnational capital, and secure the global integration of capital within its national borders. What is more important here is that fractions of capital which are willing to integrate into global relations of free trade needed state support more than ever before.

1   From the Abstract to the Concrete: A Class-Based Analysis of Business Associations

Having presented various theoretical approaches to free trade, and theories of the role of the state in the neoliberal period, this book outlined the historical consolidation of capitalism in Turkey to provide an overview of the *core research question* of the book which is: What is the role of business associations in Turkey, particularly TUSIAD, MUSIAD and TUSKON in the relationship between global free trade relations and the Turkish social formation since 2002? In accordance with the UCD approach, the book demonstrated that Turkey did not need to repeat the process of capital accumulation in advanced capitalist countries. Hence, it divided the process of capital accumulation in

Turkey into four different but connected periods which are: (i) the defining role of uneven and combined development -commercial and agrarian capital-based accumulation until the late 1950s, (ii) industrial capital-based accumulation based on the Import Substitution Industrialisation (ISI) model until the 1980s, (iii) export-led capital accumulation in the post-transition period and (iv) transnationalisation of Turkish productive capital. This periodisation is based on the shifts in the capital accumulation models which were directly affected by the shifts in the global process of capital accumulation.

The book has also examined the current characteristics of capitalism in Turkey. It has demonstrated that production in Turkey is dependent on imports, especially in the automotive sector, which underpins the expansion of assembly production in the automotive, durable consumer goods, textile and garment industries. The book suggested that in the period of the transnationalisation of productive capital in the 2000s, the larger capital groups in Turkey aimed at shifting their production from producing limited surplus value at the margins of assembly production to higher value-added accumulation and mechanisation. Accordingly, Turkey welcomed FDI at the highest rates in its history. The book indicated that FDI inflows increased from $5 billion in 2001 to $25 billion in 2007, while export volume rose from $50 billion in 2001 to $150 billion in 2012.

The book has shown that Turkish imports are dominated by intermediary goods (72.7% in 2008), whereas exports are dominated by industrial products (51.3%) and to a lesser extent consumer goods. This shows that Turkey's place in global production chains is mainly as an intermediate producer which assembles imported resources into finished goods. This has increased the dependency of Turkish capitalist classes on the global market to reproduce the social relations of production. This provides the overriding rationale behind the expansion of larger capital groups towards the international market, on the one hand, the integration of SMEs into global relations of free trade, on the other. This also explains the overarching agenda behind Turkey's neo-Ottomanist foreign policy agenda in the late 2000s and the first quarter of the 2010s.

One of the main distinctive features of this book is to provide a class-based analysis of business associations in Turkey in order to understand the historical specificity of the capitalist relations in Turkey and the expansion of Turkish capitalism towards the Middle East and North Africa in the 2010s. The book argued that business associations in Turkey are constitutively divided into class fractions. Accordingly, it argued that these business associations are not monolithic blocs without contradictions and cracks. Each association brings together several class fractions with slightly different but overlapping interests.

Also, it was argued that the fragmentation of capitalist classes in the Turkish social formation is not primarily based on religious, ideological, and cultural dynamics, rendering it misleading to speak primarily of secular and Islamist capital or of Istanbul and Anatolian capital. To a considerable extent, what differentiates capitalist class fractions is the way in which they engage in the social relations of production, what role they play in the power bloc, and their specific forms of integration into global relations of free trade, bearing in mind that they are at different scales and stages of accumulation arising from uneven development, and thus have interests corresponding to a capitalist class at different stages of its development. This means the fragmentation of business associations is not only a result of religious and cultural dynamics (such as secularism versus Islamism); such differences either reflect uneven development of different areas or particular strategies of hegemonic integration of capitalist and/or popular classes at different levels of capital accumulation (for instance, the reliance on trust-based business networks, patronage-based hegemony over workers, need for alternative sources of finance, and targeting of Middle Eastern and Central Asian markets among the "Islamist" fractions of capital). To locate the three business associations in the class structure and struggle, this book explored the component companies' class formation in relation to the social relations of production in Turkey, relations which form the material basis for the class characteristics of the business associations. In order to uncover the associations' class characteristics, the book explained the historical integration of Turkey into global free trade relations, and provided some reflections on the uneven development of capitalism in Turkey: firstly, state intervention appeared as the precondition for the emergence of the capitalist relations and the formation of the commercial bourgeoisie, and secondly, the adoption of economic regulations such as five-year plans involved a specific path of transition to capitalism. The book demonstrated that the process of capital accumulation of the larger fractions within TUSIAD was started through accumulation of commercial capital based on foreign trade. This is a result of the uneven expansion of global free trade relations, which also changed the class formation and power relations in Turkey. Accordingly, it demonstrated how the shifts in patterns of capital accumulation provided a conducive space for the emergence of business associations. The ISI model based on concentration and centralisation of capital resulted in the transformation of the commercial bourgeoisie into an industrial bourgeoisie through a reorientation to production for the internal market and capturing of smaller firms. This intervention of the state also led to the rise of the industrial bourgeoisie, such as KOÇ, SABANCI and CUKUROVA Holdings, which established TUSIAD in 1971. The form of the state was also changed by the military regime in the post-1980 period which carried out the transition to neoliberalism. Class-based politics was ended and the relationship between the state and the larger capital groups represented by TUSIAD was intensified.

The book argued that the capitalist classes in Turkey are not mirror images of the rising bourgeoisie or of the current bourgeoisie in the advanced capitalist countries. It has its own historical conditions and backgrounds, influenced by the pre-existence of advanced countries and by uneven development elsewhere (availability of cheap imports from East Asia, difficulties entering sectors already controlled by transnationalised western companies, proximity to Europe, etc). The establishment of TUSIAD represented the organised demands of larger capital groups which were united around the goal of integrating into global relations of free trade. Contrary to mainstream approaches, the book argued that neither that the emergence and/or rise of TUSIAD came at the expense of the state, nor that the state created this fraction of capital. It argued that industrial capital in Turkey has its own history and characteristics, and the relationship between the state and TUSIAD is determined and shaped by the specific circumstances. It is also influenced by the changing patterns of capital accumulation.

The book also argued that TUSIAD represents the first generation of the Turkish bourgeoisie and that the group of class fractions clustered in TUSIAD have established market dominance over other business associations in Turkey in terms of its sales, production, foreign trade and transnational networks. Accordingly, it was shown that member firms of TUSIAD create 50% of the value added in Turkey; 80% of Turkey's total foreign trade; more than 50% of the non-agricultural, non-governmental workforce; and 80% of the corporate tax revenue. The larger capital groups in TUSIAD are named as KOÇ, SABANCI, ANADOLU, CUKUROVA, ZORLU, ECZACIBASI, BOYNER, OYAK, DOGUS, DINCKOK, BORUSAN, ENKA and TEKFEN, which dominated most economic sectors and were the first capital groups in Turkey to become transnationalised. The book has demonstrated that the combined share of TUSKON- and MUSIAD-affiliated companies in the top 500 industrial companies list published by the ISO in 2009 was 7.48%, while the share of a single company, TUPRAS, owned by KOÇ Holding, was 7.56%. In the Top Exporters list in 2019, seven out of the ten top exporters are TUSIAD members. The larger groups within TUSIAD focus on energy, technology, automotive industries and finance, and have stopped their operations in secondary sectors (creating openings in lower-profit sectors for smaller firms). For instance, SABANCI holding exited from textiles, DOGUS, TEKFEN and KOÇ Holdings exited from the retail industry, and DOGUS and TEKFEN Holdings exited from the food sector. The reason for these exits is the increasing trend towards monopoly in some sectors, which has decreased the extraction of surplus value in these sectors. In short, most of the companies within TUSIAD are transnational capital which has production networks outside Turkish borders.

There are also internationally oriented companies in TUSIAD which produce for export and whose mode of production is tightly integrated into global relations of capital accumulation through subcontracting and joint venture agreements. TUSIAD, therefore, represents the companies which are socioeconomically dominant in the current social formation in Turkey, and they are the *hegemonic fraction* of the bourgeoisie in Turkey. To expand its hegemony, TUSIAD also initiated the establishment of TURKONFED which represents over four thousand SMEs. The main purpose of TURKONFED was to challenge the hegemony of MUSIAD and TUSKON over SMEs. This reflected the class struggle between different business associations.

The internationalisation of money capital in the 1990s opened new spaces for the capital groups within MUSIAD and TUSKON. They operated in the sectors which were abandoned by the larger, TUSIAD-linked capital groups. Additionally, they established business networks with the help of tariqats and religious communities, relying on mutual trust and patrimonialism. In the 2000s, some members of MUSIAD transformed into larger-scale enterprises, which became able to compete with the larger capital fractions within TUSIAD. However, the total market share of MUSIAD- and TUSKON-affiliated companies are still much lower than that of TUSIAD members. In this regard, it was argued that although there are some larger capital groups in MUSIAD and TUSKON (usually late developers in low-profit sectors), these associations mainly consist of SMEs which are mainly export-oriented producers. The book demonstrated that the majority of MUSIAD members are internationally oriented companies producing for export. These companies operate mainly in the infrastructure, construction, logistics, furniture, services, transportation, and textiles sectors. These sectors basically require low-tech production facilities with a cheap labour force, and MUSIAD members are best-placed to win state bids and to get government incentives in these sectors. Additionally, it argued that some members of MUSIAD appropriate surplus value from assembly production. Paternalistic relations are another determining feature in regulating the relations of production for MUSIAD members, as the export-oriented market is dependent on a flexible labour market and some MUSIAD members rely heavily on municipal contracts. Most member firms discourage their workers from collective bargaining or joining trade unions, ostensibly because they think there is no need for a labour code if production relations are determined by Islamic principles.

On the other hand, MUSIAD also represents larger, transnationally operating firms which operate production facilities in different countries. The transnational fraction within MUSIAD mainly operate in the metal, construction, food and beverages industries, and hence are in lower value-added sectors than comparable TUSIAD firms. To negate the mainstream argument that MUSIAD and TUSKON are the representatives of Anatolian capital, it was argued that MUSIAD has members from every geographical region of Turkey, and TUSKON members have plants elsewhere in the national market. However, Anatolian regions are overrepresented in these associations relative to their economic strength. As stated in Chapter 5, according to the top 500 industrial firms list in Turkey published by the ISO in 2008, while MUSIAD has eleven members in Istanbul and Izmir, it has sixteen members in Anatolian provinces. Similarly, although there are various members with different scales and scopes in TUSKON, like Orkide, Boydak, Ipek-Koza, NAKSAN and Ülker Group, most of the firms in TUSKON are SMEs, usually operating in textiles, construction and services.

The book argued that there are three different fractions of capital represented within TUSKON. The first fraction consists of nationally oriented companies which invest in the education, media, health and construction sectors. The second fraction consists of internationally operating capital groups which mostly produce in Turkey for export. This fraction is the dominant one within TUSKON. They mainly operate in the iron and steel, copper mining, wooden products, sugar refinery, furniture, textiles, goods, tobacco and beverages sectors. The third fraction is transnationally operating capital which engages in production relations in different countries. They are directly supported by the state in their process of capital accumulation, are dependent on a cheap labour force, and seek to invest in international markets.

The book further examines the role of the Turkish state in the process of integration of business associations into global free trade relations, and internalisation of the interests of transnational capital in Turkey. The main argument of the book is that the distinctive feature of the pre-AKP period was a lack of hegemonic power to secure and advance the interests of the different fractions of capital, and to manage contradictions between them, while disorganising the popular masses. With reference to Poulantzas, the book argued that the state is not a tool which is completely controlled by a specific class fraction. It was argued that the AKP emerged as a hegemonic power which unified different fractions of power and capital within the power bloc. It initially achieved the support of the different fractions of capital represented by TUSIAD, MUSIAD and TUSKON since the AKP eliminated the barriers and removed the obstacles to internationally operating capital, in a context of increasing global trade expectations and the possibility of win-win cooperation among the capital fractions (despite their different interests in spheres such as protectionism/liberalisation). In accordance with the theoretical arguments made in the book, the Turkish state entered global free trade relations by expanding its base of production. In practice, the AKP has restructured some ministries like the Ministry of Foreign Affairs, the Ministry of Foreign Trade and the Ministry of Finance with the purpose of improving bilateral economic relations with neighbouring countries. The capacity of the Turkish state, therefore, increased to manage the regional expansion of Turkish capital. For instance, Turkey signed FTAs and conducted High-Level Strategic Cooperation Council Meetings with many different countries. This means the state played a more active and regulatory role in the process of internationalisation of productive capital in the 2000s.

It was argued in the book that TUSIAD has always played a crucial role in the power bloc in different ways at different times. For instance, it was part of the hegemonic project applied by the military regime after the 1980 military coup. It has taken a different role in the AKP period. In this book, the relationship is explained through concepts such as fractions of capital, power bloc, and hegemony. The book argued that the AKP's coming to power was the result of a hegemonic crisis in the power bloc, and that TUSIAD gave active support to the AKP in its early years in power, particularly supporting its efforts to restructure the state in the aftermath of the banking crisis in 2001. On the one hand, TUSIAD's presence in the hegemonic power bloc was crystallised in the 2000s, but on the other, the AKP maintained relative autonomy so as to organise wider patterns of hegemony in the power bloc, often by favouring MUSIAD and/or TUSKON. It, therefore, argued that the alliance between the AKP and TUSIAD was a win-win situation for both. Indeed, TUSIAD affiliates benefited greatly from internationalisation in this period. For instance, the total assets of KOÇ Holding have risen from $7.3 billion to $51.2 billion in 2007. In the same period, the total assets of SABANCI Holding increased from $21 billion to $43.9 billion. OYAK and its shareholding companies have risen from $4.6 billion to $19 billion. Çalık Group's total assets have also grown from $1 billion to $3.3 billion, and ENKA Group's total assets have increased from $1.86 billion to $7.86 billion. Following Poulantzas, the book argued that the class struggle within the power bloc is not static, and it was demonstrated that the state cannot be examined exclusively as an instrument of capital, or on the contrary, as an agent external to it. Accordingly, the book argued that the power relations between the AKP and TUSIAD shifted in favour of the AKP in the late 2000s. In this sense, this book confirmed the argument that the concept of hegemony is not reducible to the relations between dominant and dominated classes. The power struggle between the AKP and TUSIAD represents a struggle for hegemony inside the ruling power bloc. What caused the change in power relations between the AKP and TUSIAD are, firstly, the AKP's favourable treatment of internationally oriented fractions of capital organised within MUSIAD and TUSKON, secondly, the AKP's response to the demands of the IMF in 2010, and thirdly, the constitutional referendum in the same year. However, the tensions between the AKP and TUSIAD did not persist indefinitely. Despite occasional disagreements, the state has given continued support to TUSIAD through public enterprises providing cheap materials for the private sector, tax reductions, and state-private sector partnerships. In this situation, the book argued that Poulantzian theory is useful to grasp the ways in which the relationships within the power bloc are established and changed.

In the case of MUSIAD, the book argued that the way this wing of capital interacts with the state apparatuses through the reciprocal influence of state and capital within the power bloc is different. The specific material condensation of the relationship between the AKP and MUSIAD was crystallised through municipalities, chambers in Anatolian provinces and business foundations. These proved to be the best mechanisms for MUSIAD members to realise their specific interests at the state level, and to win public procurement contracts at the local level. The Poulantzian relational approach to the state based on class struggle within and outside the power bloc is used to understand this phenomenon. The book, therefore, argued that the relationship between the state and MUSIAD is constituted by their relationship to the social relations of production. Accordingly, it was stated that the reconfiguration of specific state apparatuses, such as the Ministry of Economy, Ministry of Energy, and DEIK, enabled MUSIAD to capture a more fundamental position within the structured relations of power, which led to hegemonic dislocation in the power bloc. These state apparatuses, to a considerable extent, increased the capacity of MUSIAD-affiliated companies to realise their specific class interests. On the other hand, the AKP was in a position to construct a degree of hegemony over the popular masses, and to win the cultural and economic consent of the dominated classes, with support from MUSIAD. Hence, this book argued that the relationship between the AKP, MUSIAD and religious foundations (ENSAR, TURGEV, İlim Yayma Vakfı, ÖNDER, TÜGVA) is the means through which the ideological functionaries of the state managed to win the active consent of the popular masses and to construct the AKP's hegemony within the civil society. MUSIAD is, therefore, given a special task to maintain the active consent of the popular masses that was not obtained by the previous governments.

This book argued that TUSKON used different mechanisms and carried out manoeuvres relating to certain peculiarities in the establishment of the hegemonic project. The means the forms of integration of TUSKON-affiliated companies at the state level were also distinctive. As TUSKON was affiliated with the Gülen Movement (now termed FETO) and was strategically situated in sectors such as education and the media, the group became the most significant ally of the AKP in the production of hegemony. As a result, it had a specific kind of flexibility which allowed to perform different manoeuvres at the national and international level. For instance, TUSKON was the main participant in large-scale international business events and official visits to foreign countries. The book indicated that the Ministry of Foreign Affairs, Ministry of Industry and Trade, Undersecretariat of Foreign Trade, and TIKA were some of the state apparatuses which gave bureaucratic and technical support to TUSKON companies and sponsored its activities in foreign countries. In this sense, the book argued that the political power of TUSKON does not only stem from its relations with different power groups but also the strategy it pursues in relation to the state apparatuses.

The book also argued that both MUSIAD and TUSKON are representatives of SMEs and export-oriented capital. Although many companies have cross-membership in both MUSIAD and TUSKON, what distinguishes the two associations is TUSKON's role in the hegemonic project of the AKP government in the ten years prior to the schism in 2013–16. It was argued that the AKP's coming to power involved the integration of TUSKON into the power bloc. Following the model provided by Poulantzas, the book argued that there was a need for a hegemonic power which can unite the different interests of different fractions of capital in early 2000s Turkey, as a result of which the AKP established an alliance with the GM and the Gülen-affiliated capital which was later represented by TUSKON. Therefore, TUSKON have played a crucial role in constructing hegemony for the AKP, and acted as an institutional tool for reproducing hegemony within and outside the power bloc. More precisely, the presence of TUSKON in the power bloc was ensured by an alliance between the AKP and the GM which led to a dislocation of hegemony at the state level. It was also argued that the activities of TUSKON have expanded the AKP's hegemony using the strategic power of the GM. For instance, these dominant fractions controlled the media organs, occupied strategic positions in the state institutions, and eliminated old state elites and secular groups within the Turkish army. This means that the GM provided a basis to construct the hegemony of the AKP government and to maintain the unity of the dominant classes within the power bloc.

The book also argued that the relations between different power groups are not static, and there are always contradictions within the power bloc. As an illustration, although there was an alliance between the AKP and the GM in terms of reconfiguring power relations in 2002–13, this alliance collapsed after the 17–25 December Events in 2013. Before the tensions started, TUSKON was the most influential business association in the state apparatus, but after the 17–25 Events, TUSKON were removed from the power bloc, and the strategic positions held by TUSKON members were replaced by different capital fractions. At the centre of the conflict was the issue of control over specific state institutions such as the police, army, and judiciary. The schism between the AKP and the GM later resulted in the failed coup attempt of 15 July 2016, which was organised by the GM. This was a turning point which reconfigured the class and power relations within and outside the power bloc and gave the AKP a new lease of life by removing TUSKON and capturing its share of power. It is not just the AKP has outlived its political power, MUSIAD and TUSIAD affiliates too gained new political and economic powers in state institutions. Following Poulantzas, this book argued that the collapse of the AKP-GM alliance reflected the class struggle in the political field, and it was an accumulation of struggles which gave rise to the conflicts between the AKP and TUSKON at a time in which Turkey was experiencing a structural crisis in its economic.

As mentioned in the introduction, the question how business associations in Turkey engage in global relations of free trade was examined throughout the book. In the previous chapters, the forms of Turkish business associations' international integration and the spatial location in which they realise their commodities through free trade activities were unpacked. Accordingly, the book divided the internationalisation of Turkish capital into three periods, which are: (i) internationalisation of commercial capital (1980–1989), (ii) internationalisation of monetary capital (1989–2001), and (iii) transnationalisation of productive capital (2001-present). The kernel of the argument made in this book is that internationalisation created unevenness among business associations, which led to a fragmentation of the interests of capital. Accordingly, this book revolves around the argument that the contradictions between TUSIAD, MUSIAD and TUSKON were crystallised in the transition to the export-led development period, as the three associations' constituencies were unevenly ready to internationalise in the 1980s and later internationalised in different ways and to different degrees. Following Samir Amin, the book argued that Turkey started to produce industrial goods later than the most advanced countries, and the expansion of international capital into Turkey only occurred in the late 20th century. The way Turkey internalised the interests of transnational capital and the way Turkish capital became internationalised are important factors in understanding the different ways in which the various circuits of capital were combined and internalised. As the UCD approach predicts, internationalisation has also created unevenness within Turkey, i.e. unevenness between sectors, and between different circuits of capital. In this sense, the book argued that the companies organised under TUSIAD integrated into the global relations of free trade prior to the companies organised under MUSIAD and TUSKON, which gave them an opportunity to dominate the most valuable circuits of capital, and led to their having interests in state-level trade liberalisation much earlier. Subsequently, it was demonstrated that the monopolisation of access to the global market by TUSIAD members was the main obstacle to the development of MUSIAD and TUSKON. However, the members of these associations have become much more integrated into global free trade relations due to the internationalisation of productive capital since 2001 and the diversification of trade partners.

It was argued that TUSIAD represents the most trans-nationalised fraction of Turkish business associations. It has representative branches in Berlin, Beijing, Paris, Washington. It also established *TUSIAD International* to encourage FDI and to increase networking opportunities for its members. The larger members have plants elsewhere in the world market. The patterns of capital accumulation pursued by TUSIAD members constantly change in response to the shifting patterns of global free trade relations. It was also stated that TUSIAD has been the catalyst for the integration of Turkey into global free trade relations as TUSIAD-affiliated companies expanded into neighbouring countries, even in the aftermath of the 2008–9 global financial crisis which hit Turkish foreign trade badly. TUSIAD members expanded their base of production in countries in which costs of energy, production and labour are lower than in Turkey. For example, SABANCI Holding produces cord fabric and synthetic fibre in Iran, Indonesia, Thailand, China, and South American countries; and KOÇ and ENKA Holdings produce steel in China.

While most of the larger capital groups in TUSIAD integrated into the global market in the 1980s and 1990s, MUSIAD and TUSKON members were not ready to internationalise their base of production and therefore concentrated on producing in local provinces in this period. They started to engage in the global relations of free trade in the 2000s, simultaneously with the rise to power of the AKP. The book argued that this time-based difference created enormous imbalances between MUSIAD-TUSKON and TUSIAD members, which arose out of the uneven development of capitalist relations in Turkey. However, this imbalance also created opportunities for MUSIAD and TUSKON members. For instance, the internationalisation of monetary capital in the 1990s attracted

Saudi and Gulf capital into Turkey, and also increased the amount of remittances from Turkish workers in foreign countries. This led to the emergence of Islamic banking in Turkey, which provided credit opportunities for MUSIAD members to integrate into global relations of free trade in the Middle East and North Africa. The establishment of Bank Asya also coincided with these developments. This bank engaged in financial activities and supported the industrial activities of TUSKON-affiliated companies. In this period, most MUSIAD members targeted sectors which do not require long-term or risky operations, and which do not require high-tech investments or skilled labour, such as the tourism, retail and construction. Overall, the book argued that the rise of MUSIAD and TUSKON was a process of transformation in the pattern of capital accumulation and the uneven development of capitalism within the Turkish social formation.

What made TUSKON distinctive is also the markets they targeted. For instance, the preferred investment areas for TUSKON were (initially) Central Asian and (later) African countries. In the case of the Central Asian market, it was shown that Bank Asya played a decisive role in investing and transferring money from Turkey to these countries. In the case of the African market, it was demonstrated that the specific methods of integration are generally, subcontracting and exporting. It was also argued that Turkish schools and Trade Bridges are the most important mechanisms which TUSKON used to integrate into global relations of free trade. Turkish schools funded by TUSKON are not just ideological instruments, but also provide an economic network facility for TUSKON member companies. In this sense, the transnational networks of firms affiliated with TUSKON were not only constructed from an economic perspective, but also from a non-economic perspective.

Overall, the internationalisation of Turkish productive capital in the 2000s transformed some fractions within TUSKON from commercial capital into productive capital, and from national capital to a more international kind of capital. This was not based on an external relationship between the state and TUSKON but arose on the basis of specific power relations within the power bloc, which were designed to secure the hegemony of the AKP. After the collapse of the alliance between the AKP and TUSKON, the power relations between different business associations and power groups within the state structure were reshaped. Importantly, however, the state still plays its role in securing the long-term interests of the different fractions of capital and securing its own hegemony within the power bloc. What is more important is that different fractions of capital represented by TUSIAD and MUSIAD have benefited rather than suffered from the elimination of capital represented by TUSKON from the international market. This means some capitals have been destroyed so that others became stronger. This reflects a general mechanism through which the state can play a role in destroying smaller/weaker capitals to the advantage of larger/stronger capitals.

2 Concluding Remarks: The Changing Tendencies of Free Trade and the Transformation of the State

As the main purpose of this book is to explore the role of three Turkish business associations, namely TUSIAD, MUSIAD and TUSKON, in the integration of Turkey into global relations of free trade and also to explore the impact of global free trade on the Turkish social formation, this study also examined how concepts such as free trade, unequal exchange, uneven and combined development, and transnationalisation of production might relate to the case of Turkey. In this light, it is appropriate to say that the expansion of capital globally reproduces its contradictory characteristics in different ways in historically specific social formations. Turkey, as a late developing capitalist country, is not the only country which faced the inequalities created by the conditions of uneven and combined development, but the role of business associations in Turkey in internalising global class relations in Turkey make the Turkish case different in the Global South countries.

In recent years, global politics has undergone a process of transformation, which has affected the complex relations between the free trade regime and the role of national states. In the last decades, the process of capital accumulation which was previously restricted to the countries at the periphery, has also shifted to the advanced capitalist countries. This process has gained a momentum with the intensification of COVID-19 in 2021. However, countries at the periphery, are still of great importance for the reproduction of the global relations of production. This transformation has had different impacts on different social formations, as a direct result of the shift in the foreign trade policies of the advanced capitalist countries, and which have increased inequalities within and between countries, regions and sectors. These inequalities have resulted in various forms of protectionism in foreign trade regimes, and a return to authoritarian statism. For example, Free Trade Agreements have come under fire. The former US President Donald Trump abandoned the Trans-Pacific Partnership (TPP) trade deal which was supposed to cover 40% of world trade and create a new single market. The Transatlantic Trade and Partnership Agreement (TTIP) talks between the US and the EU were also stalled in 2016, and the North American Free Trade Area (NAFTA) was renegotiated, and it was replaced by a new free trade agreement called the United

States-Canada-Mexico Agreement. In addition to this, the UK decided to leave the EU after a referendum on 23 June 2016. In the last years, the US and China have imposed tariffs for each other's products totalling almost $750 billion. Further to this, the USA has imposed sanctions on countries and companies who are doing business with China. The USA has employed sanctions and trade tariffs as a weapon to secure its declining hegemony in the global capitalist system. It has also implemented sanctions against Turkey, Venezuela, Iran and Russia, which have seriously affected the global free trade system. (The US had previously used sanctions mainly against outlying "pariah" states unimportant to capital accumulation). These shifts reflect difficulties in securing hegemony at a national scale in a grossly uneven world market, particularly given the economic downturn following the global economic crisis amid the COVID-19 pandemic.

As is argued by theories of imperialism, the historical characteristic of capitalism is to expand internationally, but the rising tendency towards protectionism, which has arisen out of Brexit and Donald Trump's inauguration, increased TNC's worries about global free trade relations. In the case of Turkey, TUSIAD continues to be committed to a neoliberal model of free trade, with states restricted to an institutionalist role in supporting capital accumulation and supporting TNC in its activities in abroad. According to a report published by TUSIAD, protectionist policies in Western countries may cause trade wars across the world, and if the advanced capitalist countries stop producing in backward countries, this will create negative outcomes for the future of the world trade (TUSIAD, 2016:4). TUSIAD also has worries about the potential negative outcomes of Brexit since the UK is the second largest export destination for products from Turkey in 2015 and 2016 (TUIK, 2019).

The political agenda of TNC in Turkey is crucial since the expansion of capital is not only related to the realisation of value any longer. It is more important to maintain and reproduce the contemporary relations of production on an extended scale. In other words, it is more important for Turkish exporters to maintain internationalisation of transnational corporate production on an extended scale. In this regard, the recent shifts in global free trade relations were seen as obstacles which might narrow for the potential of the realisation of the value created by the TNC in Turkey. At the same time, the interests of national and internationally oriented fractions of capital have contradicted TNC's interests in times of economic crisis. These fractions needed state support more than ever before in Turkish economic history.

The recent crises in Turkey have created a need to transform state-capital relations in Turkey because parts of the national and internationally oriented fractions have lost their access to foreign markets. This has created a tension between TNC and other fractions, tensions which were not managed effectively by the ruling class. The previous alliance among capital fractions and the state was facilitated by a high tide lifting all boats (at least the boats of the three major groups of capital fractions). The global economic crisis which began in 2008 has reduced the capacity of the AKP government to unify different factions within the power bloc and to secure the different interests of the three business associations. As a result, there has been a transformation in the organisational structure of the state, including class and power relations within the power bloc. The most significant development is the failed coup attempt on 15 July 2016 which left 241 people dead and 2,194 wounded. Under the state of emergency, decrees issued by the President and cabinet was entered into law without parliamentary debate, effectively a Bonapartist situation in which the state's autonomy from class fractions was increased. This vastly empowered the executive branch against the rest of the state apparatus and the power bloc, and thus allowed the government to reorganise the organisational matrix of the state, capital-labour relations, and even traffic rules without consultation within the bloc. This also provided a pretext to disorganise the working-class and strengthen the power of capital to operate export industries based on cheap, docile labour. Since the failed coup attempt, five general strikes have been banned. The President, Recep Tayyip Erdoğan, stated in his speech at the TOBB conference to foreign investors that:

> We are using the state of emergency to provide a secure environment for business to work better. Do you have any interruption or problem in your business activities? When we came to power we had state of emergency. But, all the factories were under the threat of general strikes. Is there something similar at the moment? Actually, it is the opposite. We immediately intervene in the places which are under the threat of strike with the help of the state of emergency. We say "NO", we do not allow strikes because you cannot harm our business world.
>
> CUMHURIYET, 12 July 2017

This underlines the fact that the state used the state of emergency to get the active consent of the dominant classes, especially those which are important to its hegemonic project. This was crucial if the AKP was to reproduce its hegemony through its symbolic and material power. On the part of TUSIAD, which seeks to bring Turkey in line with Western-led international norms, it declared that the state of emergency must be ended as soon as possible, warning that foreign investments are in decline due to the ongoing state of emergency (NTV, 29 March 201). More precisely, the honorary president of

KOÇ Holding, Rahmi Koç, stated that KOÇ Holding must shift its production facilities towards the international market in light of the context in Turkey, and declared that it is going to invest mainly abroad from now on. This might be considered as a tactical manoeuvre of KOÇ Holding in the state of emergency situation. As this group represents the most transnationalised fraction of the bourgeoisie in Turkey, it extends the power struggle into the international domain and leverages its capacity to use different spaces to reproduce and reshape the power relations between the state and capital. However, since the state of emergency was issued, the profits of the companies affiliated with TUSIAD have soared. KOÇ, ENKA, TEKFEN, ANADOLU, SABANCI, and ZORLU Holdings are the most favoured companies which have profited most over the state of emergency period (Gazete Duvar, o6 February 2018). On the other hand, the president of MUSIAD stated that there has not been any negative consequence of the state of emergency for the business world and suggested that it should be used to increase incentives and to rectify imperfections in the market. As their uneven integration into global free trade relations has different impacts on the social classes in different countries, so the workers in Turkey suffered from the expansion of capitalist social relations of production which have benefited large capital, the state, and certain sections of SMEs. In all the struggles between different power groups, it is the workers of Turkey who lose out in this process without the right to be properly represented by the trade unions in the climate of the state of emergency. This means, the success of Turkey in the 2000s which has been praised by the international creditors and transnational capital is neither a fruit of the perfect management of the economy by the government or a success of neoclassical market-friendly policies. It is based on demobilisation and decomposition of the working-class, often by repressive means (though also through partial hegemony), so as to provide conditions for low-wage production.

Overall, the current stage of capitalism in Turkey is marked by the significant role of the Turkish state in the reproduction of the relations of production with respect to the current social formation. The role of the state is not limited to the management of the contradictions among different business associations or creating public consent; it also includes direct engagement with the relations of production. Therefore, its role is not limited to ideological or repressive applications. For instance, the establishment of "Varlık Fonu", the increased share of public banks in the Turkish financial system, and the increased dependency of the CBT on the president himself were results of the transformation of the state regime in Turkey after 15 July 2016, which crystallised in a transition to a presidential system after the referendum on 15 April 2017. This changed the class and power relations, which is a win-win situation for both the government and the capital groups for different reasons (though not for labour, or most of the TUSKON fraction). On the one hand, the centralisation of decision-making channels, and domination of the executive over the judiciary and parliament work in favour of whichever capital groups have influence in the power bloc, since the necessary measures are taken swiftly, without debate in the parliament. On the other hand, the organisational matrix of the state is restructured in such a way as to make it more difficult for capital fractions to criticise or resist state policy. More precisely, the hegemonic power can regulate the different interests of the different fractions of power more forcefully for the purpose of maintaining the continuation of its own hegemony. However, further research is needed to grasp the contemporary modifications in the transition to the presidential system, how this system will respond to shifts in global free trade relations, and to what extent the state now engages in the formation of new power relations.

To conclude, future research should investigate how companies organised within MUSIAD and TUSIAD will respond to the current political and economic crisis in Turkey. The economic crisis of 2020 may result in concentration and centralisation of capital as the smaller fractions will potentially go bankrupt. This is because the companies which do not operate across borders, in other words, those of which have not already transnationalised their relations of production, will be unevenly affected by the depreciation of Turkish lira. On the other hand, the larger fractions, whose production process are not heavily dependent on imports and who benefit from depreciation, may capture the resources of the bankrupted fractions. Accordingly, future research should also explore how class power and relations will be reconstructed in the power bloc, and how the state will be able to manage and mediate the different interests of different fractions of capital. This is important since the bourgeoise always needs states which can regulate social conditions and relations for the sake of the continuation of the capitalist relations of production. This also requires examining how international developments in the arena of global free trade, such as trade wars between advanced capitalist countries and protectionism in global free trade, might influence the location of Turkey in the global capitalist system.

References

Akça, İ. (2014). *Hegemonic Projects in Post-1980 Turkey and the Changing Forms of Authoritarianism*, in Bekmen, A. & Akça, İ. & Özden, B. A. (Eds.). *Turkey Reframed: Constituting Neoliberal Hegemony*. London: Pluto Press.

AGT, (2021). Effective Investment in Global Area. Retrieved from https://www.agt.com.tr/en/agt-is-at-intermob-with-new-colors-and-trends-for-2017.

Akça, İ. & Özden, B. A. (09 November 2015). AKP ve Türkiye'de Neoliberal Otoriterizmin Sınıfsal Dinamikleri [The AKP and Class Dynamics of Neoliberal Authoritarianism in Turkey]. Retrieved from http://baslangicdergi.org/akp-ve-turkiyede-neoliberal-otoriterizmin-sinifsal-dinamikleri/.

Akçay, Ü. (2007). *Kapitalizmi Planlamak: Türkiye'de Planlama ve DPT'nin Dönüşümü* [*Planning Capitalism: The Planning and the Transformation of DPT in Turkey*] İstanbul: SAV Yayınları.

Akçay, Ü. (2009). *Para Banka Devlet: Merkez Bankası'nın Bağımsızlaşmasının Ekonomi Politiği*[*Money, Bank and the State: The Political Economy of the Independency of the Central Bank of Turkey*]. İstanbul: SAV Yayınları.

Akçay, Ü. (2013). Internationalisation of Capital and Transformation of the State: Rising of Technocratic Authoritarianism, *Praxis*, 30(31), 13–43.

Akçay, Ü. (12 April 2016). Merkez Bankası'na Yeni Başkan: Faizler Düşecek mi? [New President to Central Bank: Will the Interest go down?]. Retrieved from http://baslangicdergi.org/merkez-bankasina-yeni-baskan-faizler-dusecek-mi/.

Akfel Commodities (2021). Natural Gas, Retrieved from https://www.akfel.com/en/page.php?id=23.

Akkaya, Y. (2002). Turkiye'de İşçi Sınıfı ve Sendikalar [Working Class and Trade Unions in Turkey], *Praxis,* 6, 63–101.

Al Arabiya News, (04 October 2012), South Africa Opens giant Turkish-Built Mosques Complex, Retrieved from http://english.alarabiya.net/articles/2012/10/04/241871.html.

Aljazeera (16 November 2016). Pakistan Expels Turkish School Staff over Gülen Links. Retrieved from http://www.aljazeera.com/news/2016/11/pakistan-expels-turkish-school-staff-gülen-links-161116084837457.html.

Alkan, H. & Mercan, M. H. (2013). Yeni Burjuvazi, Ekonomik Kalkınma ve Afrika: TUSKON Afrika Ticaret Kopruleri [New Bourgeoisie, Economic Development and Africa: TUSKON Africa Trade Bridges], *Marmara Universitesi Siyasal Bilimler Dergisi*, 1(1), 25–41.

Althusser, L. (1965). *For Marx*. Trans. Ben Brewster. NLB.

Altıntop, M. (18 January 2010). TUSKON'un hedefi Uzak Diyarlar [TUSKON is targeting Distant Lands]. Retrieved from http://muhsinaltintop.blogspot.co.uk/2010/01/tuskonun-hedefi-uzak-diyarlar.html.

Altun, M. (2006). *Yaşlanmadan Büyümek* [*Growing without aging*]. TEKFEN 50. Yıl, Istanbul Tarih Vakfı.

Amin, S. (1976). *Unequal development: An essay on the social formations of peripheral capitalism*. Trans. B. Pearce. New York: Monthly Review Press.

ANADOLU (2017). Group Companies, available at https://www.anadolugrubu.com.tr/ grupsirketi/25/bira-operasyonlari-anadolu-efes.

Anievas, A. & Nisancioglu, K. (2015). *How the West Came to Rule*. London: Pluto Press.

Apaydin, F. (2015). Financialisation and the Push for Non-State Social Service Provision: Philanthropic Activities of Islamic and Conventional Banks in Turkey. Forum for Development Studies, 42(3), pp. 441–465.

ARÇELIK, (2015). 2015 Faaliyet Raporu, available at http://www.arcelikas.com/UserFi les/file/2015_Yili_Arcelik_Faaliyet_Raporu.pdf.

Arçelik, (01 January 2016). Kamuoyu Aydınlatma Platformu. Retrieved from https:// www.kap.org.tr/Bildirim/498779.

Arslan, A. (2021). Relations of Production and Social Reproduction, the State and the Everyday: Women's Labour in Turkey, *Review of International Political Economy*.

Ashman, S. (2010). *Capitalism, Uneven and Combined Development and the Trnashistoric*, in Anievas, A. (Ed.). *Marxism and World Politics, Contesting Global Capitalism*, London: Routledge

Ashman, S. (2012). *Combined and Uneven Development*. In Fine, B., Saad-Filho, A., Marco, B. (Eds.). *The Elgar Companion to Marxist Economics* UK: Edward Elgar.

Atiyas, I. & Bakis, O. (2013). The Regional Dimension of Productivity and Exports in Turkey: Evidence from Firm-Level Data. Represented in Comparative Analysis of Enterprise Data Conference, September 18–20, Atlanta.

Atli, A. (2011). Businessmen as Diplomats: The Role of Business Associations in Foreign Economic Relations of Turkey. *Insight Turkey*, 13(1), 109–128.

Avci, A. (2021). The New Regime of Free Trade and Transnational Capital in Turkey, *Journal of Balkan and Near Eastern Studies*, 24(1), 78–96.

AYTAC, (2021). About Us. Retrieved from http://www.aytac.com.tr/en/content/history -vision.

Bacik, G. (2011). The Separation of Islam and Nationalism in Turkey. *Nationalism and Ethnic Politics*, 17(2), 140–160.

Basaran-Symes, C. (6 June 2016). TÜSİAD YÖNETİM KURULU BAŞKANI CANSEN BAŞARAN- SYMES'IN "OECD KAMUDA KARAR ALMA SÜREÇLERİ 2015 DEĞERLENDİRME RAPORU KONFERANSI" AÇILIŞ KONUŞMASI [The Opening Speech of TUSIAD Chairman of the Executive Board at "OECD Decision Making Processes in Public Institutions: 2015 Assessment Report]. Retrieved from http://tusiad.org/tr/basin-bultenleri/item/8868-oecd-kamuda-karar-alma-surecl eri-2015-degerlendirme-raporu-konferansi.

Başkan, F. (2010). The Rising Islamic Business Elite and democratization in Turkey. *Journal of Balkan and Near Eastern Studies*, 12(4), 339–416.

Balci, B. (2003). Fethullah Gülen's Missionary Schools in Central Asia and Their Role in Spreading of Turkism and Islam. *Religion, State and Society*, 31(2), 151–177.

Balci, B. (20 October 2013). Between Secular Education and Islamic Philosophy: The Approach and Achievements of Fethullah Gülen's Followers in Azerbaijan. Retrieved from http://carnegieendowment.org/2013/10/20/between-secular-education-and -islamic-philosophy-approach-and-achievements-of-fethullah-g-len-s-followers -in-azerbaijan-pub-54193.

Bayram, A. (2016). *Cumhuriyet Dönemi Sanayiinde Kim Kimdir? [Who is Who in Republican Era Industry]*. İstanbul: Dünya Yayıncılık.

Bedirhanoğlu, P. (2013). *Turkiye'de Neoliberal Otoriter Devletin AKP'li Yuzu [The Image of the Neoliberal Authoritarian Statism in Turkey]*. In Uzgel, I. & Duru, B. (Eds.). *AKP Kitabi [The AKP Reader]*. Ankara: Phoneix.

Bekmen, A. (2014). *State and Capital in Turkey During the Neoliberal Era*. In Bekmen, A. & Akça, İ. & Özden, B. A. (Eds.). *Turkey Reframed: Constituting Neoliberal Hegemony*. London: Pluto Press.

Benlisoy, F. (26 January 2017). Alaturka Sezarizmin Feci Sonuçlara Gebe Dengesi. Retrieved from http://baslangicdergi.org/alaturka-sezarizmin-feci-sonuclara-gebe -dengesi/.

Bieler, A. (2000). *Globalization and the Enlargement of the European Union, Austrian and Swedish Social Forces in the Struggle over Membership* London: Routledge.

Bieler, A. (2006). *The Struggle for a Social Europe: Trade Unions and EMU in Times of Global Restructuring*. Manchester: Manchester University Press.

Bieler, A. & Morton, A. (2006). *Globalization, the State and Class Struggle: A Critical Economy Engagement with Open Marxism*, in Bieler et al. (Ed.). *Global Restructuring, State, Capital and Labour*, London: Palgrave Macmillan.

Bieler, A. & Morton, A. D. (2008). The Deficits of Discourse in IPE: Turning Base Medal into Gold? *International Studies Quarterly*, 52(1), 103–128.

Bieler, A. (2012). The EU, Global Europe, and the process of uneven and combined development: the Problem of transnational labour solidarity. *Review of International Studies*, 1(23).

Bieler, A. & Morton, A. D. (2003). The Gordion Knot of Agency Structure in International Relations: A Neo-Gramscian Perspective. European Journal of International Relations, 7(5), 5–35.

Bieler, A. & Morton, A. D. (2013). The Will-O'-The-Wisp of the Transnational State. *Journal of Australian Political Economy*, 72(23).

Bieler, A. Hilary, J. & Lindberg, I. (2014). Trade Unions, 'Free Trade', and the Problem of Transnational Solidarity: An Introduction. *Globalizations*, 11(1), 1–9.

Bieler, A. & Morton, A. D. (2014). Uneven and Combined Development and Unequal Exchange: The Second Wind of Neoliberal Free Trade? *Globalizations*, 11(1), 35–41.

Birgün (19 April 2016). Retrieved from http://www.birgun.net/haber-detay/ensar-dan -gecen-yollar-akp-ye-cikiyor-ensar-vakfi-nin-iliskilerinin-haritasi-ve-analizi-109 527.html.

Boran, B. (1962). *Turkiye'de Burjuvazi Yok mu?* [Does not Turkey has a Bourgeoisie?]. *Yon Dergisi*, 39.

Boratav, K. (1990). *Inter-class and intra-class relations of distribution under 'structural adjustment: Turkey during the 1980s*. In Aricanli, T. & Rodrik, D. (Eds.). *The Political Economy of Turkey: Debt, Adjustment and Sustainability*, New York: St. Martin's Press.

Boratav, K. (2014). *Turkiye Iktisat Tarihi* [Turkish Economic History]. Ankara: İmge Kitabevi.

BORGIP, (2017). Retrieved from http://borgip.org/.

Boydak Holding, (2017a). Retrieved from http://www.boydak.com/en/p/63_alfa-mobel -vertrieb-gmbh.aspx.

Boydak Holding, (2017b). Turkiye Finans Katilim Bankasi A.S. Retrieved from http:// www.boydak.com/en/p/84_turkiye-finans-katilim-bankasi-as.aspx.

Bryan, R. ([1987]2007). The State and the Internationalization of Capital: An Approach to Analysis. *Journal of Contemporary Asia*, 17(3), 253–275.

Buğra, A. (1994). *State and Business in Modern Turkey: A Comparative Study*. Albany: State University of New York Press.

Buğra, A. (1998). Class, Culture and State: An Analysis of Interest Representations by two Turkish Business Associations. *International Journal of Middle East Studies*, 30(4), 521–534.

Buğra, A. (2002). *Political Islam in Turkey in Historical Context*, in Balkan, N. & Savran, S. (Eds.). *The Politics of Permanent Crisis: Class Ideology and State in Turkey*, New York: NOVA.

Buğra, A. (04 March 2013). Prof. Dr Ayse Buğra: Anadolu'da Gülen Cemaati Tedirginligi Var[Prof Ayse Buğra: There is an Uneasiness about the Gülen Cemaat in Anatolia], retrieved from http://t24.com.tr/haber/prof-ayse-bugra-anadoluda-gülen-cemaati -tedirginligi-var,224944.

Buğra, A. & Savaşkan, O. (2014). *New Capitalism in Turkey: the Relationship between Politics, Religion, and Business*, UK: Edward Elgar.

Bulut, A. (2008). TUSIAD Neden IMF'yi İstemiyor? [Why is TUSIAD against the IMF]. Retrieved from http://www.yenicaggazetesi.com.tr/tusiad-neden-imfyi-istiyor-562 3yy.htm.

Cakir, R. (31 January 2014). Yurt disindaki Cemaat Okullarinin Akibeti [The Aftermath of the Gülen Schools in Abroad]. Retrieved from http://www.gazetevatan.com/ rusen-cakir-605563-yazar-yazisi-yurt-disindaki-cemaat-okullarinin-akibeti/.

Cakir, R. (10 August 2016). Gülen Cemaati: Nereden Nereye? [Gülen Community: Past and Present]. Retrieved from http://www.aljazeera.com.tr/gorus/gülen-cemaati -nereden-nereye.

Capital (06 Sep 2016). Boydak Holding TMSF'ye Devredildi[Boydak Holding is transferred to the TMSF], retrieved from https://www.capital.com.tr/gundem/aktuel/ boydak-holding-tmsfye-devredildi.

Cavdar, A. (2014). Gülen Cemmati: Devlet Niyet, Sermaye Kismet [Gülen Community: The state and Capital]. Retrieved from https://tr.boell.org/sites/default/files/perspe ctives_8_tr.pdf.

CBCNEWS (02 Jun 2010). Gaza Flotilla Activists Back in Turkey. Retrieved from http:// www.cbc.ca/news/world/gaza-flotilla-activists-back-in-turkey-1.933602.

Cengiz, F. Ç. (2020). Turkey: The Pendalum Between Military Rule and Civilian Authoritarianism, Brill Publishing: Leiden, Boston.

CNN TURK, (2 November 2015), TUSIAD Toplantısında Davutoğlu'ndan Önemli Mesajlar [Critical Messages from Davutoğlu at TUSIAD Meeting]. Retrieved from http://www.capital.com.tr/is-dunyasi/sirketler-ve-yoneticiler/siz-biz-diye-ayrim -yaptilar-haberdetay-5916.

Cox, R. W. (2008). Transnational Capital, the US State, and Latin American Trade Agreements, *Third World Quarterly*, 29 (8), p.1527–1544.

CUKUROVA, (2017). CUKUROVA in Brief. Retrieved from http://www.cukurova.com .tr/en/kisaca.html.

Çınar Boru, (2018). We Are Çınar Boru. Retrieved from http://www.Çınarboru.com/ en_US/Çınar-boru/who-are-we/we-are-Çınar-boru.

Cop, B. & Zihinlioglu, O. (2017). Turkish Foreign Policy under AKP Rule: Making Sense of the Turbulence. *Political Studies Review*, 15(1), 28–38.

Cumhuriyet (23 December 2013). TUSKON'dan Yolsuzluk Aciklamasi [TUSKON's statement on corruption]. Retrieved from http://www.cumhuriyet.com.tr/haber/ turkiye/21813/TUSKON_dan_yolsuzluk_aciklamasi.html.

Cumhuriyet (17 April 2014). MIT Yasasi Meclis'ten Gecti [The MIT Law got through Parliament]. Retrieved from http://www.cumhuriyet.com.tr/haber/siyaset/61937/ MiT_Yasasi_Meclis_ten_gecti.html.

Cumhuriyet (12 July 2017). Erdoğan'dan İtiraf: OHAL'den İstifade Ederek Grevlere Anında Müdahale Ediyoruz. Retrieved from https://www.cumhuriyet.com.tr/ haber/erdogandan-itiraf-ohalden-istifade-ederek-grevlere-aninda-mudahale-ediyo ruz-779522.

DEIK & DELOITTE, 2016, Yurt Dışı Yatırım Endeksi [Foreign Investment Indeks]. Retrieved from https://www.deik.org.tr/uploads/yurtdisi_yatirim_endeksi_2016.pdf.

Demir, Ö. & Acar, M. & Toprak, M. (2004). Anatolian Tigers or Islamic Capital: Prospects and Challenges. *Middle Eastern Studies*, 40(6), 166–188.

Dinçkök, A. (03 March 2010). Siz biz diye ayrım yaptılar [We are Separated as "Us" and "You"]. Retrieved from http://www.capital.com.tr/is-dunyasi/sirketler-ve-yonetici ler/siz-biz-diye-ayrim-yaptilar-haberdetay-5916.

Doğan, A. E. (2006). Siyasal Yansımalarıyla İslamcı Sermayenin Gelişme Dinamikleri ve 28 Şubat Süreci [The Development Process of Islamic Capital and the February 28 Process]. *Mülkiye Dergisi,* xxx(252).

Dreher, S. (2015). Islamic Capitalism? The Turkish Hizmet Business Community Network in a Global Economy. *Journal of Business Ethics,* 129 (4), 823–832.

Dunya (02 Apr 2013). Retrieved from https://www.dunya.com/gundem/nijerya039ya -akfa-holding-cikarmasi-haberi-206532.

Durak, Y. (2011). *Emeğin Tevekkülü: Konya'da İşçi-İşveren İlişkileri ve Dindarlık [The Faith of Labour: The Employee-Employer Relationship in Konya]*. Ankara: İletişim.

ENKA, (2017). OUR HISTORY. Retrieved from http://www.enka.com/about-us/history/.

ENSAR Vakfı (31 March 2017). Retrieved from http://www.ensar.org/kocaelinde-42-stk -evet-icin-bir-araya-geldi_H1205.html.

Eralp, A. (1980). Turkiye'de Izlenen Ithal Ikameci Kalkinma Stratejisi ve Yabanci Sermaye [The ISI Policy in Turkey and Foreign Capital]. *ODTU Gelisme Dergisi,* 7(1–2).

Ercan, F. (2002) *The Contradictory Continuity of the Turkish Capital Accumulation Process: A Critical Perspective on the Internationalisation of the Turkish Economy".* In the Ravages of Neo-Liberalism: Economy, Society and Gender in Turkey, Nova Publications.

Ercan, F. & Oğuz, S. (2006). Rescaling as a Class Relationship and Process: The Case of Public Procurement Law in Turkey, *Political Geography,* 25 (6), 641–656.

Ercan, F. & Tuna G. (2007). *İç Burjuvazinin Gelisimi: 1960'lardan Gunumuze Bakis [The Development of Interior Bourgeoisie from the 1960s onwards]*. In Ercan et al. *Turkiye'de Kapitalizmin Guncel Sorunlari* [The Contemporary Problems of Capitalism in Turkey]. Ankara: Dipnot Yayinlari.

Ercan, F. & Oğuz, S. (2015). From Gezi Resistance to Soma Massacre: Capital Accumulation and Class Struggle in Turkey. *Socialist Register,* 51 (1), 114–135.

Ercan, F. & Gültekin-karakaş, D. & Yilmaz, Y. F. (2016). *Yeni Turkiye'de Degisen Devlet ve Sermaye Iliskilerini Tesvik Politikalari Uzerinden Okumak [The Analysis of Changing State-Capital Relations through Incentive Policies]*. In Toren, T. & Kutun, M. (Eds.). *Yeni Turkiye, Kapitalizm, Devlet Siniflar [New Turkey, Capitalism, the State, Classes]*. İstanbul: sav Yayınları.

Erdoğan, R. T. (03 April 2009). "The Global Economic Crisis and Turkey", *Transcript of the Speech Delivered by Recep Tayyip Erdoğan, Prime Minister of the Republic of Turkey,* Chatham house.

Erdoğan, (18 August 2010), Erdoğan: Bitaraf olan bertaraf olur [Those who do not take side will be eliminated]. Retrieved from http://www.milliyet.com.tr/erdogan-bita raf-olan-bertaraf-olur-siyaset-1277904/.

Erdoağan (11 September 2010). Erdoğan: Sermaye el Değğiştiriyor [Erdoğan: The Capital is Changing Hands]. Retrieved from http://www.hurriyet.com.tr/erdogan-sermaye -el-degistiriyor-15752853.

Ergüder, B. (2016). The Effects of 2008 Financial Crisis on State and Businessmen in Turkey. *Journal of Awareness*, 1(2), 17–30.

Ergüneş, N. (2007). *Sermayenin Uluslararasilasma Surecinde Yeniden Yapilanmasi [Restructuring of the Capital in the Process of Internationalisation]*. In Ercan et al. Turkiye'de Kapitalizmin Guncel Sorunlari [The Contemporary Problems of Capitalism in Turkey]. Ankara: Dipnot Yayınları.

Erkan, G. (1994). *Dünyada ve Türkiye'de Dış Ticaret Sermaye Şirketleri[Foreign trade Companies in Turkey and World]*. Unpublished master thesis, Istanbul, Istanbul University, Institute of Social Sciences.

Ersoy, N. (2013). Free Trade Agreements of Turkey. Retrieved from http://yoikk.gov.tr/ upload/IDB/FTAsCompatibilityMode.pdf.

Evans, P. (1995). *Embedded Autonomy*: States and Industrial Transformation, Princeton: Princeton University Press.

Foreign Policy, (2016, May 03). French President Says Non to TTIP. Retrieved from http://foreignpolicy.com/2016/05/03/french-president-says-non-to-ttip/?utm_cont ent=buffer5cb69&utm_medium=social&utm_source=twitter.com&utm_campa ign=buffer.

Gazete Duvar, (06 February 2018). OHAL'de Kimler Olağanüstü Kar Etti? Retrieved from https://www.gazeteduvar.com.tr/ekonomi/2018/02/06/ohalde-kimler-olaganu stu-kar-etti.

Gill, S. (Ed.) (1993). Gramsci, Historical Materialism and International Relations, Cambridge: Cambridge University Press

Göl, A. (2009). The Identity of Turkey: Muslim and Secular. *Third World Quarterly*, 30(4), 795–811.

Gramsci, A. (1971) *Selections from the Prison Notebooks*. Ed. and Trans. Q. Hoare and G. Nowell-Smith. London: Lawrence and Wishart.

Gulalp, H. (1985). Patterns of Capital Accumulation and State-society Relations in Turkey. *Journal of Contemporary Asia*, 15(3), 329–348.

Gülfidan, S. (1993). *Bid Business and the State in Turkey: the Case of TUSIAD*. Istanbul: Boğaziçi University Press.

Gültekin-karakaş, D. (2007). *Turkiyenin Yapisal Donusum Surecinde Banka Reformu [The Banking Reform in Turkey's Structural Transformation Period]*. In Ercan et al. *Turkiye'de Kapitalizmin Guncel Sorunlari [The Contemporary Problems of Capitalism in Turkey]*. Ankara: Dipnot Yayinlari.

Gültekin-karakaş, D. & Ercan, F. (2008). "Türkiye'de Uluslararasılasma Sürecindeki Sermayenin Üretken ve Para Sermaye Arasındaki Zaman Yönelimli Stratejik

Tercihi [The Strategic Choice between Money and Productive capital in the Internationalisation Process in Turkey]", *İktisat, Isletme ve Finans*, 23(262), 35–55.

Gültekin-karakaş, D. (2009). *Hem Hasimiz Hem Hisimiz: Turkiye Finans Kapitalinin Donusumu ve Banka Reformu* [*We are both Enemy and Friend: The Transformation of Turkish Finans Capital and the Banking Reform*]. İstanbul: İletişim.

Gültekin-karakaş, D. (2009b). Sermayenin Uluslararasilasma Surecinde Turkiye'de Banka Reformu [Banking Reform in Turkey in the Process of Internationalisation of Capital], *Praxis*, 19 (1), 95–131.

Gültekin-karakaş, D. & Hisarciklilar, M. & Hayta, G. (2013). *Turkiye'de Sanayilesmenin Bir Bileseni Olarak Dogrudan Yabanci Yatirim ve Dis Ticaret Iliskisi* [The Relationship between Foreign Trade and FDI as a constituent part of the Industrialisation]. In Asici, A. A. & Hisarcikliliar, M. (et. Al.) (Eds.). *Umit Senesen'e Armagan Paylasimlar: Sayilarla Turkiye E Ekonomisi* [in the Memory of Umit Senesen: Turkish Economy in Numbers]. İstanbul: Literatur Yayinlari.

Gürakar, E. & Esfahani, H. S. (2013). Fading Attraction: Turkey's Shifting Relationship with the European Union. *The Quarterly Review of Economics and Finance*, 53 (4), 64–379.

Gürakar, E. Ç. (2016). *Public Favouritism in Public Procurement in Turkey*. New York: Palgrave Macmillan.

Gürel, B. (2015). *Islamism, A comparative historical Overview*. In Balkan, N. & Balkan, E. & Öncü, A. (Eds.). *The Neoliberal Landscape and the Rise of Islamist Capital in Turkey*. New York: Berghahn.

Güzelsarı, S. & Aydın, S. (2010). Türkiye'de Büyük Sermayenin Örgütlü Yükselişi Siyasal ve Yönetsel Süreçlerin Biçimlenmesinde TÜSİAD [The Organised Rise of the Big Bourgeoisie in Turkey: The role of TUSIAD in Shaping the Political and Administrative Processes], *Abant Izzet Baysal Üniversitesi Journal of Social Sciences*, 10(20).

HABAS, (2021). HABAS TOPLULUĞU. Retrieved from http://www.habas.com.tr/.

Haberturk (21 Dec 2013). MUSIAD'dan Sorusturma Aciklamasi[MUSIAD's Statement on Corruption], retrieved from http://www.haberturk.com/ekonomi/is-yasam/haber/905586-musiaddan-sorusturma-aciklamasi.

Hamsici, M. (4 December 2013). Bayram Balci: Cemaat CHP'yi Desteklemez (The Cemaat Will not Support the CHP). Retrieved from http://www.bbc.com/turkce/haberler/2013/12/131203_akp_gülen_balci_int.

Hanieh, A. (2009). Hierarchies of a Global Market: The South and the Economic Crisis. *Studies in Political Economy*, 83 (1), 61–84.

Hart-Landsberg, M. (2013). *Capitalist Globalization: Consequences, Resistance and Alternatives,* New York: Monthly Review Press.

Hendrick, J. D. (2009). Globalization, Islamic Activism, and passive revolution in Turkey: the case of Fethullah Gülen. *Journal of Power*, 2(3), 343–368.

Hendrick, J. D. (2013). *Gülen: The Ambiguous Politics of Market Islam in Turkey and the World*, New York: New York University Press.

Hoşgör, E. (2011). Islamic Capital/Anatolian Tigers: Past and Present. *Middle Eastern Studies*, 47(2), 343–360.

Hoşgör, E. (2016). New fragmentations and new alliances in the Turkish Bourgeoisie, *Journal Fur ENTWICKLUNGSPOLITIK*, XXXII (1/2), 114–134.

HT Ekonomi, (01 August 2016). Gediz Holding yönetim Kurulu Başkanı Hülya Gedik Bloomberg HT'de [Hulya Gedik, the Chairman of the Executive Board of Gedik Holding,is at HT Ekonomi]. Retrieved from http://www.haberturk.com/ekon omi/is-yasam/haber/1274995-gedik-holding-yonetim-kurulu-baskani-hulya-gedik -bloomberg-htde.

Hürriyet, (05 June 2003). Retrieved from http://www.hurriyet.com.tr/dedigim-tutma zsa-kendimi-asarim-151215.

Hürriyet (06 November 2009). Retrieved from http://www.hurriyet.com.tr/islam-ulkel eri-arasindaki-ticaret-540-milyar-dolar-12871489.

Hürriyet, (29 December 2013). Erdoğan: "Orada bir yanlis yaptik" [Erdoğan: We made a mistake tAbout Here]. Retrieved from http://www.hurriyet.com.tr/erdogan-orada -bir-yanlis-yaptik-25465765.

Hürriyet, (30 September 2014). Retrieved from http://www.hurriyet.com.tr/deik-in -yeni-baskani-omer-cihad-vardan-27291024.

Hürriyet (29 July 2017). Retrieved from http://www.hurriyet.com.tr/olpak-deik-baskanl igi-konusunda-bilgim-yok-40534886.

IÇDAŞ (2017). History. Retrieved from http://www.icdas.com.tr/pages/5752/3725/f/en -US/History.aspx.

Institut du Bosphore, (2012). Paris Boğaziçi Enstitüsü, İstanbul'daki yıllık toplantısında krizdeki Avrupa'nın yarattığı fırsatları ve sorunları ele alacak. Retrieved from http:// tusiad.org/tr/tum/item/5950-paris-bogazici-enstitusu-istanbuldaki-yillik-toplan tisinda-krizdeki-avrupanin-yarattigi-firsatlari-ve-sorunlari-ele-alacak.

Interview 1, [Zafer Ali Yavan], the General Secretary of TUSIAD between 2009 and 2016, Interview Info: 18 August 2016.

Interview 2 [Ahmet Turan Ergüt], MUSIAD Sivas Branch, Interview Info: 04 August 2016.

Interview 3 [Name Withheld], MUSIAD Sivas Branch, Interview Info: 04 August 2016.

ISO (2017). The Top 500 Enterprises Magazines. Retrieved from http://www.iso500.org .tr/iso-500-dergileri/birinci-500-dergileri/.

ISO (2020). The Top 500 Enterprises Magazines, available at https://www.iso500.org .tr/sunum-ve-konusma-metni/iso-500/.

Jessop, B. (1982). *The Capitalist State: Marxist Theories and Methods*. Oxford: Martin Robertson & Company Ltd.

Jessop, B. (1985). *Nicos Poulantzas: Marxist Theory and Political Strategy*. Macmillan.

Jessop, B. (2010). The return of the National State in the current crisis of the world market. *Capital & Class*, 34(1), 38–43.

Jessop, B. (2014). Althusser, Poulantzas, Buci-Glucksman: Elaboration of Gramsci's Concept of the Integral State. Retrieved from https://bobjessop.org/2014/02/01/althusser-poulantzas-buci-glucksmann-elaborations-of-gramscis-concept-of-the-integral-state/.

KARAR (12 March 2018). FETÖ'nün 1 Numaralı Para Kayanğı. Retrieved from http://www.karar.com/ekonomi/fetonun-1-numarali-para-kaynagi.

Kastamonu Entegre, (2018). Company Profile, retrieved from http://www.kastamonu entegre.com.tr/en/keas-corporate/3/company-profile.

Keyder, C. (1987). *The Political Economy of Turkish Democracy*. In Schick, C. I. & Tonak, E. A. *Turkey in Transition, New Perspectives*, Oxford: Oxford University Press.

Keyman, E. F. (2007). Modernity, secularism and Islam: The case of Turkey. *Theory, Culture & Society*, 24(2), 215–234.

Keyman, E. F. & Öniş, Z. (2007). *Turkish Politics in a Changing World: Global Dynamics and Domestic Transformations*. İstanbul: Istanbul Bilgi University Press.

Kiely, R. (2010). *Rethinking imperialism*. London: Palgrave.

Kiely, R. (2012). *Globalization and Imperialism*. In Fine, B., Saad-Filho, A., Marco, B. (Eds.). *The Elgar Companion to Marxist Economics*. UK: Edward Elgar.

KOÇ, (2017). Automotive. Retrieved from http://www.koc.com.tr/en-us/activity-fields/sectors/automotive.

Koralturk, M. (1999). *Imparatorluktan Cumhuriyete Turkiye'de Sanayi Sermayesinin Orgutlenmesi* [*The Organization of Industrial Bourgeoisie from the Empire to the Republic*]. In Baydar, O. & Dincel, G. *75 Yilda Carklari Dondurenler* [*Leading ones in 75 Years*]. İstanbul: İstanbul Tarih Vakfı Yayınları.

Koyuncu, B. (2014). Kuresellesme ve MUSIAD: Bir Musluman Isadami Derneginin Kuresellesmeye Eklemlenmesi. *Sosyoloji Dergisi*, 25 (1), 26–36.

Kurt, Y. (ET. Al, 2016), Spirituality as an Antecedent of Trust and network commitment: The Case of Anatolian Tigers. *European Management Journal*, 34 (6), 686–700.

Lenin, V. I., (1999). *Imperialism: The Highest Stage of Capitalism*, Sydney: Resistance Books.

Lorasdağı, B. K. (2010). The Relationship between Islam and Globalisation in Turkey in the post-1990 period: The Case of MUSIAD, *BILIG*, Winter(52), 105–128.

Luxemburg, R. ([1913] 2003). *The Accumulation of Capital*. London: Routledge.

Marois, T. (2012). *States, Banks and Crisis: Emerging Finance Capitalism in Mexico and Turkey*. UK: Edward Elgar Publishing.

Martin, J. (2008). *The Poulantzas Reader: Marxism, Law and the State*. London: Verso.

Marx, K. (1973). *Grundrisse*. London: Penguin Classics.

Marx, K. ([1976] 1990). *Capital: A Critique of Political Economy*, Volume III. Trans. David Fernbach. Harmondsworth: Penguin Classics.

Marx, K. ([1885] 1978). *Capital Vol II*. Harmondsworth: Penguin Classics.

Marx, K. & Engels, F. (1894). *Collected Works*, Hamburg: Volume 37.

Mert, S. (2013). Poulatzas'la Donusume Bakmak [Analysing the Transformation with Poulantzas]. Yol Dergisi, Summer. Retrieved from https://www.yolsiyasidergi.org/poulantzasla-donusume-bakmak-sinan-mert.

MFA (Ministry of Foreign Affairs) (2011a) *Relations between Turkey and Lebanon*. Retrieved from http://www.mfa.gov.tr/relations-between-turkey-and-lebanon.en.mfa.

MFA (Ministry of Foreign Affairs) (2011b). Relations Between Turkey and Iraq. Retrieved from http://www.mfa.gov.tr/relations-between-turkey-and-iraq.en.mfa.

MFA, (Ministry of Foreign Affairs) (2016a). Retrieved from http://www.mfa.gov.tr/high-level-cooperation-council-meeting-between-turkey-and-greece.en.mfa.

MFA, 2016b, Participation of Foreign Minister Cavusoglu in Turkey-GCC high Level Strategic Dialogue Meeting. http://www.mfa.gov.tr/participation-of-foreign-minis ter-cavusoglu-in-turkey_gcc-high-level-strategic-dialogue-meeting-of-foreign -ministers.en.mfa.

Milliyet (15 November 2008). TUSIAD: Kamu Ihale Kanunu AB'ye Aykırı Hale Geliyor [Public Procurement Law is Against the EU]. Retrieved from http://www.milliyet .com.tr/tusiad--kamu-ihale-kanunu-ab-ye-aykiri-hale-geliyor-ekonomi-1016347/.

Milliyet (29 April 2014). Retrieved from http://www.milliyet.com.tr/corum-icin-ensar -vakfi-ve-musiad-tan-corum-yerelhaber-171970/.

Ministry of Economy (2014). Turkey-South Korea Free Trade Agreement. Retrieved from https://www.ekonomi.gov.tr/portal/faces/oracle/webcenter/portalapp/pages/cont ent/htmlViewer.jspx?contentId=UCM%23dDocName%3AEK-208280&parentP age=dis_iliskiler&_afrLoop=26626399676299634&_afrWindowMode=0&_afrW indowId=null&_adf.ctrl-state=1dpafvuu6t_1#!%40%40%3F_afrWindowId%3Dn ull%26_afrLoop%3D26626399676299634%26contentId%3DUCM%2523d DocName%253AEK-208280%26parentPage%3Ddis_iliskiler%26_afrWindowM ode%3D0%26_adf.ctrl-state%3D1dpafvuu6t_5.

Ministry of Economy, (2016). Uluslararası Doğrudan Yatırımlar 2015 Yılı Raporu [Foreign Direct Investments 2015 Report]. Retrieved from http://www.ekonomi.gov.tr/por tal/content/conn/UCM/uuid/dDocName:EK-231834.

Ministry for EU Affairs (04 July 2007). Devlet Bakani Babacan Bruksel'de [The State Ministry Babacan in Brussels]. Retrieved from https://www.ab.gov.tr/40880.html.

MUSIAD (1999). Türkiye Ekonomisi Raporu. [Turkey's Economy Report]. Retrieved from http://www.musiad.org.tr/F/Root/burcu2014/Ara%C5%9Ft%C4%B1rmalar%20 Yay%C4%B1n/Pdf/Ekonomi%20Raporu/Turkiye_Ekonomisi_1999.pdf.

MUSIAD (2003). Türkiye Ekonomisi Raporu. [Turkey's Economy Report]. Retrieved from http://www.musiad.org.tr/F/Root/burcu2014/Ara%C5%9Ft%C4%B1rmalar%20 Yay%C4%B1n/Pdf/Ekonomi%20Raporu/Turkiye_Ekonomisi_2003.pdf.

MUSIAD (2009). Türkiye Ekonomisi Raporu. [Turkey's Economy Report]. Retrieved from http://www.musiad.org.tr/F/Root/Pdf/Ara%C5%9Ft%C4%B1rma%20Rapor lar%C4%B1/T%C3%BCrkiye%20Ekonomisi%20Rapolar%C4%B1/Turkiye_Eko nomisi_2009.pdf.

MUSIAD (2011). 2011 Türkiye Ekonomisi Raporu [Turkey's Economy Report in 2011]. Retrieved from http://www.musiad.org.tr/F/Root/Pdf/Ara%C5%9Ft%C4%B1rma%20R aporlar%C4%B1/T%C3%BCrkiye%20Ekonomisi%20Rapolar%C4%B1/Turkiye_Ek onomisi_Raporu_2011.pdf.

MUSIAD (2012). Turkiye Ekonomisi Raporu. Retrieved from http://www.musiad.org. tr/F/Root/Pdf/Ara%C5%9Ft%C4%B1rma%20Raporlar%C4%B1/T%C3%BCrk iye%20Ekonomisi%20Rapolar%C4%B1/Turkiye_Ekonomisi_Raporu_2012.pdf.

MUSIAD (2017a). MUSIAD Arastirma Raporlari, Deger Tabanli Teknolojik Donusum. Retrieved from http://www.musiad.org.tr/F/Root/Pdf/deger-tabanli-teknolojik -donusum.PDF.

MUSIAD, (2017b). Library Shelves, http://www.musiad.org.tr/en/musiad-library/mus iad-special-sublications.

MUSIAD Ankara (2017c). Katma Değerli Üretim İçin ARGE'ye Verilen Önem Artmalı. Retrieved from http://www.musiad.org.tr/tr-tr/haberler/duyuru-haber/katma-dege rli-uretim-icin-ar-geye-verilen-onem-artmali-815?Branch=ankara.

MUSIAD (2017d), Branches, retrieved from http://www.musiad.org.tr/en/branches.

OSCE, (16 September 2009). *The unprecedented fine imposed on Doğan Media Group Threatens Media Pluralism in Turkey, says OSCE Media Freedom Representative.* Retrieved from http://www.osce.org/fom/51313.

NAKSAN, (2021). Retrieved from http://www.naksan.com/en/index.php.

NTV (29 March 2019). TUSIAD'tan OHAL Çağrısı, available at https://www.ntv.com.tr/ turkiye/tusiaddan-ohal-cagrisi,-r8-q7cMKkGh_djejzmBBw.

ODA TV, (18 December 2013). Dershaneler Hakkinda Bilmek Istediginiz Her sey [All You Want to know about the Dershanes]. Retrieved from http://odatv.com/ders haneler-hakkinda-bilmek-istediginiz-her-sey-1811131200.html.

Oğuz, S. (2008). Globalisation and the Contradictions of State Restructuring in Turkey, PhD Thesis, Toronto, York University.

Oğuz, S. (2011). Turning the Crisis into an Opportunity: Turkey's Policy Responses to the 2008 Crisis, *TODAIE's Review of Public Administration*, 5(1), 1–33.

Oğuz, S. (2013). *Turning the Crisis into an Opportunity: Turkish State's Response to the 2008 Crisis.* In Karaagac, B. (Ed.). *Accumulations, Crises, Struggles Capital and Labour in Contemporary Capitalism.* Vien: Verlag.

Oğuz, S. (2016). *"Yeni Türkiye'nin Siyasal Rejimi" [Political Regime of New Turkey].* In Tören, T. & Kutun M. (Eds.). *Yeni Türkiye'de Kapitalizm, Devlet ve Sınıflar [The State and Capitalism in New Turkey].* İstanbul: SAV Yayınları.

Ollman, B. (1993). *Dialectical Investigations.* New York: Routledge.

Ollman, B. (2015). Marxism and the Philosophy of Internal Relations; or how to replace the mysterious paradox with contradictions that can be studied and resolved. *Capital & Class,* 39(1), 7–23.

Ollman, B. & Badeen, D. (2015). Preface to the Special Issue: Dialectics and the Gordian Knot. *Capital & Class,* 39(1), 3–5.

Öniş, Z. (1997). The political economy of Islamic resurgence in Turkey: the rise of the welfare Party in perspective. *Third World Quarterly,* 18(4), 743–766.

Öniş, Z. & Turem, U. (2001). Business, Globalization and Democracy: A Comparative Analysis of Turkish Business Associations, *Turkish Studies,* 2(2), 94–120.

Öniş, Z. & Bakır, C. (2007). Turkey's Political Economy in the Age of Finacial Globalization: The Significance of E U Anchor. *South European Society and Politics,* 12(2), 147–164.

Öniş, Z., & Kutlay, M. (2013). Rising Powers in a Changing Global Order: the political economy of Turkey in the age of BRICS. *Third World Quarterly,* 34(8), 1409–1426.

Orkide Dunyasi, (2013a). Retrieved from http://orkide.com.tr/Files/Journal/Orkide%20dergi-26baski.pdf.

Orkide Dunyasi (2013b). Retrieved from http://orkide.com.tr/Files/Journal/orkide%20dergi%20osayi%2027-baski.pdf.

Orkide Dunyasi (2014). Retrieved from http://orkide.com.tr/Files/Journal/orkide%20dergi%2028%20obaski.pdf.

Ozbudun, E. (2000). *Contemporary Turkish politics: challenges to democratic consolidation.* USA: Lynne Rienner Publishers.

Ozbudun, E. (2015). Turkey's Judiciary and the Drift toward Competitive Authoritarianism. *The International Spectator,* 50(2), 42–55.

Özcan, G. B. (2015). Energy Privatizations, Business-politics Connections and governanceunder political Islam, *Government and Policy,* 33(6), 1714–1737.

Özdemir, Ş. (2006). *Anadolu Sermayesinin Dönüşümü ve Türk Modernleşmesinin Derinleşmesi [The Transformation of Anatolian Bourgeoisie and the Deepening of Turkish Modernism].* Ankara: Vadi Publishing.

Özdemir, S. (2014). *Islam ve Sınıf [Islam and Class].* Ankara: Nika Publishing.

Özdemir, (27 January 2014). Saflar Yeniden Tutuluyor [The Sides are changing]. Available at http://www.hurriyet.com.tr/saflar-yeniden-tutuluyor-25661094.

Özden, B. A. & Akça, İ. & Bekmen, A. (2017). *Antinomies of Authoritarian Neoliberalism in Turkey: The Justice and Development Party Era.* In Tansel, C. B. (2017). *States of Discipline: Authoritarian Neoliberalism and the Contested Reproduction of Capitalist Order.* London: Rowman & Littlefield International.

Özel, I. (2013). Is it none of their business? Business and Democratization, the case of Turkey, *Democratization,* 20(6), 1081–1116.

Özel, I. (2015). *State-Business Alliances and Economic Development, Turkey, Mexico and North Africa* London: Routledge.

Ozgenturk, J. (10 January 2016). TUSKON Eksiliyor MUSIAD Buyuyor [TUSKON Falls Away, MUSIAD Rises. Retrieved from http://www.hurriyet.com.tr/yazarlar/jale -ozgenturk/tuskon-eksiliyor-musiad-buyuyor-40038361.

Ozilhan (03 October 2003). Özilhan Merkez Bankasını Övdü [Ozilhan Praises the Central Bank]. Retrieved from http://www.hurriyet.com.tr/ozilhan-merkez-bankas ini-ovdu-38501625.

Özkale, U. & Yüksel, M. K. (2016). TÜRKİYE'DE BÜTÇE HARCAMALARI: FARKLI DAĞILIMLARIN EKONOMİK BÜYÜMEYE ETKİSİ [Budget Spending in Turkey: the Impact of Different Distributions on Economic Development]. KOÇ UNIVERSITY-TÜSIAD ECONOMIC RESEARCH FORUM WORKING PAPER SERIES, Working Paper 1603.

Özkan, M. (2012). A new actor or passer-by? The Political Economy of Turkey's Engagement with Africa, Journal of Balkan and Near Eastern Studies, 14(1), 113–133.

Özkan, M. (2013). Does Rising Power Mean Rising Donor? Turkey's Development Aid inAfrica, Africa Review, 5(2), 139–147.

Özkan, F. (14 May 2010). Kamplasma Sermayede de Basladi [The Intra-Capital Polarization is Started]. Retrieved from http://www.radikal.com.tr/yazarlar/funda -ozkan/kamplasma-sermayede-de-basladi-996685.

Özgür, Ö. (1972). 100 Soruda Türkiye Kapitalizminin Gelişmesi, İstanbul: Gerçek Yayınevi.

Öztürk, Ö. (2011). Turkiye'de Buyuk Sermaye Gruplari: Finans Kapitalin Olusumu ve Gelisimi [Larger- Scale Capital Groups in Turkey: The Emergence and Development of Finance Capital]. İstanbul: SAV Yayınları.

Öztürk, Ö. (2014). Türkiye Finans Kapitali [Finance Capital in Turkey]. In Savran et al. (Eds.). Marksizm ve Siniflar: Dunyada ve Trukiye'de Siniflar ve Mucadeleleri [Mraxism and Classes: Classes and Class Struggles in the World and Turkey], pp. 227–251. Ankara: Yordam Kitap.

Öztürk, Ö. (2015). The Islamist Big Bourgeoisie in Turkey. In Balkan,N. & Balkan, E. & Öncü, A. (Eds.), The Neoliberal Landscape and the Rise of Islamist Capital in Turkey. New York: Berghahn.

Palloix, C. (1977). The Self Expansion of Capital on a World Scale. Review of Radical Political Economics, 9(2), 1–2.

Panitch, L. & Gindin, S. (2004). Global Capitalism and American Empire, Socialist Register, 40(40).

Panitch, L. & Gindin, S. (2012). The Making of Global Capitalism, The Political Economy of American Empire, London: Verso.

Poulantzas, N. ([1968] 1978). Political Power and Social Classes, London: Verso.

Poulantzas, N. ([1974] 1975). Classes in Contemporary Capitalism. London: NLB.

Poulantzas, N. ([1978]2000). State, Power and Socialism. London: Verso Classics.

RMT (Republic of Turkey Ministry of Trade 2019), Free Trade Agreements, available at, https://ticaret.gov.tr/dis-iliskiler/serbest-ticaret-anlasmalari, (accessed on 01 April 2019).

Robinson, W. & Harris, J. (2000). Towards A Global Ruling Class? Globalization and Global Ruling Class, *Science & Society*, 64(1), 11–54.

Robinson, W. I. (2001). Social Theory and Globalisation: The Rise of a Transnational State, *Theory and Society*, 30/2, 157–200.

Robinson, W. I. (2004). *A Theory of Global Capitalism: Production, Class, and State in a Transnational World.* Baltimore: Johns Hopkins University Press.

Robinson, W. (2010). *Beyond the Theory of Imperialism: Global Capitalism and the Transnational State*, in Anievas, A. (Ed.). *Marxism and World Politics, Contesting Global Capitalism.* London and New York: Routledge.

Rogers, F. H. (2010). The global financial crisis and development thinking. *World Bank Policy Research Working Paper Series*, 5353.

Saad-Filho, A. & Fine, B. (2004). *Marx's Capital.* London: Pluto Press.

Saad-Filho, A. (2015). *The rise of the South.* In Marois, T. & Lucia, P. (Eds.). *Polarising Development: Alternatives to Neoliberalism and Crisis*, Pluto Press.

SABANCI, (2017). The Sabancı Group in brief. Retrieved from https://www.sabanci .com/en/sabanci-group/sabanci-group-in-brief/the-sabanci-group-in-brief/i-128.

Sakallioglu, U. C. (1991). Labour: the battered community. *Strong State and Economic Interest Groups: The post-1980 Turkish Experience.* Berlin: Walter de Gruyter.

SARKUYSAN, (2018). About us, available at http://www.sarkuysan.com/en-EN/about -us/119.aspx.

Savran, S. (2008). *Kod Adi Kuresellesme, 21. Yuzyilda Emperyalizm [Code Name is Globalisation, Imperialism in 21st Century].* Istanbul: Yordam Kitap.

Savran, S. (2002). *The Legacy of the Twentieth Century.* In Savran, S. & Balkan, N. (Eds.). *The Politics of Permanent Crises Class, Ideology, and the State in Turkey,* New York: Nova Science Publishers.

Savran, S. (2010). Türkiye'de Sınıf Mücadeleleri Cilt 1: 1908–1980, Yordam Kitap: Ankara.

Savran, S. (2015). *Class, State and Religion in Turkey.* In Balkan, N. & Balkan, E. & Öncü, A. (Eds.). *The Neoliberal Landscape and the Rise of Islamist Capital in Turkey.* New York: Berghahn.

Sawaya, R. (2018) Subordinated Development, Subordinated Development in the Process of accumulation of Latin America and Brazil, Brill Publishing: Lieden-Boston.

Saygili, S. (2003). Bilgi Ekonomisine Geçiş Sürecinde Türkiye Ekonomisin Dünyadaki Konumu, Ekonomik Modeller ve Stratejik Araştırmalar Genel Müdürlüğü Stratejik Araştımalar Dairesi Başkanlığı, July, 2003.

Saygili, S. (et. Al. 2010). Turkiye Imalat Sanayinin Ithalat Yapisi [The Import Structure of Manufacturing Industry of Turkey]. TCMB Calisma Tebligi No: 10/02.

Shaikh, A. (2007). *Globalization and the myth of free trade: history, Theory and Empirical Evidence*. Routledge.

Schick. I. C. & Tonak, E. A. (1987). *The International Dimension: Trade Aid and Debt*. In Schick, C. I. & Tonak, E. A. *Turkey in Transition,New Perspectives*, Oxford: Oxford University Press.

Sklair, L. (2001). *The Transnational Capitalist Class*. Oxford: Blackwell.

Smith, J. (2016). *Imperialism in the 21st Century: The Globalisation of Production, Super-Exploitation, and the Crisis of Capitalism*. New York: Monthly Review Press.

SOL (20 January 2011). Ve Erdoğan TUSIAD'ın Onur Konuğu [And Erdoğan is the Honoured Guest of TUSIAD]. Retrieved from http://haber.sol.org.tr/devlet-ve-siya set/ve-erdogan-tusiadin-onur-konugu-haberi-38253.

SOL, (16 September 2011). Bienal'e Koç'un Evren'e yazdığı mektup damga vurdu, available at http://haber.sol.org.tr/kultur-sanat/bienale-kocun-evrene-yazdigi-mektup -damga-vurdu-haberi-46467.

Sönmez, M. (2010). *Turkiye'de İş Dünyasının Örgütleri ve Yonelimleri [Business Groups in Turkey and their Strategies]*, İstanbul: Friedrich-Ebert-Stiftung Derneği Türkiye Temsilciliği.

Sönmez, M. (2014). *AKP-CEMAAT Catismadan Cokuse [The AKP-The Cemaat From Conflict to Crackdown]*. Ankara: NOTA BENE.

State Planning Organisation (SPO), 2000. Eight Five-Year Development Plan http:// www.bilgitoplumu.gov.tr/wpcontent/uploads/2015/01/sekizinci_kalkinma_pl ani.pdf.

Strauss, D. (28 April 2011). Turkey: Inspiring or Insidious, *Financial Times*. Retrieved from https://www.ft.com/content/650452e8-71c6-11e0-9adf-00144feabdco.

Syed Ali, S. (2007). Financial Distress and Bank Failure: Lessons From Closure of Ihlas Finance House in Turkey. *Islamic Economic Studies*, 14(1& 2).

T24 (21 February 2014). *7 Subat'ta Gul Hakan Fidana 'İfade Ver' dedi; Erdoğan 'Gitme' dedi* [Gul told Hakan Fidan to give a statement on 7 February, but Erdoğan said No]. Retrieved from http://t24.com.tr/haber/7-subatta-gul-hakan-fidana-ifade-ver-dedi -erdogan-gitme-dedi,251631.

Tanyılmaz, K. (2015). *The Deep Fracture in the Big Bourgeoisie in Turkey*. In Balkan,N. &Balkan, E. & Öncü, A. (Eds.). *The Neoliberal Landscape and the Rise of Islamist Capital in Turkey*. New York: Berghahn.

The Guardian (02 June 2010). Flotilla Raid: Turkish Jihadists Bent on violence attacked troops, Israel claims. Retrieved from https://www.theguardian.com/world/2010/ jun/02/flotilla-raid-turkish-jihadis-troops-israel-claims.

The Economist (25 March 2010). Ottoman Dreaming. Retrieved from http://www .economist.com/node/15772860.

Thicke, A. (28 April 2017). The Rise and fall of the Gülen Movement (and Turkey). Retrieved from https://washingtonhatti.com/2017/04/28/the-rise-and-fall-of-the -gülen-movement-and-turkey/.

TIM (2019). İhracatta İlk 1000 Firma, available at https://www.tim.org.tr/tr/ raporlar-ilk-1000-ihracatci-arastirmasi-dosyalar-2019

Timur, T. (1987). *The Ottoman Heritage*, in Schick, C. I. & Tonak, E. A. *Turkey in Transition, New Perspectives*. Oxford: Oxford University Press.

Tosyalı Holding, (2021). Our Facilities. Retrieved from http://en.tosyaliholding.com.tr/ tesislerimiz/detay.aspx?SectionID=Yjg4oC6LN%2fhyRdXobN3zcw%3d%3d.

Tuğal, C. (2009). *Passive Revolution: Absorbing to Islamic Challenge to Capitalism*, Stanford: Stanford University Press.

TUIK (2016), Foreign Trade by Years, http://www.tuik.gov.tr/PreTablo.do?alt_id=1046.

TUIK (2019). TUIK Foreign Trade Statistics. Retrieved from http://www.turkstat.gov.tr/ UstMenu.do?metod=temelist.

TUIK (2021). TUIK Labour Statistics. Retrieved from https://data.tuik.gov.tr/Bulten/ Index?p=%C4%B0%C5%9Fg%C3%BCc%C3%BC-%C4%B0statistikleri-Haziran -2021-37482&dil=1.

Tuna, G. (2009). Birikim Sürecinde TOBB'un Tarihsel Gelişim Uğrakları [The Historical Development Moments of TOBB in Accumulation Process]. *Praksis*, 19(1).

Tur, O. (2011). Economic relations with the Middle East under the AKP trade, business Community and reintegration with Neighbouring zones, *Turkish Studies*, 12(4), 589–602.

Turkiye Finans, (2017). About Turkiye Finans. Retrieved from https://www.turkiyefin ans.com.tr/en-us/about-us/about-turkiye-finans/Pages/about-turkiye-finans.aspx.

TUSIAD, (1979). TUSIAD 1979 Gazete Ilanlari [TUSIAD 1979 Newspaper Advertisements]. Retrieved from http://tusiad.org/tr/basin-bultenleri/item/9376-tusiad-1979-gazete -ilanlari.

TUSIAD, (2002), Bağımsız Düzenleyici Kurumlar ve Türkiye Uygulaması [Independent Regulatory Agencies and Turkish Case], Publication No. TUSIAD-T/2002-12/349. Retrieved from http://tusiad.org/tr/yayinlar/raporlar/item/1883-bagimsiz-duzenley ici-kurumlar-ve-turkiye-uygulamasi.

TUSIAD, (2003). Turkiye Ekonomisi [Turkey's Economy], Publication No. TUSIAD-T/ 2003-12-371. Retrieved from http://tusiad.org/tr/yayinlar/raporlar/item/1817-turk iye-ekonomisi-2003.

TUSIAD & OECD, (2003). Türkiye'de Düzenleyici Reformlar: Ekonomik Dönüşüme Yaşamsal Destek [Regulatory Reforms in Turkey: A Crucial Contribution to the Economic Transformation] Publication No. TUSIAD-T/2003/9/359. Retrieved from http://www.tusiad.org/tr/yayinlar/raporlar/item/1909-turkiyede-duzenleyici -reformlar-ekonomik-donusume-yasamsal-destek.

TUSIAD, (22 June 2016). TÜSİAD Parlamento ve Kamu Kurumları ile İlişkiler (PARKUR) Heyeti Ankara Temaslarının İkincisini Gerçekleştiriyor [TUSIAD PARKUR Committee is having second contact in Ankara], Publication No. TS/Kİ-= BÜL/ 16-40. Retrieved from http://tusiad.org/tr/basin-bultenleri/item/8877-parlamento -kamu-kurumlari-ile-iliskiler-parkur.

TUSIAD (16 December 2016), TUSIAD Çin'i Anlamak & Çin ile İş Yapmak konulu bir konferans düzenledi [TUSIAD organised a conference titled as Understanding China Doing Business with China]. Retrieved from http://tusiad.org/tr/basin-bul tenleri/item/9560-tusiad-cin-i-anlamak-cin-ile-is-yapmak-konulu-bir-konferans -duzenledi.

Trotsky, L. ([1930] 2000). The History of the Russian Revolution. Retrieved from https:// www.marxists.org/archive/trotsky/1930/hrr/cho1.htm.

Trotsky, L. ([1936] 1996). The third International after Lenin: The Draft Programme of the Communist International A Criticism of Fundamentals, https://www.marxists .org/archive/trotsky/1928/3rd/3rd.pdf.

ÜLKER Holding, (2021). Dünya'da Ülker. Retrieved from http://www.ulker.com.tr/tr/ ulkerle-tanisin/hakkimizda/dunyada-ulker.

UNCTAD, (2011). World Investment Report 2011: Non-Equity Modes of International Production and Development, New York, UN.

UNCTAD, (2012). Investment Country Profiles Turkey. Retrieved from http://unctad .org/en/PublicationsLibrary/webdiaeia2012d6_en.pdf.

UNCTAD, (2016). World Investment Report. Retrieved from http://unctad.org/en/Publ icationsLibrary/wir2016_en.pdf.

Uysal, G. (2021). Turkey's Sub-Imperialism in Sub-Saharan Africa, *Review of Radical Political Economists*, 04866134211003995.

Vardan, Ö. C. (2012) *Islam ve Cihad [Islam and Jihad]*. Istanbul: Timas Publishing.

Yaka, O. (2011). TUSIAD as a Hegemonic Force in Turkish Politics: A Gramscian Analysis of the Promotion and Limits of EU Membership as a Hegemonic Project, Unpublished PhD Thesis, Department of Sociology, Lancaster University.

Yalman, G. (2002). *The Turkish State and Bourgeoisie in Historical Perspective: A relativist Paradigm or a Panoply of Hegemonic Strategies*. In Savran, S. & Balkan, N. (Eds.). *The Politics of Permanent Crises Class, Ideology, and the State in Turkey*, New York: Nova Science Publishers.

Yalman, G. (2012). *Politics and Discourse under the AKP Rule: The Marginalisation of Class-Based Politics, Erdoganization and Post-Secularism*. In Yucesan- Özdemir, G. & Cosar, G. (Eds.). *Silent Violence: Neoliberalism, Islamist Politics and the AKP Years in Turkey*, Ottawa: Red Quill Books.

Yankaya, D. (2012). 28 Şubat: Yeni İslami Burjuvazinin İktidarı Yolunda bir Milat [The February 28: A milestone for the Hegemony of the New Islamic Capital]. *Birikim*, 278–279, 29–37.

Yaşlı, F. (21 April 2016). Retrieved from http://www.birgun.net/haber-detay/birgun-un -ses-getiren-interaktif-haritasini-yasli-boyle-yorumluyor-cikarlari-birbiriyle-ortu sen-bir-sermaye-sebekesi-var-109634.html.

Yavuz, H. (2003). *Islamic Political Identity in Turkey*. Oxford University Press.

Yavuz, H. (2009). *Secularism and Muslim Democracy in Turkey*. Cambridge: Cambridge University Press.

Yavuz, H. M. (2013). *Toward an Islamic Enlightenment: The Gülen Movement*. Oxford: Oxford University Press.

Yavuz, H. M. & Koç, R. (2016). The Turkish Coup Attempt: The Gülen Movement Vs. The State, *Middle East Policy*, XXIII, 136–148.

Yeldan, E. (2011). *Kuresellesme Surecinde Turkiye Ekonomisi [Turkish Economy in the Globalisation Period]*. İstanbul: Iletisim Yayinlari.

Yıldız, Y. (1999). Istanbul Menkul Kıymetler Borsasaında Grupların Hakimiyeti: 10988-1998 [The Hegemony of Groups in Istanbul Stock Exchange Market: 1988–1998], unpublished master thesis, Ankara, Gazi University, Institute of Social Sciences.

Yildirim, K. (11 December 2017). Liberal Otoriteryan Legalizme Karsi Hukukun Ustunlugu mu? [Is it the Superiority of Law against the Liberal Authoritarianism?]. Retrieved from https://devletvesiniflar.blogspot.co.uk/2017/12/liberal-otoriteryan -legalizme-kars.html.

Yukseler, Z. & Turkan, E. (2008). Transformation of the Turkish Production and External Trade Structure: Global Orientations and their Reflections, TUSIAD- KOC University Economic Research Forum, 02/453. Retrieved from http://eaf.ku.edu .tr/sites/eaf.ku.edu.tr/files/rapor2008_uretim_ve_disticaret_yapisindaki_donu sum.pdf.

Index